820.9

GEORGE H

IDEA AND IMAGE

GEORGE HERBERT
Idea and Image

A Study of *The Temple*

SISTER THEKLA

Published by
The Greek Orthodox Monastery of the Assumption, Filgrave,
Normanby, Whitby, North Yorkshire YO22 4PS, England nd. 1974

© Sister Thekla

PRINTED IN GREAT BRITAIN
BY THE FAITH PRESS LTD.
LEIGHTON BUZZARD LU7 7NQ
ISBN 0 903455 18 8

All references are taken from:

The Works of George Herbert. Ed. F. E. Hutchinson.

Reprinted. Oxford 1970

George Herbert
Born.　April 3rd 1593
Died.　March 1st 1632

There is no fruitfull yeare, but that which brings
That last and lov'd, though dreadfull day.

Home

CONTENTS

	page
Introduction	11
PART I. The Work of Faith	19
CHAPTER I. Priest of the Church of England	21
CHAPTER II. World of Grace and World of Nature	39
i. Redemption	40
ii. Faith	42
iii. Grace	45
iv. Imputation of Righteousness	57
CHAPTER III. Theology in Practice	70
i. The Saints	70
ii. The Bible	73
iii. The Eucharist	77
iv. Suffering	87
CHAPTER IV. The Angry God	96
PART II. The Work of Love	117
CHAPTER I. The Person of Christ	119
i. Christ: the Redeemer	119
ii. Christ: the Beloved	133
CHAPTER II. Participation in Christ	152
i. Sin	152
ii. Repentance	156
iii. Morality	163
iv. Death	171
CHAPTER III. The Offering of Praise	178
i. The duty of praise	178
ii. Language of sacred verse	186
iii. Verse as the medium of devotion	191
iv. Verse as the work of devotion	193
v. Self-dedication to devotional verse	197

PART III. Key-Poems of the Mystery   207

      i. The Mystery of God: *Divinitie*   209
     ii. The Mystery of continuity: *The Flower*   212
    iii. The Mystery of success: *The Answer*   215
    iv. The Mystery of freedom: *The Collar*   216
     v. The Mystery of presence: *Miserie*   219
    vi. The Mystery of praise: *Jordan* (II)   222
   vii. The Mystery of affliction: *Josephs Coat*   224
  viii. The Mystery of renewal: 225
           Love unknown   225
           The Pulley   232
    ix. The Mystery of Eternity: 234
           Mans medley   234
           Home   237
           The Pilgrimage   241
           Hope   244

PART IV. Synopsis of the Imagery   247

      i. Introduction to Imagery   249
     ii. Index to diagrams   250
    iii. Examples of use of diagrams   251
    iv. Key-words   260

Diagrams   261

Conclusion   277

An Essay by Mother Maria: *George Herbert: Aspects of his theology*   279

Index of Poems   306

INTRODUCTION

A few years ago, Mother Maria was concerned in a discussion on George Herbert. How far could his poetry, in particular, *The Temple,* be interpreted as the mystical expression of a spiritual ascent of sanctification, and how did his poetry stand vis à vis the Anglican position as defined by Hooker? Where would his attitude differ, in philosophical foundation, from that of the Cambridge Platonists? One outcome of the discussion was her Essay, *George Herbert: Aspects of his Theology,* published 1972. A further outcome is this present book, *Idea and Image,* which closely follows the theological line first drawn in the Essay. The connection is indeed so close that we have, as a matter of obvious interest, re-printed the Essay together with *Idea and Image.*

As far as *Idea and Image* is concerned, I have taken as the initial working hypothesis that a poet, however much he will speak in his peculiar poetic image, yet may mean strictly and soberly what he says in the same category of truth, as, for example, a scientist, however much he may speak in different idiom. Thus, as the hypothesis for further enquiry, I have taken a fully non-exclusive attitude to literature, and have included poetry into the whole realm of truth, as we understand truth in our daily lives. This means, that, as foundation, I have unreservedly accepted Herbert's own statement that his poetry was written for God, and, from this premise, I have then attempted to follow the simple statement into the consequent complexities of experience.

On another level, I have also kept in mind that Herbert was not only a student of Cambridge, but an Orator, and thus highly skilled in every nicety of the art of disputation, and this pattern of disputation, argument, counter-argument, conclusion, has helped considerably in distinguishing apparent even uncontrolled emotion from a formal inner structure of logical exposition within the poetic image. It has become more and more evident to me that what so often may seem a personal lament of pain, grief, doubt, can be accepted as the stylised image of a theological initial argument, to which comes the counter-argument, again perhaps in apparent emotional terms, and, thence, the conclusion, once again within the image of an emotional resolution. The inevitable solution at the end of poem after poem can not allow for the preceding lamentations *as* lamentation and nothing else. Lamentation *as* lamentation would never find a solution on each occasion of conflict. Thus, on one level, the repeated conflicts must be seen as image of the idea.

It would therefore seem that a wider pattern opens out for *The Temple* than the sole expression of Herbert's personal experiences. There emerges an even systematic exposition of the Anglican theological standpoint, in the direct line from Hooker and persisting to our own times in spite of every possible space for deviation. Thence, the consequences emerge of such a standpoint, with the practical problems inherent, and then the next logical step: the taking of the theory, the system in image form, into the daily application, even to the exposition of a moral and pietistic code. But, above all else, there would seem to emerge the direct confrontation with God, in its strictest theological relevance.

It is in this last stage, through the passage of the theological system, and its consequences both practical and moral, that there emerges, as the very centre and heart, the Person of Christ. And, here, Herbert transcends dogma in all its aspects, not relinquishing the doctrine of his Church, nor denying it, but gathering it up, and offering to God the theology of his Church, as a Mystery of love.

The step from doctrine into Mystery is obviously common to all the Churches, but I would suggest that in Herbert may be traced the peculiar grace of the Church of England, the non-assertion, which both exposes the faithful to the suffering of personal conflict and decision, but also gives the freedom of integrating the theological teaching, as far as it is assertive, and, at the same time, surpassing it, relying in the last count on the inexplicable Mystery of the love of God. It is here, in the day-to-day even unconscious awareness of the limitation of reason, and thence the immediate presence of the Mystery, that the Orthodox and Anglicans are so near to each other in attitude, whatever the dogmatic differences. Of course, on certain essential points, the Orthodox Church refuses any form of ambiguity, strictly adhering to the Tradition and to the teaching, but, equally, the Orthodox Church, in common with the Church of England, holds fast to the undefined latitude of Mystery.

This, then, was my first shock in my re-entry into Herbert's poetry: the realisation that, on one level, *The Temple* may be regarded as a treatise, in verse, on Anglican theology on the explicit pattern of disputation, the evident personal pain and conflict being the formal image for the argument. From here, I moved on to the awareness of the mystical confrontation, which goes beyond dogma. This transcending of rationalisation is particularly apparent in a few poems, which I have considered in greater detail on their own, and which I have called the *key poems*. But, a third aspect gradually became more and more clear during the process of analysis.

In the consistent repetition of certain words and phrases, their synonyms and their derivatives, and their inter-relationship, in the meticulous choice of vocabulary, it began to emerge that Herbert was as austerely systematic in his imagery as he was in the connotation of his ideas. He consciously rejects, as far as it was possible, all the words which for him are too grossly associated with sensuality in any form, or with the scintillation of court wit, and he fastidiously selects and preserves a distilled company of words, which he considers the most fitting instrument for his intercourse with God. The words, in themselves, are consistently simple, but there emerges an inner coherence between themselves, verging sometimes on what nearly seems a kind of secret code. This even esoteric combination of words considerably enhances the force of any apparently isolated word or phrase for it brings with it all the underlying related connotations found in a different context. In the appreciation of the inter-relationship of the images, the poems stand out more and more as a closely knit unity, and I have therefore added as the last Part of the book a synopsis of at least some of Herbert's most representative imagery. Thus, I have attempted to demonstrate, not by evaluation, but by actual presentation, the brilliance of his poetic craftsmanship. It is the attempt to suggest that the dichotomy of thought *or* poetry is a fallacious approach. In Herbert the two realms of thought and poetry are *not* one, and he deliberately offers his poetic gift as the vehicle of his worship, thus dissociating himself from the possible misunderstanding that he confuses the mind and the heart. But, there is a true balance to be found in Herbert between the idea and the image, and the value of the image which he so carefully offered constantly eluded him. It was Herbert's grief that he feared lest his creative genius was not sufficient as the practical expression of his love.

To sum up: I have attempted to suggest that the mystical way of sanctification is not to be attributed to Herbert in the light of the evidence of *The Temple*, but, that he is, in the truest and finest meaning, didactic to the furthest limit of systematic dogmatism. I have also attempted emphatically to contradict myself in suggesting how Herbert may be seen as, above all else, a mystical thinker. Thus, I am suggesting that the contradiction of dogmatism and mysticism may be approached as no contradiction, in as much as the mystical thinker is the greatest realist. Idealism and mysticism are poles apart. A true mystical thinker is the most practical of all men, seeing and accepting the daily reality, and working with the reality whether in the philosophical, religious, social or moral field. But, whatever he does, the true mystical thinker refuses to rest in the work, involved and trapped in the immanent purpose. His aim is ever transcendent, the reality beyond the reality, the truth beyond the truth, the beauty beyond the beauty. There can be no art for art's sake in any sphere.

This is the double life of the mystical thinker, the two realities of his life, and often he may try to hide the one beneath the other, precisely as Herbert frequently does.

It is this double movement which I have tried to lead towards in my exploration of *The Temple,* that is, the reality of Herbert's allegiance to his Church, the Church of England, on earth, with all the consequences, and, then, the reality of the love which can not be contained in the Church on earth, or indeed within the confines of the created world. But, this double movement, I am convinced, can never be seen as a progress in time, as some kind of sanctifying and developing ascent; if it were, it would cease to be the double movement, for the Mystery of the co-presence of time and no-time would be finally denied.

In connection with the suggestion that Herbert's poetry, on one level, can be seen as an exposition of Anglican theology in verse, it may be of interest to insert here some extracts from the Articles of Religion, to which Herbert would have subscribed at his Ordination. I am only giving short extracts relating to points which would seem particularly relevant to the themes of *The Temple.* The aspect of didacticism should of course not be overstressed, but nevertheless it is as well not to ignore the solid theological foundation which Herbert knew and accepted and asserted. The Articles also show the basis for the inevitable conflict and, equally, for the latitude which allows space for resolution of doubt in the final Mystery.

Articles of Religion

Article II   Of the Word, or Son of God, which was made very Man
... Christ ... who truly suffered, was crucified, dead and buried, to reconcile his Father to us, and to be a sacrifice, not only for original guilt, but also for all actual sins of men.

Article VI   Of the Sufficiency of the holy Scriptures for salvation
Holy Scripture containeth all things necessary to salvation: so that whatsoever is not read therein, nor may be proved thereby, is not to be required of any man, that it should be believed as an article of the Faith, or be thought requisite or necessary to salvation. ...

Article VII   Of the Old Testament
The Old Testament is not contrary to the New . . . no Christian man whatsoever is free from the obedience of the Commandments which are called Moral.

Article X   Of Free-Will
The condition of Man after the fall of *Adam* is such, that he cannot turn and prepare himself, by his own natural strength and good works, to faith, and calling upon God: Wherefore we have no power to do good works pleasant and acceptable to God, without the grace of God by Christ preventing us, that we may have a good will, and working with us, when we have that good will.

Article XI   Of the Justification of Man
We are accounted righteous before God, only for the merit of our Lord and Saviour Jesus Christ by Faith, and not for our own works or deservings: Wherefore, that we are justified by Faith only is a most wholesome Doctrine, and very full of comfort . . .

Article XVI   Of Sin after Baptism
. . . the grant of repentance is not to be denied to such as fall into sin after Baptism. After we have received the Holy Ghost, we may depart from grace given, and fall into sin, and by the grace of God we may arise again, and amend our lives. And therefore they are to be condemned, which say, they can no more sin as long as they live here, or deny the place of forgiveness to such as truly repent.

Article XVII   Of Predestination and Election
. . . As the godly consideration of Predestination, and our Election in Christ, is full of sweet, pleasant, and unspeakable comfort to godly persons, and such as feel in themselves the working of the Spirit of Christ. . . .

Article XVIII   Of obtaining eternal Salvation only by the Name of Christ
. . . For holy Scripture doth set out unto us only the Name of Jesus Christ, whereby men must be saved.

Article XX   Of the Authority of the Church
. . . Wherefore, although the Church be a witness and a keeper of holy Writ, yet, as it ought not to decree any thing against the same, so besides the same ought it not to enforce any thing to be believed for necessity of Salvation.

Article XXII   Of Purgatory
The Romish Doctrine concerning . . . invocation of Saints, is a fond thing vainly invented, and grounded upon no warranty of Scripture, but rather repugnant to the Word of God.

Article XXVIII   Of the Lord's Supper
The Supper of the Lord is not only a sign of the love that Christians ought to have among themselves one to another; but rather it is a Sacrament of our Redemption by Christ's death: insomuch that to such as rightly, worthily, and with faith, receive the same, the Bread which we break is a partaking of the Body of Christ; and likewise the Cup of Blessing is a partaking of the Blood of Christ. . . . Transubstantiation . . is repugnant to the plain words of Scripture. . . . The Body of Christ is given, taken, and eaten, in the Supper, only after an heavenly and spiritual manner. And the mean whereby the Body of Christ is received and eaten in the Supper is Faith.

Article XXXV   Of Homilies
The second Book of Homilies, the several titles whereof we have joined under this Article, doth contain a godly and wholesome Doctrine, and necessary for these times, as doth the former Book of Homilies, which were set forth in the time of *Edward* the Sixth; and therefore we judge them to be read in Churches by the Ministers, diligently and distinctly, that they may be understanded of the people.

1. *Of the right Use of the Church*
2. *Against peril of Idolatry*
3. *Of the repairing and keeping clean of Churches*
4. *Of good Works: first of Fasting*
5. *Against Gluttony and Drunkenness*
6. *Against Excess of Apparel*
7. *Of Prayer*
8. *Of the Place and Time of Prayer*
9. *That Common Prayers and Sacraments ought to be ministered in a known tongue*
10. *Of the reverend estimation of God's Word*
11. *Of Alms-doing*
12. *Of the Nativity of Christ*
13. *Of the Passion of Christ*
14. *Of the Resurrection of Christ*
15. *Of the worthy receiving of the Sacrament of the Body and Blood of Christ*
16. *Of the Gifts of the Holy Ghost*

17. *For the Rogation-days*
18. *Of the state of Matrimony*
19. *Of Repentance*
20. *Against Idleness*
21. *Against Rebellion*

Acknowledgment

I am most grateful to Father Dominic SSM, who is himself at present working on a thesis on Herbert to explore the Biblical and theological use of the title image, *The Temple,* for bringing to my notice a reference book of the highest value: *Cameron Mann: A Concordance to the English Poems of George Herbert.* The Folcroft Press Inc. 1970. First pub. The Riverside Press, Cambridge, 1927.

PART I

THE WORK OF FAITH

CHAPTER I

Priest of the Church of England

We do not know very much of the life of George Herbert beyond the few facts for which we have documentary evidence. Other than for these few facts, we rely on surmise arising out of the meagre contemporary or near-contemporary comments available. One of these apparently incontrovertible facts is that of Herbert's becoming a Priest, a modest country Parson. Another fact would seem to be that there was no necessity, in worldly terms, for this step of self-effacement. We have no evidence to claim, even if we wished to do so, that Herbert became a Priest because in some way or other he found himself a failure in the world. But, equally, we can not claim, as an objective and proved fact that he became a Priest because for him there was no alternative possibility of truth. But, we can, at least, take as a hypothesis that Herbert made the decision of leaving worldly ambition and becoming a Priest, and, if we are careful only to accept this hypothesis without any continuation into the speculative field of evaluation of his motives or spiritual achievement, then we become free to follow his poetry in the full interest and fascination of its self-revelation.

What Herbert writes suggests a conscious denial of the world, of worldly values, worldly comforts, worldly successes or achievement. He would seem in no way inhibited in such denials, emphatic and unequivocal. There is no suggestion that he feels himself called to any form of involvement with the world, other than in the normal course of parish duties. Consistently, he turns away from the world and all that the world signifies. But such a violent denial, in its actual experience of aggressiveness, must bring with it the suggestion of the contrary latent within itself. If he denies the world so emphatically, then the passage away from the world would not appear a predominantly easy one.

It was a *merrie world* in *The Quip* which, with a gang of toughs, attacked him unawares and defenceless *where I lay*. His assailants jeered at him for his impotence, for his not seizing upon beauty with sensual grasp, not singing the songs of avarice, not glancing at success, nor making his mark by intellect. To each, there was only the repeated reply, the self-denial into the Person of his Lord:

But thou shalt answer, Lord, for me.

At the end, the tables are turned. The answer will come. At *the houre of thy designe,* at the precise moment of God's choosing, and only then, neither within the circumstance nor choice of any human being, God will claim him as his own, and this answer will enter finally, deeply, inescapably, as a sword-point, into the very hearts of his traducers:

>   say, I am thine:
> And then they have their answer home.

In *Vanitie* (II) comes the warning of the erroneous evaluation. The delights of earth are *flat;* they lack all transcendent aim, all soaring quality of the Spirit. Souls, which are not fashioned of earth, must be ill at ease in the world:

> For they can never be at rest,
> Till they regain their ancient nest.

The nest is the home, before forced or voluntary expulsion into an alien and dangerous yet natural setting. And the nest is the home of the Spirit, for is not the Spirit a bird, a Dove?

> Then silly soul take heed; for earthly joy
> Is but a bubble, and makes thee a boy.

In *The Rose,* the world is seen as a place of *sugred lies,* seemingsweet deception. The deception is in the delusion of the pleasures which Herbert rejects. He is content with the *strict, yet welcome size* of his allotment of worldly delight. The reason for this would seem his denial that there is any pleasure. What appears pleasure remains merely disguised tribulation. But, even if there were any pleasure, it would mean nothing to him, who has renounced his claim. His answer to worldly pleasure lies in this symbol of the rose. Fair as the rose may seem, its nature is medicinal, and where medicine is necessary, illness must be inherent. The rose condemns worldly joys as a pestilence, requiring the cleansing of repentance. He would prefer health to remedy, and so:

> But I health, not physick choose:
>   Onely though I you oppose,
> Say that fairly I refuse,
>   For my answer is a rose.

The *sugred lies* of *The Rose* become *Embroider'd lyes* in *Dotage.* Pleasures and sorrows are equally delusions of foolish misorientation:

> But oh the folly of distracted men,
> Who griefs in earnest, joyes in jest pursue . . .

How can man keep his gaze consistently downwards, instead of looking up into the clarity of eternity? Heaven is:

> Where are no sorrows, but delights more true
> Then miseries are here!

The Size goes further in poverty. The demand is here of denying not only the material comforts of the world, but so too the spiritual reassurance. The poverty he advocates is not a blind poverty, but as the fore-taste of great riches. His heart need not be greedy now. The faintest trace of spice to bring some savour to immediate despondency should be sufficient, for is not such a trace the promise of the whole which it represents?

> If thou hast wherewithall to spice a draught,
> When griefs prevail;
> And for the future time art heir
> To th' Isle of spices, is 't not fair?

How can Herbert dare to claim in the world what God, himself, did not claim? If in utmost self-limitation, God condescended to worldly poverty on every level, then:

> Wouldst thou his laws of fasting disanull?
> Enact good cheer?
> Lay out thy joy, yet hope to save it?

He disclaims emphatically the possibility of worldly happiness now, and, then, of future joy. Christ refused this possibility:

> Thy Saviour sentenc'd joy,
> And in the flesh condemn'd it as unfit,
> At least in lump . . .

Herbert counsels himself to forget all hopes of immediate happiness. As a Christian he must rejoice not in corpulence but in being *thinne and spare*. He must not attempt to grasp too much, lest he lose everything:

> Then close again the seam,
> Which thou hast open'd: do not spread thy robe,
> In hope of great things.

Thus he rejects the achievement of the world. And, he turns his back even on spiritual satisfaction in this echo of Christ's rebuke: *But all their works they do for to be seen of men: they make broad their phylacteries, and enlarge the borders of their garments* (Matt. 23, 5).
And, he calls to mind the initial inspiration of the Passion of his Lord:

>   thy dream,
> An earthly globe,
> On whose meridian was engraven,
> *These seas are tears, and heav'n the haven.*

Self-condemnation seems to sum up this conscious and emphatic turning away from the world:

The *Thou* at the opening of the poem is himself. Herbert accuses no-one except himself for the worldly tendency which holds within itself the denial of Christ. He sees the hypocrisy of the self-righteousness which would blame the murderers of the Incarnate Christ, and yet continue as the murderers in spirit of the Risen Christ, and of the Body of Christ, the Christian Church. The *Thou*, who dares to condemn the Jews for preferring Barabbas, a murderer, before *the Lord of glorie,* is advised to look at his own condition before he persists in accusing others. The eye of judging accusation, *that busie wanderer,* ever spying out the mote, must be re-called. Careful self-examination may lead to the startling and unpleasant truth, that he, who condemns, has made precisely the same choice, preferring a murderer to Christ. Is not the world a murderer?

> The world an ancient murderer is;
> Thousands of souls it hath and doth destroy
> With her enchanting voice.

But, the Christian, he, himself, is far more culpable than the Jews who called for the life of Barabbas. The Jews only preferred the murderer, whilst the Christian both sells Christ and prefers the murderer in uniting his soul with gold. Such a union is, as it were, adultery to the highest degree, for the Church is the Bride of Christ. And now the Christian has made the second, perfidious marriage:

>   a sorrie wedding
> Between his soul and gold . . .

This treacherous commercial transaction, a mercenary unfaithfulness to the Beloved, is revealed in the climax of the double-epithet:

> For he hath sold for money his deare Lord,
> And is a Judas-Jew.

The Day of Judgment can be brought forward in time. If we look clearly at our own perfidy, if we remove the obscuring diversions of sin and passion by means of relentless self-examination, then the light reveals the sin. Here there would seem some entrance into the practical working of Herbert's spirituality. The denial of the sin, conscious and willed, can not remove the sin, but it can open it out to its full extent and thus lead to the self-condemnation, the possible basis for work, as yet not expressed:

> That light, which sin & passion
> Did before dimme and choke,
> When once those snuffes are ta'ne away,
> Shines bright and cleare, ev'n unto condemnation,
> Without excuse or cloke.

So Herbert denies wealth and career, and he denies it positively, whatever the struggle, because he takes the denial into the active channel of his Ordination.

> Quitting both his deserts and all the opportunities that he had for worldly preferment, he betook himself to the Sanctuarie and Temple of God, choosing rather to serve at Gods Altar, then to seek the honour of State-employments. (Extract from *The Printers to the Reader*)

And, in entering the Priesthood, Herbert takes upon himself fully the responsibility of Priest and Church. He brings due honour to the Church as Institution, and to the Priest, as mediator of the Church.

There would seem in Herbert no suggestion of split as far as the Church and the Priesthood were concerned. In *The Temple*, there can be traced no doubt whatsoever in the validity of the Church as a Divine Institution, and, thence, as a means of salvation. The holiness of the Church is extended into the Priest, to whom the same reverence is due and should be paid according to his calling, although not necessarily to him as a person outside his calling. The important emphasis would seem to lie on the fact that Herbert sees the Church as *a* means of salvation, and certainly not in any sense as the absolute one. But, by being *a* means, it does not imply that the Church may be seen as an alternative, that is, that it can be dispensed with in favour of another means. The position is not precisely defined, and, thereby, in Herbert's approach to the Authority of the Church there is nothing exclusive. The personal responsibility, in all its implication, and the sacramental ministry of the Church remain side by side, but with the emphasis, other than for the Sacraments, strongly devolving upon the personal spirituality. Yet, as Guardian and Administrator of the Sacraments the Church may not be ousted, nor circumvented, nor, in any sense, belittled. In the Sacramental sphere the Church rests supreme, however much its power may seem, or be, otherwise denied in favour of individual responsibility.

Moral and didactic in tone, as it is clearly meant to be, and is, *The Church-Porch,* the entry into *The Temple,* demands the duty owing to the Church, both in material contribution and in worship. Church and God are not to be separated:

> Restore to God his due in tithe and time . . .

With-holding of tithes will meet the punishment of sin:

> A tithe purloin'd the whole estate.

And absence from Church means self-deprivation of God, and of heaven:

> Sundaies observe: think when the bells do chime,
> 'Tis angels musick; therefore come not late.
> God then deals blessings: If a king did so,
> Who would not haste, nay give, to see the show?

Thus, the obligation becomes a much sought-after privilege. *The King,* no mere human king, is present in His Church. The common meals of the week merge into the sacred meals of the Church Services. Is there not an underlying note of dry irony in:

> Fast when thou wilt but then, 'tis gain not losse.

In this connection, private prayer is seen as an eccentricity, and in no wise to be taken as a substitution or excuse for absence from Church. The command of public worship is not to be ignored, and in this context Herbert even seems to under-estimate any other form of prayer. He is intent on pressing home his point of the importance of the Church within the personal life, the private routine.

> Though private prayer be a brave designe,
> Yet publick hath more promises, more love:
> . . .
> Leave thy six and seven;
> Pray with the most: for where most pray, is heaven.

The respect and awe felt for the Church, as the Temple of God, must continue into behaviour inside the Church. The worshipper should be bare-headed. He must kneel. He must forget his worldly high estate:

> All equall are within the churches gate.

The attraction of Church should not primarily be the interest or even the edification of the sermon. Here, Herbert emphatically diverges from the Protestant inclination towards the sermon as the focal point of the Service. Service is, first and foremost, worship, and so:

> Resort to sermons, but to prayers most:
> Praying's the end of preaching.

Nothing should keep, nor delay us from punctual attendance, and the spiritual behaviour in Church should be of the most rigorous self-recollection. The time in Church is a time of searching investigation into one's own innermost being, a focussing upon the heart, the seat of grace and the seat of sin:

> In time of service seal up both thine eies,
> And send them to thine heart; that spying sinne,
> They may weep out the stains by them did rise.

The condition in Church should be one of intense concentration on this work of worship and examination. All thoughts of the world outside must be shut out:

> Christ purg'd his temple; so must thou thy heart.

It is no light warning that follows. Bad behaviour in Church can lead, according to Herbert, to actual damnation. Such behaviour clearly for him is analogous to sin against the Holy Spirit, who inspires the Church as He did at the first Pentecost. How can we dare to misbehave in the presence of God?

> Look to thy actions well:
> For churches are either our heav'n or hell.

Only in purity of heart, of mind, of intention, should we dare to enter the Church. Taught and admonished on our responsibility to the occasion, then, and only then, we can, as it were, safely pass through the porch into the Temple within. Then, and only then, we can answer the invitation:

>   approach, and taste
> The churches mysticall repast.
>   (*Superliminare*)

The warning is couched in terms of dread:

> Avoid, Profanenesse; come not here:
> Nothing but holy, pure, and cleare,
> Or that which groneth to be so,
> May at his perill further go.

If the Church is taken seriously, then the Servants of the Church, the direct descendants of the Apostles, have their indubitable place within the scheme of Salvation. If the Church is not to be discounted in the fullness of her inspiration, then the Priest may not only not be discounted, but he must be afforded solemn respect. Again, in *The Church-Porch*, comes the stern command to treat the Priest seriously in his function as preacher, not to mock what he says, nor how he speaks. The respect is due to him as the direct emissary of God, and he bears within himself the power of condemnation. Herbert will not claim for the Priest the absolute power of granting or denying absolution, but turns the question back upon the person, that is, the man who ignores or mocks the Priest, is condemned, not by the act of the Priest in refusing absolution, but by his own action. In the last count, there can be no definite statement, nor explanation of Grace. God remains the One and final Arbiter:

> Judge not the preacher; for he is thy Judge:
> If thou mislike him, thou conceiv'st him not.
> God calleth preaching folly. Do not grudge
> To pick out treasures from an earthen pot.
>   The worst speak something good: if all want sense,
>   God takes a text, and preacheth patience.

And, the judgment will follow without doubt if we deride Church and Priest: for the Church is of God's making, not of man's:

> None shall in hell such bitter pangs endure,
> As those, who mock at Gods way of salvation.

Whether Herbert has the Holy Communion specifically in mind here, or whether he writes in image, or both, is not clear, but the purport is none the less uncompromising in its threat of the punishment which follows impure participation in the Mystery of the Church, in the willed denial of her means of healing and cleansing:

> Whom oil and balsames kill, what salve can cure?
> They drink with greedinesse a full damnation.

For Herbert, in this context, it appears clear that we are damned if we cling to the personal self-importance and deny the authenticity of the Church. The Law, for us, comes in the preaching of the Church, and as the Jews denied the vehicle of thunder, we, in our turn, deny the vehicle of foolishness. Jews and Christians are the children of God, each in their turn carefully guarded, each, in their turn, scorning the offer of love:

> The Jews refused thunder; and we, folly.
> Though God do hedge us in, yet who is holy?

Exodus 20, 18: And all the people saw the thunderings . . .
1 Cor. 1, 21: . . . it pleased God by the foolishness of preaching to save them that believe.
Or perhaps, the synthesis: *St. John 12, 29:* The people therefore, that stood by, and heard it, said that it thundered . . .

So, from the more generalised basis of *The Church-Porch*, Herbert's stand, where Church and Priest are concerned, becomes more pointed. Inevitably, as already suggested, it is a stand which might be, and has often been, seen as compromise, but, as always, if it is compromise, then it is positive compromise. The spiritual work only begins on this basis of doubt, and it is, in fact, forced onwards, strengthened by the dogmatic unassertiveness. This *willed* and positive undogmatic dogma becomes even more explicit, as should appear later, in the consequences of such an attitude to the Church.

In *The Priesthood*, Herbert sees the priesthood as:

> Blest Order, which in power dost so excell,
> That with th' one hand thou liftest to the sky,
> And with the other throwest down to hell
> In thy just censures . . .

Thus, at once, comes this inexplicable Mystery of *the power* of the Priest. There is, in fact, no *actual* categorical power. But, in the

Grace of the Mystery of the Spirit within him, the Priest has an indefinable yet none the less salutary effect on the sinner. The Priest is the wielder of the sword of Scripture. It is as if the power of the Word is imputed to him. And, this would appear one aspect of the whole question of imputed Righteousness. Filled with the Spirit, the Priesthood seems to Herbert far beyond his temerity to approach. But, immediately, he withdraws from any form of exaggerated respect, very much in the same way as he withdraws from the Mother of God and from the Saints. Worship and veneration are only for God, Priests are of clay, and only to be respected as the instruments of God:

> Their hands convey him, who conveys their hands.

There can be no question of Church absolute Authority in its own vested right, nor of a constant Spirit within the Church and within her Priests. All is at the single Will of God, unpredictable and inscrutable and in no way permanently delegated to any man. But, the Will of God still includes the Church and her Priests. The laying-on of hands persists and, hence, the Apostolic succession, although, somehow, at the same time, there is no continuity, the Grace must come to each seeker after Priesthood as a personal, and new dispensation from God alone. The apparent dichotomy is overcome by a total abandonment of self before God:

> Onely, since God doth often vessels make
> Of lowly matter for high uses meet,
>   I throw me at his feet.
>
> There will I lie, untill my Maker seek
> For some mean stuffe whereon to show his skill:
> Then is my time.

The suggestion of the duality of approach possible in *The Priesthood,* of a position which allows for the indisputable continuity of the Church on the one hand, but, equally disallows the categoric assurance either of the continuity, or of the spiritual resting within the certainty, goes even more emphatically further in *The Windows.*

Again comes the dreadful doubt, which is only relieved from despair by submission and trust. The Priest is ordained, but it seems as if his Ordination can not be regarded as final. The Grace of the Inspiration must be renewed and the time of such renewal is not within the power of the Priest himself. There is no assurance of continuity by any effort in himself. How can the Priest be the vehicle of God's *eternall word?* Is the Priest not human, frail, erratic?

> He is a brittle crazie glasse . . .

But, he is granted the favour, through Priesthood, of showing the Word. He is the passage of the light, the vehicle of the illumination. Yet, and this is the hasty qualification of the claim, only:

> through thy grace.

There is no promise of continuity within the Church. The richer the flow of immediate Grace, the more the Priest reflects the glory of his Lord. It is only for the Priest to submit to be the instrument of transmission. His part is thus relegated to negativity, yet to positive negativity, for he must wish to be the instrument to the highest capacity of his spirit:

> . . . then the light and glorie
> More rev'rend grows, & more doth win:
> Which else shows watrish, bleak, & thin.

If the life and light of infused Grace are present, then:

> Doctrine and life, colours and light, in one
> When they combine and mingle, bring
> A strong regard and aw . . .

But, if the light and life are lacking, then:

> speech alone
> Doth vanish like a flaring thing,
> And in the eare, not conscience ring.

This uncertainty of tenure is the accompaniment to the whole body of Herbert's spirituality and becomes more distinct at every fresh example of his theological stand. All depends on the descent of Grace, but when the Grace, which can in no wise be earned nor anticipated, is experienced as present, then the dread of *the sudden* is at least temporarily allayed, and the joy of the Priesthood bursts out in all its reality of glowing pride. The Priest takes on his fullest measure as the brilliant instrument of the Divine Light. Then, all Priests are one within the majesty of *Aaron:*

> Holinesse on the head,
> Light and perfections on the breast,
> Harmonious bells below, raising the dead
> To leade them unto life and rest:
> Thus are true Aarons drest.

It is the *harmonious* bells, which alone can lead to God; again and again, the serene one-ness with God, when the one-ness is experienced as present, is realised by Herbert in some image of harmony. Where harmony is, there is God. And, man, for once, at peace.

Again the acknowledgment of the total unworthiness in himself *as* himself: a confession of unworthiness which is not the common and proper acknowledgment, nor even the over-sensitive repentance of the intensely religious man, but, which is a confession of objective theology, of the anti-pole of the doctrine of Inner Grace. There is no road of worthiness, only the imputed Righteousness of Christ, and, thus, once again, into *the sudden*. For who can know from moment to moment whether or not he is in Grace?

>   Profanenesse in my head,
>   Defects and darknesse in my breast,
> A noise of passions ringing me for dead
>   Unto a place where is no rest:
>   Poore priest thus am I drest.

But, *the now* is, for this moment, fully certain. Unworthiness *is* worthiness, a worthiness which alone can surpass any worthiness to which any merit might attain. It is the eternal worthiness imputed to him, according to his measure, but radiating beyond him:

>   Onely another head,
>   I have, another heart and breast,
> Another musick, making live not dead,
>   Without whom I could have no rest:
>   In him I am well drest.

Dying into Christ, his whole creative being submitting and merging into Christ, he finds himself fitted for the Priesthood:

>   Christ is my onely head,
>   My alone onely heart and breast,
> My onely musick, striking me ev'n dead;
>   That to the old man I may rest,
>   And be in him new drest.

Having put on Christ, mind and spirit are cleansed and ready for work: his thoughts are holy, and his heart transparent to the Word: his teaching shaped and moulded by Christ. Christ possesses him, the living Christ in his receptive soul. Then, only then, the sweetly attuned Instrument of Christ, the bearer of Christ, he has the power and the right to summon the people to join with him in due adoration:

>   Come people; Aaron's drest.

Such a rare moment is indeed a moment of unspeakable delight, but is not the cost heavy? How is it possible to endure a joy entirely outside one's own volition or reason, a joy which would seem to depend entirely on the Divine Will, beyond one's comprehension, to which, in faith, one must submit or perish? And, yet, for Herbert, it is a joy. Of that, there can be little doubt in the resonance of the verse.

The joy, through Christ alone, can be extended into the Church, and, once again, the personal inadequacy becomes adequate in *Church-Musick*, through the heavenly inspiration of the music. It was of as Herbert, once more, was lifted out of himself, now into the music, unease replaced by ease:

>   ... when displeasure
>   Did through my bodie wound my minde,
>   You took me thence, and in your house of pleasure
>   A daintie lodging me assign'd.

He is assimilated into the music, whose cadence, in its rising and falling, strongly suggests the whisper of the presence of the Holy Spirit:

>   Now I in you without a bodie move,
>   Rising and falling with your wings:
>   We both together sweetly live and love,
>   Yet say sometimes, *God help poore Kings.*

God help poore Kings: a compassionate and proud co-incidence with Lear's promise to Cordelia, that they would sing alone in prison, and together perhaps spare a thought for the trials of the world. Without the music, he will not survive. This is his comfort. But, with the music, his way lies straight to heaven, in the breath of the Communion of Saints, the Church:

>   But if I travell in your companie,
>   You know the way to heavens doore.

To the Church, therefore, there has been given, somehow, some form of continuous inspiration, although Herbert denies any such absolute form. And he traces back his trust in the Institution of the Church to the Feast of Pentecost.

Whitsunday suggests what the Church once experienced. This would seem the crux: the Church *once* experienced it. And because of the historical emphasis, the Church can only be *a* way of salvation for Herbert, and not the assured way. The experience of Pentecost was, again, for him, the *sudden* vertical descent of the Spirit on that one particular occasion. The descent must ever be repeated to be a valid inspiration. The continuity may not be assumed.

The opening lines of *Whitsunday* are a prayer for the descent of the Spirit that he may even begin to express what is in his heart. The Spirit is the Dove, and the Spirit alone can descend and bring to life, actually hatch out, the latent life. Without the Gift of the Spirit, Herbert knows himself as some unhatched egg, doomed to death. Hatched by the Spirit, he too will be in the Spirit, and fly with Him:

> Listen sweet Dove unto my song,
> And spread thy golden wings in me;
> Hatching my tender heart so long,
> Till it get wing, and flie away with thee.

It seems as if the only human contribution to the experience is the offering of the *tender* heart, the submitting to God of a heart malleable and pliable: again, the willing instrument upon which the Spirit may play his music. Herbert longs for the fire which *once* descended upon the Apostles. Then the Church, indeed, was the Church, without any doubt:

> thou didst then
> Keep open house, richly attended,
> Feasting all comers by twelve chosen men.

At the Feast of Pentecost, in the first days of the Church, the abiding presence of the Spirit made heaven of earth: the stars would have sought service then on earth, and the sun was ashamed before the radiance of twelve suns. But, the time is over. Men destroyed the only men who had the consistent power of healing them. The First Church was *the pipes of gold,* through which could pour, unabatingly, the *cordiall water to our ground.* The time is over. Christ finds his place now only within. An objective assurance of salvation in the Church is no longer possible. The members of the Church forfeited the right. But, the hope remains in Christ:

> The same sweet God of love and light . .

God, alone, can bring back its fullness of continued grace to the Church, and for this Herbert prays:

> Restore this day, for thy great name,
> Unto his ancient and miraculous right.

Yet, still, somehow, the final word would seem to be not a despondence in this direction, where the Church is concerned, but a certainty that the Church, in a mysterious way, has this indisputable part in the scheme of salvation and Herbert, in all the tenderness of his heart, would wish all to participate.

The Jews must come to life again, for were they not the first from whom we took our life?

> Poore nation, whose sweet sap and juice
> Our cyens have purloin'd, and left you drie:
> Whose streams we got by the Apostles sluce,
> And use in baptisme, while ye pine and die . . .

Herbert prays ardently for the Jews, he can not endure their exclusion. The miracle may happen, as some pre-view of the Day of Judgment. An Angel may blow a trumpet, and the Church, in repentance, prostrate before Christ, imploring as Christ told us to implore, until He grants the request, and life, creative life of faith, will once again flow in the veins of His People:

> And by that crie of her deare Lord obtain,
>   That your sweet sap might come again!

Herbert's love of the Church, and his faith in the Institution of the Church, finds perhaps its most affectionate expression in *The Invitation*. He must share with others what he himself enjoys and knows to be true. He must search, as it were, the highways and bye-ways and bring all in to share in the Supper. This feast may not be for him alone. The Invitation is to *All*. *All* must come to a banquet which *is* God. This is a real feast. Let *All* repent of the wine which they have drunk in dissipation, and drink the wine which is the blood of Christ. *The Invitation* summons *All* to come: to come without fear. Such a glad summons is very near to the words of St. John Chrysostom read at Easter in all Orthodox Churches. Herbert's summons catches the same unearthly joy of the one instant when life really seems to transcend itself and touch Eternity. Let sin be afraid. Not man. *All* must come: The sinful, and the pleasure-seekers. What greater pleasure than here? *All* must come: The Lovers. What greater love than here? A love, which surpasses death. Herbert has opened to the uttermost. He has searched and called, and he will continue to search and call. Is not the Church the Temple of Christ?

> Lord I have invited all,
> And I shall
> Still invite, still call to thee:
> For it seems but just and right
> In my sight,
> Where is All, there All should be.

But, for Herbert, the Church was not an undefinable body. The Church was the Church of England. His adherence to the Church of England produced his worst poetry, aggressive and polemical, yet it may not be ignored. However bad the verse, it gives the clue to the devoted single-mindedness which lay at the root of his spiritual experience.

In *The Church Militant*, Herbert differentiates between the Churches, and sketches a somewhat unhappy picture of the journey of the Church from East to West, in direction analogous to the movement of the sun. When Sin arrived in Greece, apparently he was much encouraged by what he found there:

> But all was glorious cheating, brave deceit,
> Where some poore truths were shuffled for a bait
> To credit him, and to discredit those
> Who after him should braver truths disclose.

Rome, however, was far worse than Greece:

> Sinne being not able to extirpate quite
> The Churches here, bravely resolv'd one night
> To be a Church-man too, and wear a Mitre . . .
> . . .
> So now being Priest he plainly did professe
> To make a jest of Christs three offices . . .

The hypocrisy of Rome is exposed, in Sin, personified:

> He took fine vizards to conceal his crimes:
> From *Egypt* Anchorisme and retirednesse,
> Learning from *Greece*, from old *Rome* statelinesse . . .

Rome sat, and others came to her. Rome would not move:

> It did not fit his gravitie to *stirre*,
> Nor his long journey, nor his gout and furre.

The vituperation reaches its climax:

> And having conquer'd, did so strangely rule,
> That the whole world did seem but the Popes mule.
> As new and old *Rome* did one Empire twist;
> So both together are one Antichrist . . .

And, it is not surprising to see Rome then epitomised as the *Western Babylon*. However, England does not escape censure:

> Religion stands on tip-toe in our land,
> Readie to passe to the *American* strand.

Would the passing mean simply the passing on of the Church of England as a mission to America, where the Church would find safe lodging because of the poverty? This would indeed seem a strange logic of Providence, to permit a people to be submitted to forced impoverishment that it might be the safe custodian of the Church of England!

> Then shall Religion to *America* flee:
> They have their times of Gospel, ev'n as we.
> My God, thou dost prepare for them a way
> By carrying first their gold from them away:
> For gold and grace did never yet agree:
> Religion alwaies sides with povertie.

Yet, America, too, will not finally escape, and *The Church Militant* ends on the eschatological note of the journey completed, damnation suggested equally to all the Churches in their corruption:

> But as the Sunne still goes both west and east;
> So also did the Church by going west
> Still eastward go; because it drew more neare
> To time and place, where judgement shall appeare.

The particularisation of the Church of England, the love for her, and the grief felt in her inner unrest is brought out more fully in *Church-rents and schismes*. The Church of England is the rose. The sweet flower of Christ, red in the true blood of Christ. But, her throne of supremacy, her glory, has been viciously assailed from within, for it is a worm which has gnawed her. Piece by piece, she is being torn surreptitiously asunder, until now, almost imperceptibly, the destruction has been completed and:

> . . . Onely shreds of thee,
> And those all bitten, in thy chair I see.

Martyrdom was a strength, blood shed for Christ did not enfeeble, but blood, shed internally, kills:

> Your colour vaded, and calamities
>   Turned your ruddie into pale and bleak:
>   Your health and beautie both began to break.

And, her enemies were not slow to see the weakness of this sickness within:

> They rushed in, and cast them in the dirt
> Where Pagans tread.

Desolation fills Herbert in pity for the source and nourisher of his religion; there is hardly enough water throughout the continents of the world to suffice for the tears of compassion to flow from his two, inadequate eyes:

>   . . . since it is night,
> And much of Asia and Europe fast asleep,
> And ev'n all Africk; would at least I might
>   With these two poore ones lick up all the dew,
>   Which falls by night, and poure it out for you!

Compassion turns to pride in *The British Church*. Here, Herbert rejoices in his Mother, the one Church, in his estimation, of precise and balanced proportion. In dogma and ritual:

> Neither too mean, nor yet too gay,
>   Shows who is best.

Rome is discarded as insincere, false, seductive, and gaudy:

> Hath kiss'd so long her painted shrines,
> That ev'n her face by kissing shines,
>   For her reward.

As for the Protestant Church, *She in the valley,* she goes to the other extreme of over-modesty, and with super-conscious simplicity, she *nothing wears.* The Church of England, *dearest Mother,* wins the contest, serene she takes up her position between the two exaggerated opponents, and her *praise and glorie* is *the mean.* God has bestowed on the Church of England alone this double grace: she is firmly entrenched within the best of each of the two extremes. And, only to her, has God granted this unique position:

> Blessed be God, whose love it was
> To double-moat thee with his grace,
> And none but thee.

Herbert wrote, *Blessed be God,* and, thereby, he expressed his willing and glad submission to his Church, the Church of England. He opened himself fully, not merely as a formality, to all that membership of the Church of England implied, and, as a Priest of the Church of England, he took upon himself the whole weight of accepting the doctrine. *Blessed be God:* the unswerving acceptance in the divine institution of the Church of England. What, then, did such an acceptance involve? And with what consequences for Herbert in particular?

CHAPTER II

WORLD OF GRACE AND WORLD OF NATURE

The conflict of the Anglican position, or perhaps, more precisely, the professed contradiction, seems so integral a part of Herbert, as was indeed the solution of the balance already within the expressed suffering, that hardly any aspect in which he writes of spiritual experience is free from the double premise: world of grace—world of nature: continuity—renewal: way—reception.

At times, this double premise, of the Inner Grace which may grow within the measure of the personal progress as opposed to the imputed Righteousness, whence Grace, outside our volition, comes down upon us as a mighty force of the Absolute, only to be withdrawn, reveals itself in Herbert in a violent expression of suffering and outburst of incomprehension of the ordeal. At other times, the same experience finds its expression in serenity within the grief. Or, again, even of triumph. But, whatever else, the idiom of conflict may never be seen in any negative connotation, the *via media* is no compromise.

The Temple would seem to express the positive, living, day-to-day balance and resolution of a theology, which might seem inherently antithetical. Thus, in one sense, the avowed conflict is in itself the solution. Beyond the integration of the conflict, there lies no further solution. There is no question of an immanent answer to the doctrinal split between the Church of England and Rome. The solution is the active work in the endurance, and the denial of any passivity or sentimentality. There is no trace in *The Temple* of the hound of heaven, no chase ending in sensuous surrender. The image of conflict is not the preliminary to the next step, but it *is* the Faith, in the shape and form in which Herbert's Church has chosen to live it.

Out of the bulk of Herbert's poems, it is possible to choose a few where the consistent judgment theme, the dreaded question of the assurance of salvation, and, the consequences of such a question, is particularly explicitly expressed. Without the criterion of the Church on the one hand, and the criterion of Faith (the Elect) on the other, we become, on this level, inevitably, in some form, our own criterion. We are faced with judging the efficacy of our faith, both in this life and at death. A two-fold judgment accompanies us. Are we making progress now? How will we meet God at the Judgment? Sickness or weariness of mind, the *dry* times of prayer, unfruitfulness in every and any spiritual or creative field, even physical affliction, all take on the devilish temptation of despair, because we do not know their meaning. We have no criterion and are left tossing in the bewilderment. Are such assaults to be taken as signs of God's displeasure? As tokens of our sin? Of being out of Grace? Must we perish? Or is there still a way open to growing sanctification here, and salvation here-after?

The only immediately apparent bulwark to this despair would seem therefore the theology of redemption through Christ. The actual fact of the crucifixion, the actual fact of the Cross, held up between our sins and God.

i. *Redemption*

The World of Nature is separated from the World of Grace. But, even so, in Herbert there can be traced the consciousness of what may be seen as human potentiality towards redemption. There is no general redemption. The split is wide. But, yet, there comes the hint of the awareness of something of life, of goodness within the world of death and sin.

The growth of human depravation is outlined in *The World*. First the creation, by *Love*: then followed civil war: *Fortune*, autonomous human will, overcome by *Wisdome*, participation in the Truth. *Pleasure*, the decorated Church in Herbert's view, seducing the faithful, overcome by *laws*, the threatening Reformed Church. *Sin*, from within, destroying the whole structure stealthily, and *Grace* alone able to prune the vicious off-shoots of the Fall. And, finally, the vile combination and conspiring of Sin and Death totally to annihilate the whole dear building of Love. Who could withstand them? Only Christ, he alone can destroy Sin and Death in his Glory, and so, in the manifest Trinity of the Father, who built, in Love, and the Spirit, who inspired in Truth, and the Son, who redeemed in Glory, destruction has become creation:

> But *Love* and *Grace* took *Glorie* by the hand,
> And built a braver Palace then before.

Or, again, in *Vanitie* (I), once more there is the suggestion of immediate presence of eternal life within a world of fleeting death. Science reigns supreme in the immanent world. In his field of action, the Astronomer is swiftly expert in locating and identifying the stars; he watches them closely, even possessively. He can forecast their movements, when they will be fully visible, or more elusive:

> he sees their dances,
> And knoweth long before
> Both their full-ey'd aspects, and secret glances.

The expert and skilful Diver cleaves the waters of the sea, seeking out the hidden pearl, risking mortal danger, to plumb the secret depths; God has carefully buried the pearl to prevent his risking his life, and to safe-guard the stupid woman; and, yet, the diver finds the pearl, for her:

> Who with excessive pride
> Her own destruction and his danger wears.

As for the Scientist, he knows the innermost structure, the secrets of the anatomy in its elementary simplicity. He knows the bird in its nest before it has the feathers to cover its basic form. He knows the birds without the attractive plumage, but as they really are, before anyone else is admitted for an audience. The *callow principles* are his intellectual domain. For others, the skeletons are obscured, for him they are evident:

>   before
>   They appear trim and drest
> To ordinarie suitours at the doore.

All is man's empire of knowledge. And, yet, in one direction, at his highest scientific peak, man is still thwarted:

>   What hath not man sought out and found,
>   But his deare God? who yet his glorious law
>   Embosomes in us, mellowing the ground
>   With showres and frosts, with love & aw,
>   So that we need not say, Where's this command?

In his graciousness, God does not make it difficult for us to discern his greater empire, the whole empire of creation around us. The life of God surrounds us. Our dominion only reaches to death. This speaks of eternal life, and this message is always present:

>   Poore man, thou searchest round
>   To finde out *death,* but missest *life* at hand.

And, again, a more delicate and, somehow, loving hint that any spiritual effort of ours in this life must have an eternal value: Herbert sees the temporal death around him in *Vertue*: the day, however pleasant, however serene a union of earth and sky, must end with the dew-drops of night: the rose, red and inflamed with fever, speaks already in full flower of its innate wilting: and, as for Spring, the enclosure of fragrance, of delicacy, of delight in every form, its notes must also reach their last. What then remains:

>   Onely a sweet and vertuous soul,
>   Like season'd timber, never gives;
>   But though the whole world turn to coal,
>   Then chiefly lives.

ii. *Faith*

In this same context of the hint of the acceptable effort of man, working for his own redemption and not merely appearing some passive object torn between arbitrary irruptions and withdrawal of Grace, comes Herbert's assertion on the potency of *Faith*. Faith, might, perhaps, have even seemed to him a possible solution for the dilemma of salvation, as it had proved for the Protestants. But, as a solution, in itself, it did not satisfy him.

Herbert is deeply moved by the condescension of God, who justly angry at man's sin, yet himself provides man with the one weapon for renewed sovereignty:

> Lord, how couldst thou so much appease
> Thy wrath for sinne as, when mans sight was dimme,
> And could see little, to regard his ease,
> And bring by Faith all things to him?

Then comes the suggestion of the part of Faith in the Eucharist. He was hungry, but objectively there was no meal. So, the Roman theology of transubstantiation is flatly rejected. But, when, in faith, he believed the feast to be there, then, indeed it was, in all reality, in the mystery of the reception:

> I had it straight, and did as truly eat,
> As ever did a welcome guest.

This is followed by the further question of sanctification. He could not be assured of salvation, the healing power of Christ, through the mediation of the Church, which was no longer unquestionably his. But, by faith, he could grasp this same power of Christ, which, by faith, so entered into him, that he could still make his ascent of sanctification:

> That I can walk to heav'n well neare.

His sin, the load of debts weighing him down, which would cast him into prison, again, is, in faith, forgiven. Believing in the redeeming intercession of Christ, he believes that he owes nothing. And, because of his faith that he owes nothing, Christ does stand between him and God and:

> my creditor
> Beleeves so too, and lets me go.

Faith draws him up from the deepest hell to the highest glory: from Adam to Christ. There is nothing in the life of man which has not been pre-lived by Christ and therefore redeemed:

> If I go lower in the book,
> What can be lower then the common manger?
> Faith puts me there with him, who sweetly took
> Our flesh and frailtie, death and danger.

Christ has fulfilled all our weaknesses before they came to be. If we have Faith, there can be no inadequacy, because through Christ,

Grace brings the short-comings of nature to the requisite measure for salvation. The World of Grace and the World of Nature meet in Faith, which allows Grace, through Christ, to make up our defects. We, again, other than for the active Faith which we exercise, are passive:

> If blisse had lien in art or strength,
> None but the wise or strong had gained it:
> Where now by Faith all arms are of a length;
> One size doth all conditions fit.

> A peasant may beleeve as much
> As a great Clerk, and reach the highest stature.
> Thus dost thou make proud knowledge bend & crouch,
> While grace fills up uneven nature.

But, the question can not remain unasked. What is this Faith of which Herbert speaks with such faith? And, it becomes even distressingly apparent, within this context, that the Faith, however active it may seem in action, still, somehow, remains outside our human volition. The Faith, to have the Faith, is already within the disposal of the imputative power bestowed by the Father upon the Son; and on whom the imputation of Righteousness may fall, no-one can tell. The dilemma can only be solved, it would seem, in the rare moment of joy, when a man, as Herbert in this poem, simply knows that he has, at least temporarily, this undefinable Faith, which ensures salvation for him. Then, he experiences the condition of which Herbert now writes. Man, in himself, is dark. He is sinful. To the Son, alone, has been given the power to bestow his own light, in part, to enlighten man's darkness:

> When creatures had no reall light
> Inherent in them, thou didst make the sunne
> Impute a lustre, and allow them bright;
> And in this shew, what Christ hath done.

But, in this rare moment of assurance, the enshrouding darkness, the undergrowth blurring the vision, of a sudden disperses, and in the graceful presence of Faith, murky gloom transforms to glorious sky. And, still within this assured inner consciousness of being in Grace, comes the certainty of salvation to be. He will be among the elect unto the resurrection of life:

> What though my bodie runne to dust?
> Faith cleaves unto it, counting ev'ry grain
> With an exact and most particular trust,
> Reserving all for flesh again.

iii. *Grace*

It is not surprising, that, on such a premise of no-assurance, fear and despondency must more frequently replace the rare instances of inner certainty. Times of despondency prevail and of indecision. Any period of so-called idleness is particularly to be dreaded. (It is interesting how the identification of sin and idleness must have persisted, if we think of Keats's revolt against this concept of idleness as sinful impassivity.)

In *Businesse*, for example, Herbert sharply rebukes himself for lapsing from ceaseless repentance. If he has no *sighs or grones*, it were better for him that he had no *flesh and bones*. And, the reason for this demand is the Person of the Incarnate Son, who alone has the power to save him:

> But if yet thou idle be,
> Foolish soul, Who di'd for thee?

The soul should fear to cease to labour, knowing that if the Son had not assumed his body, if the Son had not died *most wretchedly*, then he would have been damned, with two deaths: the first death in life, and the second death in Judgment. If the Son had lived, he would have died. He should not dare to be idle, but seeing his Saviour's death as the discovery of precious mineral rock, he should repent, become fully conscious of his sin, and of his Saviour:

> Who in heart not ever kneels,
> Neither sinne nor Saviour feels.

Businesse allows for the effort of repentance, but other poems reveal far more strongly the inevitable terror of the arbitrary, inexplicable coming and withdrawing of Grace. Grace and Faith, without which nothing can be achieved, are neither constant, nor, in one sense, his. And, again and again, Herbert's poems betray this torment as he implores God for some security of tenure. It is as a prison, a circular tread-mill. Without salvation, we are damned. But what is the assurance? The Grace of our faith. Through the Grace of our faith, we are imputed righteous by the ransom of Christ crucified. But, how do we come by the Grace? By the faith. By the descent of the Grace outside our volition. But how, then, does the Grace descend? Through the imputation of Righteousness by the Cross of Christ crucified upon those of us who are in Grace. With the denial of the Church as the assurance of salvation to the faithful, all continuity and certainty has gone.

All depends on faith in the single person and, hence, the multiplicity of ramifications from the demand of such faith. It would have been a different matter, or, at least, spared much suffering, if the question of assurance had never been asked, nor answered. So, Herbert implores for any sign of continuity.

In *The Familie*, Herbert sees the heart as a household; and, as a household, it contains warring and discordant factions. Its members grow noisy and unruly. Where noise is, and multiplicity reigns, there can be no room for Grace. The mark of the Spirit of God is unity and peace. The Spirit must descend to prepare a seemly place for himself and Herbert begs him to do so:

> Turn out these wranglers, which defile thy seat:
> For where thou dwellest all is neat.

Where there is harmony, then of a surety the Spirit has put order into disorder. But, where the harmony is lacking, then the Spirit will not stay. Grace comes and goes:

> And where these are not found,
> Perhaps thou com'st sometimes, and for a day;
> But not to make a constant stay.

The point is that the house of the Spirit can only be prepared by the Spirit, and Herbert can merely pray the Spirit to come and make this preparation.

The Temper (II) shows the deepest suffering of this uncontrollable inconsistency. The joy, which Herbert recognises in *Faith*, so that he could be sure of his faith, has left him, as inevitably it must, if our capacity of love is interpreted as ruled by the arbitrary irruption of the Absolute, inexorably returning to itself. The few simple lines live as the monument to the inevitable suffering implicit in the professed allegiance to his Church:

> It cannot be.

The emphatic opening denial carries with it the indisputable reality of the fact. *It cannot be*: the identical words which men so often use when faced with a sudden death, some unexpected disaster, or grievous shock. It is the cry of incredulity at the actual possibility of any such inexplicable intrusion into the accepted order of serene and enjoyable life. And, Herbert's image of bewilderment is directed at the blow, not of mortality, but of mutability. Only an instant previously, the passing of time hardly discernible, he had been filled with a *mightie joy*. The joyous Grace of God had reigned within him in all its transcendent power. It was the joy not of the world which had seized and held him in its potency. This gracious joy had taken him, in his totality, fulfilling him as in *Faith*. The image of the sudden catastrophe is taken further into the suggested identification of God and Death. If God must enact Death with his dart, Herbert begs him to refrain from destroying the joyous Grace within him, and, thus, him. Can not God/Death turn his dart upon Sin? Destroy the sin, and thereby leave the living space for Grace which will give Herbert his life?

> Lord, if thou must needs use thy dart,
> Save that, and me; or sin for both destroy.

The incomprehensible puzzle lies in the contradiction. The material World of Nature, which God has created, remains static and predictable. It remains consistent to its created structure, its shape and form, and intended purpose in the creation:

> The grosser world stands to thy word and art . . .

But, the impact of the World of Grace upon Man, the work of the Spirit of God, is wholly, from the human point of view, inconsistent. It would even seem that God, himself, destroys what he constructs. Over and over again he would seem to send forth his Spirit, only to re-call the breath of Grace, and to begin again. There can be no comprehension on Man's part of Grace, no possibility of prognostication of its coming or of its going. Man, in the face of Grace, is faced with only the consistency of inconsistency. The hope of faith in *Faith* is shown to be fallacious. The joy of the faith is within the same relentless movement of unpredictable erection and destruction as a besieged city:

> But thy diviner world of grace
> Thou suddenly dost raise and race,
> And ev'ry day a new Creatour art.

Herbert implores for some consistent continuity. If Man can not focus the multiplicity of his spiritual and intellectual energy upon the One God, then he is lost within the dissipation of his faculties. Only in worship of the King, Man can be certain of his own integrity. But, if the throne is absent, where is he to look? He longs for the indication of some possibility to concentrate his love within himself upon God whose presence he need not doubt. The one evidence at his disposal for the presence of Grace, that is of God, is the sudden light of joy within himself to tell him so. He yearns for other evidence:

> O fix thy chair of grace, that all my powers
>   May also fix their reverence:
>   For when thou dost depart from hence,
> They grow unruly, and sit in thy bowers.

Herbert begs God, as it were, by force to give Man the unity which he so desires; if God would even seem to be dividing and putting him to rout, in effect the result would be the same, for it would still mean the presence of God, and, thence, the unity. All apparent change is thus irrelevant:

>   Scatter, or binde them all to bend to thee:
>   Though elements change, and heaven move . . .

Nothing else matters, provided that the Grace remains:

>   Let not thy higher Court remove . . .

It is a higher Court, this glory of God in the heart of man. It comes directly from on high, vertically entering into his soul, and it is, in every sense, the supreme Court. All fades into insignificance if only God remains within him, the King of Glory, the bestower of Grace, the source of sanctification. All else may remove, every outside influence be transitory and mutable, if only, *within* him, God remains immutable:

>   But keep a standing Majestie in me.

The Temper (II) epitomises the condition of the faithful soul in, what may sometimes seem, the theological impasse. *The Glimpse* is very close in content to *The Temper* (II).

The Glimpse suggests the identical condition of deserted surprise. What had just been, is suddenly no longer there. Grace is now not in the image of joy, but of delight:

>   Whither away delight?

Delight had only been present, this very instant. Where would it have gone? And, even more, why should it have gone?

>   Thou cam'st but now; wilt thou so soon depart,
>   And give me up to night?

God is the true light. The Spirit inspires and enlightens. Without the presence of the Spirit, all is darkness; and, conversely, if there is spiritual darkness, then there would seem no reason but the absence of the Spirit. The Spirit, alone, is the Comforter; there is rest only in the Spirit. And, the Spirit, again, is tormentingly inconsistent:

> For many weeks of lingring pain and smart
> But one half houre of comfort to my heart?

It is ever the incomprehensibility of the difference between the World of Grace and the World of Nature which constitutes the problem. Grace should move in harmony with nature, and, thus, be more foreseeable. Winds, waves, flowers, vary in longevity, but are consistent to themselves. The rapidity of the coming and going of wind and wave is of as little consequence as the greater durability of flowers. But, the duration of the presence of Grace is not only unpredictable, but of graver consequence:

> Thy short abode and stay
> Feeds not, but addes to the desire of meat.

The fleeting presence of Grace increases the yearning for the constant presence. Grace is the Spirit, and the flame of the Spirit sets the heart afire with longing for the Spirit even as quick-lime generates more inward heat by the application of water. The choice of quick-lime for the image would appear significant, for lime is deadly. The heat within the lime kills. It is as if Herbert sees man parched and burned up in the paradox of the absence of the fire of the Spirit. The fire refreshes, its absence burns. *Hope* is for Herbert most frequently a word of misleading connotation. Hope is a delusion, and in the deluding hope of a constant presence, he endures the absence of the Spirit. His heart:

> Pickt here and there a crumme, and would not die . . .

Wherever he can, he tries to find some particle of food for his hope, as a bird, perhaps, picking at a crumb here and there, as a man, perhaps, tasting to his full capacity the Grace of the Eucharistic bread, the crumb which he sees as his portion of the Promise. Hope refuses to accept that the Spirit would ever only stay temporarily, and persists, in the face of fear, to dare to think that Man can provide, of his own dexterity, the means of retaining the Spirit:

> But constant to his part,
> When as my fears foretold this, did replie,
> A slender thread a gentle guest will tie.

But, even if the hope of a constant stay is a delusion, there remains a hope which is no delusion. This is the hope of accepting the departure of the Spirit, and yet praying incessantly for the return. We were told to knock and knock again:

> Yet if the heart that wept
> Must let thee go, return when it doth knock.

Our treasure is in heaven, and the fullness of the Spirit reigns only in glory in heaven. Our reward may only be after death. But, even so, the prayer persists, and must persist, that out of this vast treasure of Grace, some fragments may come to us here and now, without damaging or depleting the fullness. (St. Matthew 15, 27: *and she said, Truth, Lord: yet the dogs eat of the crumbs which fall from their masters' table*.) Does not this suggest that Herbert left more space for the participation in the Mystery of the Whole, here and now, than would always appear evident? And, even more, if the treasure is untouched in its fullness does it not also suggest that his denial of the Saints in heaven, as will be seen in *To All Angels and Saints*, is not quite as categorical as it appears? For the fullness of the prerogative of Christ still remains untouched, whatever the apparent drain:

> Although thy heap be kept
> For future times, the droppings of the stock
> May oft break forth, and never break the lock.

The Spirit descends, from out of the fullness, into Man. And, Herbert makes his last plea. If he is to work positively, and creatively, if he is meant still to work, then, surely, he must be granted the condition for work. He can, as it were, just manage to keep going, provided that the delay in the return of the Spirit is not excessively prolonged:

> If I have more to spinne,
> The wheel shall go, so that thy stay be short.

The image of the spinning, of the repetitive turning of the wheel in anticipation of the renewal of strength, suggests all the force of the monotony of the day-to-day work, the conscientious fabric of life, in the half-gloom awaiting the full light. But, this apparently uninteresting spun-out cloth is his work, and for his work, again, Herbert claims the necessity of peace and harmony. Without the serenity he can not even do this work, and without the serenity, the Spirit will not re-enter. Grief and Sin are the intruders, when

Grace is absent. They are the noise, who exclude Grace. But, Grief and Sin are members of the family, and, thereby, somehow, included in him, redeemed in his powers by Grace. His dispersed faculties, at whose mercy he now is, would instantly gather out of the multiplicity into the one, if the Spirit once again inspired him, and, being one, from mocking they would turn to worship of the King:

> O make me not their sport,
> Who by thy coming may be made a court!

The heavenly stock of God, with which he must work, can lie barren and useless. In *Grace,* Herbert is, within the World of Nature, totally severed from the World of Grace. Of his own, he has no autonomous capacity for growing and multiplying. And there is no other driving power of cultivation but the refreshing rain from the World of Grace, from above:

> My stock lies dead, and no increase
> Doth my dull husbandrie improve:
> O let thy graces without cease
> Drop from above!

Again, the *without cease.* It is the unpredictable inconsistency wherein lies the torment. The World of Nature, where Man is concerned, can not work in continual darkness. The light of Grace, through the beams of the sun, must bring its radiant warmth down, from above, or leave Man to the dread darkness of the imprisonment of sin:

> If still the sunne should hide his face,
> Thy house would but a dungeon prove,
> Thy works nights captives: O let grace
> Drop from above!

Once again, comes the contrast between the continuity of the working of the created natural world, and the discontinuity of the Spirit in relation to Man. The dew drops regularly, every morning. Can the dew really be intended to out-rival and out-run the refreshment of the Spirit, which can not be summoned on demand?

> The dew doth ev'ry morning fall;
> And shall the dew out-strip thy Dove?
> The dew, for which grasse cannot call,
> Drop from above.

Death and Life confront each other. Death burrows as a mole from beneath, gnawing away Man's life with the removal of each layer of protective soil, as a worm may gnaw away the root of a flower. The only possible anti-dote to this systematic destruction is in the re-action of the soul, made potent by Grace, dropping from above, and working within. Grace and Sin would then confront each other. Sin, preparing for Death, is ever *hammering my heart;* Sin is forging the indestructible armour of steel, which will allow no relieving chink through which Grace/Love might yet creep. It is *a hardnesse, void of love.* Only God can save the situation. If only God would send the Grace from above, then Grace would thwart Sin, un-do the hardness, make the heart tender and attainable to Love, and give space to life within itself:

> Let suppling grace, to crosse his art,
>   Drop from above.

Yet, it is a weary struggle, from moment to moment, hour to hour. It is a struggle where frequently there seems no response, and where always there can be no evidence of victory even in the future. In such a climax of weariness, Herbert makes the entreaty. Why can not God at least remove him from this scarred battleground? If God will not send a re-inforcement of Grace from above, will He not in mercy take him there, where he need no longer plead? All is in the disposal of the Almighty, and if the solution is not obvious here, there is no doubt of the solution in Eternity:

> O come! for thou dost know the way:
> Or if to me thou wilt not move,
> Remove me, where I need not say,
>   *Drop from above.*
>
> Bright spark, shot from a brighter place,
>   Where beams surround my Saviours face,
>   Canst thou be any where
>   So well as there?

So, in *The Starre,* the sense of wearied defeat in *Grace* is transformed into eager anticipation. It is the same essential condition of the alienation of Man, in the World of Nature, from the World of Grace, but the longing for death as the outcome of the final despair, with only the hint of death as the beginning, the solution, is here fully translated into a positive longing of fulfilment and life. There is no quarrel. Herbert gives the Star/Grace the freedom to come, if it so wishes. He does not implore its presence. But, if the Star is willing, then he invites it to take up an unworthy dwelling in his heart, and, thereby, *make it better*. The double property of the Spirit, fire and light, purging and illuminating, is the work of the Star if it condescends to enter his heart. And the third property of the Spirit is also the Star's, for after the purging and illumination comes the possibility of awakening to the life of the Spirit, the reciprocal animation:

> Touch it with thy celestiall quicknesse,
>   That it may hang and move
>   After thy love.

Thus animated by the three-fold properties of the Spirit, the soul can take its flight to heaven. The position is reversed and fulfilled. Where the prayer had been for the constancy of God's *Standing Majestie* (*The Temper* (II)), now, through the Grace of the Spirit, he envisages his place, within the radius of worshippers around the throne of his Saviour. That he too, as a star, may glitter, and join in the celestial dance of adoration, twisting, turning, forwards, backwards, before the Son. Death is not the final despair of defeat in the awareness of the elusiveness of Grace, but it is the victory of union. Barren and unproductive in the World of Nature, by Grace, Herbert claims that he will return *home,* bearing the harvest of fruit, of which he had not even been aware. Barren and fertile, in the World of Grace, are one. Heaven is the hive, and the bees, who have toiled, if they return to the hive, must return with honey, or they would not return. The hive is light, and water, which need not drop down. And does not God rejoice in the one sinner who repents?

> Sure thou wilt joy, by gaining me
> To flie home like a laden bee
>   Unto that hive of beams
>   And garland-streams.

However, whether Herbert sees death as the only yet feared alternative, or whether he greets it as a friend; whether he sees his spiritual sterility as a sin, or as a potential fertility, the fact remains unaltered. There are two worlds which can not essentially be one. God and Man remain divided, except in the unexpected and involuntary, on the part of Man, irruption of Grace, or in the dream of union in death.

In *A Parodie,* Herbert suggests yet another possibility to avoid the torment of absence. He wonders if perhaps the whole problem rests on a question of appearance of absence due to a temporary aloofness, and whether, in fact, Grace may not really remain constant within him, although sometimes in less evident a form. It is the *It cannot be* of *The Temper* (II) taken now out of the realm of shocked surprise, of acceptance of the inevitable departure of Grace, into the realm where it is possible to see the departure only as an *appearance* of departure. How can Grace have departed in reality when the relationship with Grace is so intimately related? Without Grace, man is nothing:

>   Souls joy, when thou art gone,
>   And I alone,
>   Which cannot be,
>   Because thou dost abide with me,
>   And I depend on thee . . .

Herbert now insists that the light, the joy, can not really go. The *effect* is precisely of their going. There is the weight of dark depression, there is the terror, and the blackness. But, the cause is only *thy eclipsed light*. The discontinuity is merely the obscuring of the continuity. It seems that, somehow, God withdraws the evident presence of Grace, which yet persists, and thereby, by the apparent removal, encourages Sin to grow bold. Sin is deluded into thinking that Grace is really absent and behaves accordingly. In the seeming absence, Sin beats and raves, misled into the false assumption that Grace has gone, and the soul is lost and bereft. But only God knows what life remains for the soul even in such an erroneous assault. The doubt of Sin's assertiveness besets as a reality. The warmth of Grace is no longer Herbert's, he is cold, sterile, uncreative, precisely in the identical condition as of being actually deserted by Grace. And, yet, in the throes of the manifest agony:

>   Thou com'st and dost relieve.

The coming is made more possible, because it is only a coming into his awareness. There has, in fact, been no abandonment.

A Parodie would seem an isolated sustained effort at a convincing rejection of the premise of the two worlds. But, still, it remains unconvincing. It is an uneasy explanation in as much as such an explanation can hardly be considered as theologically sound. Does the obscuring, for example, come from God? Or from the side of the soul? If from God, for what reason, and on what Scriptural evidence? It would seem that *A Parodie* offers a solution which is by way of a personal flight of fancy and can hardly be acceptable.

The Search, in direct contradiction to *A Parodie,* and considerably more forcefully convincing, again begins with the desolation of abandonment, but, this time, even more poignantly. The loss of Grace is now personified into *My Lord, my Love*:

>   My searches are my daily bread;
>   Yet never prove.

The *daily bread* immediately brings the suffering into the field of salvation, for as daily bread it is the gift of the Lord in his own prayer, but, so too, the reference to the bread may be a hint, in the context of *search,* to the acceptance of the doctrine of non-assertion in the objective physical reality of the Body of Christ in the Eucharist. In prostration of grief and adoration, Herbert seeks for an assurance of the presence of Grace. He is now seeking not as much for the actual presence, as for the assurance that the presence is real and objective, not an appearance of absence or presence. But, neither the World of Nature, nor the World of Grace can give him the reassuring answer which he demands. As far as he is concerned, he can not be given the certainty of continuity as a comprehensible reality. Again, he is faced with the two worlds, both constant and complete within themselves, while he alone is distraught. Grass burgeons, and stars glitter. World of Nature and World of Grace both know the clue to assured serenity, *while poore I pine.* He tries every means within his power to find the seat of Grace. First a quiet sigh of grief, and then the deeper groan of active penitence, for it was *tun'd,* but the result remains the same. A strange explanation enters his mind, of another new world, where God has taken up his dwelling, leaving the old, desolate in sin. But, this he discards. The question bursts out anew. He knows God is somewhere, the light is there, it can only be eclipsed (as in *A Parodie,* but outside himself), but, where? And why?

>   Where is my God? what hidden place
>   Conceals thee still?
>   What covert dare eclipse thy face?
>   Is it thy will?

If it is the will of God to withstand him, then he is lost. Anything else he can and will break through to reach his God. Brass, steel, mountains, whatever encloses God he will surmount (Herbert can not resist the same pun on *will* as Shakespeare's Mark

Antony in the funeral oration!). But, God's will is a fortification which can not be circumvented in thought or physical assault or any art or cunning. If the distance is God's will, then the distance is further than anything that man can conceive, and as incapable of meeting as East and West, the Poles, parallels. And his grief emulates in proportion the distance from which God separates himself from him. With an echo of Psalm 126 anticipated, Herbert pleads:

> O take these barres, these lengths away;
>   Turn, and restore me . . .

He implores that God, in his Almighty power, ceases to be his contrary:

> Be not Almightie, let me say,
>   Against, but for me.

And when God turns, even as the fortunes of Sion, his whole life will be reversed. The distance will become so much a no-distance that not the finest blade could sever their unity. Conflict would indeed be resolved as the lack of distance takes on the image of the dividing sword:

> When thou dost turn, and wilt be neare;
>   What edge so keen,
> What point so piercing can appeare
>   To come between?

The triumph is complete. Even as God's distance surpasses any distance conceivable by man, so his nearness equally surpasses any conceivable nearness:

> For as thy absence doth excell
>   All distance known:
> So doth thy nearenesse bear the bell,
>   Making two one.

In the common phrase, *bear the bell,* the winning of the prize, could there again be the hint of the Eucharistic presence? If the search at the opening of the poem were also the search within the Eucharistic bread, could the discovery also be within the Eucharistic feast, at the ringing of the Communion bell?

Making two one.

But this is the merest of slight suggestions, with no palpable evidence whatsoever.

iv. *Imputation of Righteousness*

It seems, then, that we, with Herbert, have reached the final point in the exploration of the spiritual journey which began at the premise of the two worlds: the World of Nature, which we know, constant and somehow peacefully directly connected with God, and the World of Grace, which we do not know, in which God holds court. Man belongs to neither and to both. He is assured of nothing, either now or for the future. He only experiences the presence of God, the World of Grace, as the rare invasion of joy, which inevitably leaves him sterile and forsaken. Any effort to find out where the Grace goes, how it comes, and why it comes or goes, is beyond his understanding. In himself, therefore, man can have no assurance whatsoever of the possibility of sanctification while he lives, nor of the possibility of salvation when he dies. The assurance is not in the Church. Thus, only one assurance remains, as a theological possibility, and that is imputed Righteousness. The assurance can only be in the ransom paid by Christ for our sins, so that, without any sanctifying virtue, as such, in ourselves, we may, in the first place, live, and, in the second place, die, holding his Cross as our justification.

> Having been tenant long to a rich Lord,
> Not thriving, I resolved to be bold,
> And make a suit unto him, to afford
> A new small-rented lease, and cancel th' old.
>   (*Redemption*)

The Old Law, the Old Church, his own early life, all seem fruitless. A new stage must be made, and the only direct way is through redemption, Christ, the Saviour, must be sought out and petitioned. But, Christ was not aloof in heaven, he was in fact within the very world which he had long ago *dearly bought*. The distance between Man and God had been bridged by the Son of God. He did not wait in heaven for his subjects to bring their petitions to him, as Rome sat, but he had come, himself, *to take possession*. The suitor returned, down to his own world, and with his own worldly standards, he sought his Lord where his Lord should reasonably be found:

> and knowing his great birth,
> Sought him accordingly in great resorts;
> In cities, theatres, gardens, parks, and courts . . .

But, the Lord of the world was not in the world. How could he be needed or recognised by those who valued their possessions in the world? It took some time, but:

> At length I heard a ragged noise and mirth
> Of theeves and murderers . . .

The scoundrels were making merry, shouting and laughing: a tavern scene, an Elizabethan secret lair of rogues and vagabonds with their false patches, self-inflicted wounds, and hooks for pilferings. And, in the midst, as one with the carousing motley crowd of outcasts, the respectable petitioner for a new lease, finds his landlord: *there I him espied*. There was no mistaking him. There is no question of who the One is among the many. It can only be He, isolated in majestic glory, unnoticed by the merry-makers, yet with them in the Passion of his redeeming action. Their laughter was his Agony. They could not know that as He sat with them, He died for them, paying for their life with drop after drop of his blood. But, He knew. He also saw the one petitioner amidst the crowd and recognised him, and knew his necessity as He had known each single necessity in His ministry on earth. He did not waste a second. The single need was His Hour:

> Who straight, *Your suit is granted,* said, & died.

This is the only steadfast safety-line of continued assurance. Only in the knowledge of the Cross, is it possible to have any certainty for daily survival.

The Altar, the table of sacrifice, makes very clear Herbert's insistence on the meeting-point of Man with God, within the Sacrifice.

The Altar would seem the actual Altar erected in the Church for the Priest to celebrate the sacrifice of the Eucharist, and at the same time it is the Altar of the inner sacrifice of repentance. The real stone of the Altar is reflected in the hardness of the heart. The *broken Altar* of repentance is fashioned by the heart, and held together by a cement watered with tears. And, each particular part of the inner Altar is directly contrived by God himself:

> No workmans tool hath touch'd the same.

Once again, therefore, comes the conviction of the impossibility of any inner spiritual motion which is not moved into activity by God (Grace) himself:

> A Heart alone
> Is such a stone,
> As nothing but
> Thy pow'r doth cut.

And, inspired by Grace, the sinful hardness of the heart can join in the worship enacted on the actual Altar, and, even more, find a substitute in the objective worship of the celebration on the actual Altar for any deficiency in itself:

> That, if I chance to hold my peace,
> These stones to praise thee may not cease.

This, however, is only possible because of the first and all-powerful Sacrifice of Christ. The worship of the sacrifice offered on the Altar would be entirely worthless if it were not imputed value by *the* Sacrifice. The sanctity lies only in the Mystery of the repeated efficacy of the redeeming Sacrifice:

> O let thy blessed SACRIFICE be mine,
> And sanctifie this ALTAR to be thine.

Church-lock and key has a similar theme to *The Altar* in as far as the distance from God, through sin, is again suggested as not of Man's own volition but of God's: that is, once more, the vexed problem of Grace. Without the in-flow of Grace, it is not possible to overcome the condition of sin. But, the further step is now taken. In contradiction to the apparent with-holding of God's Will to inspire Man with the Grace of repentance, Herbert presents the crucified Christ, whom God can not deny. The imagery in the poem is precise and exacting in evoking the experience of the mutual inter-acting relationship.

Herbert knows that it is his sin which prevents God from hearing him:

> which locks thine eares,
> And bindes thy hands...

It is his sin which cries out more loudly than his pleading, and drowns his tears, thus suppressing his own efforts at repentance.

There is also the possibility that his demands are not strong enough:

> Or else the chilnesse of my faint demands.

But the weakness is seen as coldness, a *chilnesse,* and therefore immediately suggesting that this weakness is brought about by lack of the warmth of the fire of the Spirit, of Grace.

This suggestion is taken further in the lines that follow. Cold hands, in the first instant, while they are still very cold, suffer from the heat of the fire, and yet continue to build it up in order to diffuse the warmth and over-come the pain. Thus, it is not in any fault of his intention which causes his pleading to be unanswered. He may be cold (sinful) but not because he denies the fire (Grace). It can only be in God's refusal to hear him:

> Yet heare, O God, onely for his blouds sake
>   Which pleads for me . . .

The water of his own tears, which was drowned by the mightier waters of the absence of Grace, and the coldness of sin, where the fire of Grace was lacking, now is transformed in redemption to blood instead of water, and blood which is warm, flowing from the Redeemer's side. The hardness of the sins, which would have been the lock for exclusion, now become the key for entry, washed by this flow of interceding blood. Herbert and God together are powerless before this transference of Grace, made more effective *because* of Herbert's sins, not in spite of them:

> For though sinnes plead too, yet like stones they make
> His blouds sweet current much more loud to be.

Ephes. 4.30 follows the same trend of thought, but with some difference. Here Herbert is concerned, not with God who withholds Grace from him, but God, Love, grieved at his sin. Herbert, in his sinfulness, feels the pain of the Holy Spirit at his rebellious and perverse behaviour, when he is *sowre*. And, he is deeply touched at the consciousness that God should care for such a worm, as he, himself, would carelessly crush. He knows that, somehow, only in weeping, he can gain eternal life for himself. The lasting joy lies within the sorrow of the world:

> Weep foolish heart,
> And weeping live . . .

Where there is no repentance, there must be death, and death has no connection with tears, the sign of repentance:

> For death is drie as dust.

Drie as dust: a warning of the dust to which we return in death but which will resurrect to life, if not for the sin which may not be forgiven. The prayer is to die, if death must be, into the blackness of night, but with the hope of the reviving forgiveness of the Spirit:

> Yet if ye part,
> End as the night, whose sable hue
> Your sinnes expresse; melt into dew.

The soul must deny the seeming joys of the world, the sins are God's grief. The music must be tuned only to songs of repentance. Surely his heart, his bowels of compassion, can not be so dried up by sin as to be even less impressionable than the hardest stone?

> Marbles can weep; and surely strings
> More bowels have, then such hard things.

So, Herbert decrees ceaseless repentance to himself. And, in so doing, forthwith denies its validity in itself and presents the one incontrovertible alternative. Is it not for him to persevere unendingly in spite of his impurity, *I am no Crystall*, in continued repentance, when there exists *a cleare spring*, which never ceases to flow on his behalf? But, what is more, Man, that he is, how can he even guarantee that he can sustain this continued repentance? Suppose, his *flesh would fail*? Suppose his worthlessness overcame his effort and stopped the flow, outmatching his tears? Then, still he can demand the greater forgiveness, not in his own right:

> Lord, pardon, for thy Sonne makes good
> My want of tears with store of bloud.

The clear spring is unfailing, for it is Christ's blood.
Conscience: the connotation of conscience for Herbert would seem primarily not the derived meaning of reasonable awareness in the sphere of morality, but more simply the rational worldly vigilance, which may impede the immediate spurt forward of a spiritual or creative urge. Hence, conscience, in this context, would seem the spirit-less intruder into the peaceful energy of his focussed

mind. Conscience distracts, and makes a quibbling noise which upsets his normal power of judgment:

>By listning to thy chatting fears
>I have both lost mine eyes and eares.

He must have uninterrupted silence in order that he can gather himself into the stillness of unity, to bring the balanced synthesis into his separate or antithetical threads of thought:

>My thoughts must work, but like a noiselesse sphere;
>Harmonious peace must rock them all the day:
>No room for pratlers there.

How, then, can this intrusion of the materialistic, sub-spiritual world of ratiocination and busy speculation be withstood? How can he defend himself from his meddling conscious self? The answer can only be, again, in the one assurance to which he can hold. He claims proudly, but the pride is not in himself:

>If thou persistest, I will tell thee,
>That I have physick to expell thee.

The false values of the world, the noise, not of the Spirit, could have filled him to the exclusion of the Spirit. Spirit, the essential *dynamis* of the harmony of creation, linked to the World of Grace, might yet not find room in him because of the discordant elements of *Conscience*, whose origin is the rational faculty, linked to the World of Nature. World of Grace and World of Nature confront each other in him. He, in himself, is powerless to come to the aid of Grace. But, he has his Champion, who is all-victorious. He holds the prescription for the only medicine: *My Saviours bloud*. One drop from the Eucharistic chalice, and his soul is cleansed within him. The World of Nature is routed, dumbfounded:

>No, not a tooth or nail to scratch,
>And at my actions carp, or catch.

Moreover, Herbert now pushes the war into the enemy's camp. The World of Nature has been put to flight by the medicine which Herbert has drunk and with which he has been purged. Yet, he can go further. The self-same medicine, which gave him health, can turn to destroy the world. Did not Christ come to save, but did he not also bring a sword? The Cross of blood is the medicine to heal and the only weapon which can be turned by the Spirit against the Flesh:

> The bloudie crosse of my deare Lord
> Is both my physick and my sword.

Thus, the way of sanctification is, once more, not Herbert's way in his own right of growth, but, only in the constant right of the Sacrifice made for him.

In *Good Friday*, Herbert actually addresses the Person of the Crucified Christ, on whom alone he can rely, in whom alone he sees his assurance of overcoming sin, through him alone.

Christ is Herbert's *chief good*, the greatest source of all benefit, which is measureless in Grace, and in suffering. The favour to Man and the agony endured would seem related to each other in the context of redemption, nearly a commercial transaction, *My chief good* continues into:

> How shall I measure out thy bloud?
> How shall I count what thee befell,
>   And each grief tell?

Herbert seeks to find a comprehensible measure for the suffering of Christ, but, even in image, this would not seem possible. Enemies, stars, leaves, fruits, none can compare with the One Sacrifice. Dedication alone can answer such Ransom. Every hour of his life, Herbert prays, may enclose within itself one pain, one agony that Christ suffered, so that his whole being may be permeated and made radiant in the glory of the One Sun:

> Then let each houre
> Of my whole life one grief devoure;
> That thy distresse through all may runne,
>   And be my sunne.

His nourishment is Christ. And, as every minute of the day is synonymous with a sin, he also sees it as his sins experiencing, or even animating the pains, and, in the experience, knowing that these pains of Christ are their healing, or, as in *Conscience,* their *physick.* If a beast, which has no reason, can instinctively know what will heal him, so can his brutish sins recognise the remedy of Christ's pain:

> Or rather let
> My severall sinnes their sorrows get;
> That as each beast his cure doth know,
>   Each sinne may so.

Now, comes a very fine point of transference. Whereas, otherwise, Herbert has pleaded for the direct in-coming of Grace, on this occasion, he opens his heart to the redeeming Christ. If the crucifixion of Christ, if His saving blood, drop by drop, will write His history in Herbert's heart, then the imputation, from *outside*, in effect becomes the Grace *inside*, by means of the agony of Christ. The battle-ground of the heart is there: Sin and Grace unable to live together. Sin jostling out Grace by its vile and noisy presence. But, in his heart, there is Herbert's own ink (his own blood), and if once Christ writes His crucifixion with Herbert's blood, in Herbert's heart, imputation will turn to Grace:

> Since bloud is fittest, Lord, to write
> Thy sorrows in, and bloudie fight;
> My heart hath store, write there, where in
> One box doth lie both ink and sinne . . .

And where Grace is victorious, Sin is banished. Sin can not withstand the immediate presence of the suffering Ransom:

> That when sinne spies so many foes,
> Thy whips, thy nails, thy wounds, thy woes,
> All come to lodge there, sinne may say,
> *No room for me,* and flie away.

Yet, however much Herbert may try to bend imputation of Righteousness into Inner Grace, which can remain constant, and grow, Grace begetting grace for Grace, he does not achieve the identification fully and incontrovertibly. And, it may well be, that he would not have wished to do so. The solution must remain open, the open-ness for his Church, being the solution. The doubt of the assured stability of Grace remains. The plea continues, the same plea in effect as for *standing Majestie*:

> Sinne being gone, oh fill the place,
> And keep possession with thy grace . . .

There is no certainty of anything but the inevitable empty darkness to follow the immediate joy of presence:

> Lest sinne take courage and return,
> And all the writings blot or burn.

Blot or burn: not only an erasing action, but a razing action, the plunder and looting of a besieged city captured by a merciless foe.

In one way, for Herbert, Sin/Evil seems to be something *outside* himself, even as Grace is, and therefore so difficult to integrate into good. Sin/Evil seems the direct counterpart of Grace/Good, and thence of autonomous power. In this context, there is even a hint of duality where Evil and Good face each other as equal combatants, as if, in this condition of blind suffering, Herbert becomes oblivious of the relativity of Evil faced with the One Good.

The epitome of the single concentration on the imputation of the Righteousness of Christ to the exclusion of all else, in the day to day life, may be seen in *The Holdfast*.

I threatned: the poem opens even with defiance, a challenge on Herbert's part that he will overcome, in his own right, his own incapacity. But, the very word *threatned* already holds within itself the suggestion of failure. Had there been victory there would have been no threat as the initiation. The threat, in a strange sort of way, is directed against his own leniency to himself as well as to God, for the threat is to *observe the strict decree* of his dear God, to the uttermost of his capacity. The conflict is yet again re-established as the premise. His dear God has laid down a rule which Herbert can not observe, but struggles to assume the possibility. The struggle is declared useless at the very instant of its initiation:

> But I was told by one, it could not be . . .

There it stands, simple, and isolated, the flat contradiction to Man's potency for good in himself. It *could* not be, not that it was not permitted, nor that it was permitted but difficult, but, plainly, it *could* not be. Herbert was told this by *one*. At this stage, it seems, that the *one* is an undefined and unrecognised presence, a voice which, however, Herbert can not help but obey and follow. The *one* then suggests to him that there was an alternative; even if he could not, in his own potentiality, follow the way of God, yet, he could trust *in God to be my light*. Unreasoning faith was possible, the same trust which for an instant claimed him joyfully in *Faith*. The fact, that this possibility is immediately taken from him suggests that the *one* is the condition which Herbert often calls *hope*. Hope invariably suggests a step which appears eminently reasonable for the achievement of that for which he longs, and invariably proves the step an illusion, possibly for the very reason that it is comprehensible and gives the semblance of achievement, where no achievement can be. This hope, then, of achievement through faith alone, is at once taken from him:

> Nay, ev'n to trust in him, was also his . . .

So, once again, the unceasing doubt of the circle: without Grace he can not act, he can not reach towards God, but the Grace comes from God, and the Grace is not at his disposal. Achievement is impossible, but acknowledgment of total failure *is* possible:

> We must confesse that nothing is our own.

Is this a straw upon which it is possible to seize? Can perhaps the journey after all be achieved by unqualified humility, by denying any form of progress? Can the progress be made through the denial of the progress?

> Then I confesse that he my succour is . . .

The confession of human impotency is made. God is Man's one help. Can Herbert, now, negatively, proceed on his way of sanctification, basing his ascent on the rungs of humility? But, the answer comes back, even sharply, plumbing the depth of the attempted evasion:

> But to have nought is ours, not to confesse
> That we have nought.

How precisely Herbert has replied to his own attempted evasion: the humble confession of nothing as a starting-point remains fixed, that we really have nothing and, therefore, can not leave the starting-point, even on the strength of the confession of nothing:

> I stood amaz'd at this,
> Much troubled . . .

He was in the impasse. But, suddenly, the mist cleared and he heard and he saw:

> till I heard a friend expresse,
> That all things were more ours by being his.

A friend: the Comforter: the Spirit: or Christ himself in his compassion. But, the promise of true, not illusionary, hope lay in those words. Christ died as a ransom for us: his was a righteousness which words could not express; how could we, on our own, therefore have anything even beginning to compare with what we have in him? In Christ, lies our salvation, here and now, safe and unassailable, inside the fallen world of sin:

> What Adam had, and forfeited for all,
> Christ keepeth now, who cannot fail or fall.

Righteousness of Man is safely preserved by Christ, Christ the immutable. There lurks no fear in this. But can the fear be long absent, once the question has been asked? If our salvation must be explained and it is explained by Christ's ransom, is it possible to avoid the further fear of doubt, the necessity to face the *conditions* of election for being chosen to be saved by Christ's ransom?

The way, as a way, of sanctification, of ascent by spiritual effort in the growing strength of an inner Grace which steadfastly develops in the measure of the sanctification, making the ascent consistent, is not possible in life. Of this way of sanctification, of the growing inner Grace, there is no assurance. The World of Nature confronts the World of Grace and Man belongs to both, he is helpless in his own way of salvation during his life-time. And, he is equally helpless, after death, in justifying himself before God. Once the question of assurance is asked in regard to life, then we can not escape the same need, and even more vitally, for death. The question pursues us, in speculation, to the Day of Judgment. And, here, Herbert holds to the same hope: the Righteousness of Christ crucified, transferred to man.

The double orientation and, as it were, pull of nature and of Grace, comes out precisely in *Coloss. 3.3*. The pull is experienced through life, but it is in death that the consequences of the pull are realised. In Christ, in death, and through Christ, in life and in death, only is the reward of salvation possible:

> *My* words & thoughts do both expresse this notion,
> That *Life* hath with the sun a double motion.

Sun would forthwith appear to have the double connotation of the actual sun and the Sun of Righteousness, Christ:

> The first *Is* straight, and our diurnall friend,
> The other *Hid* and doth obliquely bend.

Why obliquely? Possibly, because no life towards Christ can be anything but indirect in the worldly sense, possibly also a reference to the oblique anagram which becomes apparent by the end of the poem.

By nature, our life *wrapt In flesh* has a downward movement, into the earth, into death and dissolution. Yet, through the birth of Christ, that is, in his life, not in his death, nor in his resurrection, we are taught, in imitation of him, to be aware of the other world, which is not of this world. In the flesh, we are flesh, and it can only be *one eye*, (again the oblique movement) while we live, which can turn to heaven. But, that one eye can be fixed upon heaven in resolute purpose. As the star of Grace may shoot down from heaven to us, thus the light of our single eye *can aim and shoot at that which Is on high*. The image, is, here, not only of the shooting star, but, again, of conflict. We attack heaven regularly with the artillery provided by the Incarnation. And, strong in Christ, we toil day to day to abandon the world, and, through his power alone, the abandoning is assured of success:

> To gain at harvest an eternall *Treasure*.

The Day of Judgment, when seen with the eyes of love and not of fear, becomes the sure harvest for the grain, which will not be cast out, worthless, into the furnace. And, so, where *your* has become *our* in the sub-heading of the poem, *our-your* goes the further intimate step into the *my* of the acrostic:

> My Life Is Hid In Him, That Is My Treasure.

The reward is the treasure, but the treasure *is* Christ. In him, and through him, the fulfilment *is* he.
Judgement is, at its most explicit, the carrying of the imputation of Righteousness into death.
The scene is set. The Day of Judgment. The unhappy creature faces God, all-powerful and dreadful Judge. The most hardened sinner, with a heart not even of stone, Herbert's favourite epithet of toughened sin, but of iron, must tremble. From every man God demands that single man's own, particular written statement of accounts. There can be no opportunity for cheating. The book had been given by God to each one to keep as his personal responsibility, and account must be rendered back to God:

> Almightie Judge, how shall poore wretches brook
>   Thy dreadfull look,
> Able a heart of iron to appall,
>   When thou shalt call
> For ev'ry mans peculiar book?

It is beyond Herbert's powers of imagination even to guess what others will do in this last and most terrible predicament. But, he has heard somehow and somewhere that some may even attempt to placate God by their own efforts of merit. With delicate irony Herbert comments on the foolishness and presumption. Who can show so white a paper?

> That some will turn thee to some leaves therein
>   So void of sinne,
>   That they in merit shall excell.

With this glancing reflection on Roman Catholic chances, as he saw them, of salvation, Herbert turns to his own intention:

> But I resolve, when thou shalt call for mine,
>   That to decline . . .

How, at the Judgment Seat, Herbert intends to disobey a command from the Almighty Judge is not immediately apparent. But, even as he refuses, he will:

> . . . thrust a Testament into thy hand:
>   Let that be scann'd.

He will substitute for his own book, the Testament: that is, the New Covenant of the Gospel, of the blood of our Saviour. And, then, the disobedience of his action becomes pre-eminently obedience. Was not the Son of God sent by God to redeem Man? Were not the sins of Man taken upon himself by the Son of God? So, Herbert, in full submission to the New Covenant of the ransom paid for him, thrusts the Testament into the hand of the Judge. His salvation is assured, if he holds the Testament *to* thrust into the hand of the Judge, for, to hold the Testament, the Covenant, could only have been granted to him by the Son of God. In the Grace of the Son, his sins are bought by the Son, sent by the Father. They are no more *his* sins:

> There thou shalt finde my faults are thine.

This is again one of the rare moments of temporarily assured joy. But, as long as Herbert puts his hope in the imputation, neither the assurance nor the joy can endure, for he can never know when, why, or how, the Testament will be in *his* hand to thrust back to God. Imputation is not at his disposal. So, it would appear, that Herbert must bear with the consequences of the two unconnected worlds, the World of Nature and the World of Grace. The single hope, for salvation, in the imputation of Righteousness, brings with it heavy labour and tribulation in the daily life of the working spirit.

CHAPTER III

THEOLOGY IN PRACTICE

How can the split between the World of Grace and the World of Nature, and the reliance, in whatever seeming form, on the imputation of Righteousness, be seen in terms of daily, practical theology? Of the potentiality of creative spiritual living? What, in effect, is the consequence in principle of such a super-imposed division?

It would seem that the consequence in principle finds its most tender spot of vulnerability in the question of the Mystery. Acceptance of the Mystery, *as* Mystery in its purest sense, that is, the joy of the incomprehensible, and, in the same movement, the acknowledgment of the limitation of reason as a positive, not negative, factor of spirituality, would obviate the whole speculative field on the question of the assurance of salvation, and the often barren suffering in the wake of such speculation. But, if the assurance is demanded, in whatsoever form or to whatsoever degree, the Mystery is somehow, however unconsciously or unwillingly, denied. What remains is, as it were, a shorn and enfeebled Mystery, brought down from its transcendent connotation and hobbled to the immanent. In effect, questions of assurance of salvation, may lead to the salvation ceasing to be essentially a Mystery, and the Mystery may cease to be the consistent self-limiting answer. The Mystery may not necessarily be denied explicitly, but the position, which remains without the Mystery in the foreground, can not help but be equivocal and see-saw. And, again, once the Mystery of the Church in its objective reality has been questioned, however slightly, or the Mystery of the Sacraments refused a full objective reality, however much latitude is still allowed for retaining the Mystery, then, the question of personal assurance of salvation must rear its head of tempting doubt.

In Herbert's attitude to the Saints, to the Bible, to the Eucharist, and, in the last count, to the meaning of suffering, there can be seen, at its most sensitive, the consequence of the precipitation of the Mystery into the immanent sphere, in the attempt to balance the Church as the guarantee of salvation. If salvation is taken out of the realm of Mystery, then it only remains to probe and probe again at the same wound, for which the healing oil has been mislaid.

i. *The Saints*

Apart from the anagram on the name of Mary, in which Herbert incidentally with academic neatness makes his point by returning to the Greek *pitched his tent* instead of the English *dwelt,* there is only one poem directly confronting the problem of the Saints. The uneasiness of the Articles of Religion are strongly reflected in Herbert's uneasiness as a conscientious member of the Church of England. The very fact of there only being the one poem emphasises the uneasiness. What could Herbert, with his warm and generous heart, with his capacity of love, and wish to love, do in such a quandary? If he agreed to the premise of Grace, which must again and again come anew for each person, denying the Mystery of continuity in the Church, and, hence, severing the Mystical Body of Christ from its incontrovertible unity with Christ, as Christ in a form which we can not define, but none the less *as* Christ, then how was he to approach the Saints? If the question of the veneration of the Saints is put as one of rivalry with Christ, then of course the veneration must be rejected. But, the effort of rejection in Herbert does not sound convincing, and the reason given for the denial is far from impressive.

Herbert even seems to want to get this task of renunciation over as quickly as possible, so he addresses his poem *To all Angels and Saints.* He can not help but praise them in their glory. Are they not in heaven, face to face with God? They no longer see through a glass darkly, to them is revealed God as Love. No anger. They have been judged worthy, these glorious Spirits to:

> See the smooth face of God without a frown
> Or strict commands . . .

Their place in heaven is royal:

> Where ev'ry one is king, and hath his crown,
> If not upon his head, yet in his hands . . .

Why has Herbert added *yet in his hands?* Could he be referring to *Rev. 4, 10-11?* Here the four and twenty elders cast their crowns before the Lord God Almighty, that is, they remove the crowns from their own heads and throw them before their Lord, proclaiming him as the sole Creator, and sole object of worship: *Thou art worthy, O Lord, to receive glory and honour and power: for thou hast created all things, and for thy pleasure they are and were created.* If this is the reference, which Herbert has in mind, then he is using the Saints as his justification for denying them. However, he goes on more openly, apologetically:

> Not out of envie or maliciousnesse
> Do I forbear to crave your speciall aid . . .

He would particularly rejoice to seek comfort and refreshment from the Mother of God. Was she not entrusted with the precious treasure of God Incarnate? Herbert's frequent image of *box*, as the container of the human spirit, becomes the more delicately fashioned *cabinet* for the pure womb in which *the jewell lay*. He is drawn to the Mother of God, it seems with a nearly irresistible longing of love. The step to peace was not a difficult one, but it would, for him, have been a peace of short duration and unfaithfulness to his Church. The step would have removed Herbert from the sphere of dogmatic contradiction, which he had freely accepted and to which he rigorously adhered. One motion of weakness, as he would see it, might relieve suffering, but would bring in its train the worse suffering of perjury and treachery, not only to his Church, but to his God. Herbert denies the Mother of God, even more emphatically than he denied the Saints, on the grounds of her own evidence. She, above all, obeyed her God without question in her hymn of self-renunciation, how can he not imitate her in this immanent self-denial, in order to rise with the Spirit? Christ has not directly ordered the veneration of Saints, and so:

> But now, alas, I dare not; for our King,
> Whom we do all joyntly adore and praise,
> > Bids no such thing:
> And where his pleasure no injunction layes,
> ('Tis your own case) ye never move a wing.

The Day of Judgment will come. And the man, who has dared to deny one tiny fraction of worship to the One God, will meet his punishment. On one level, this sounds mean beyond words, as if God, who is Love, will measure love! But, of course, more was at stake. Herbert seems to be fighting, against every inclination in himself, to preserve the concept of only one irrefutable possibility of salvation, that is in the Person of Christ. With the Church no longer the absolute guarantee, even a side-step into her tradition, would result in a dissonance of doubt. The suffering of balance must be retained, and the Saints rejected:

> Therefore we dare not from his garland steal,
> To make a posie for inferiour power.

But, even as Herbert rejects the Saints as an object of veneration, their place in heaven he does not deny, nor their power of receiving his message, if not his prayers. He leaves it to the Saints, even somehow defiantly, to put the situation right by their understanding of his quandary. The Saints will know that if they could have proved their position, veneration would be forthcoming:

Since we are ever ready to disburse,
If any one our Masters hand can show.

To All Angels and Saints is not a comfortable poem. The balance, for once, verges on the disagreeable. To invoke the Mother of God and the Saints in order that they may appear to deny themselves savours of sophistry, and might well seem politically cynical, if it were possible to think of Herbert in the context of cynicism. But, even so, the poem suggests how untenable a spiritual position, founded on balance, may come to be if it once seeks for proof in rationalisation, and forsakes active and mute carrying of the contradictions.

ii. *The Bible*

The Bible, Old and New Testaments, also holds, of necessity, this ambivalent position in Herbert's theology. It seems that here again he could even reach the point of seeing the Bible as a possible rival to Christ, if such a suggestion were not too absurd to be considered. The Bible has its place in the scheme of salvation, but, again, it can not be granted the final objective Mystery of the reality of Grace. If there were this space for Mystery, then the objective reality would afford no difficulty, but without the Mystery, the objective reality must be subjected to Grace, that is to the ever arbitrary descent at the Will of God, enlightening with its presence which is temporary, and only fleetingly joining the World of Nature to the World of Grace during the period of its inexplicable and unaccountable presence. In the Bible, therefore, *in itself,* there can be nothing assumed, that is, the Mystery does not allow the assurance of an incontrovertible permanent reality; the reality depends on Grace, and the Grace is a Mystery but not *the* Mystery. Acceptance of *the* Mystery means acknowledgment of continuity. Acceptance of Grace as a Mystery may mean, as it does for Herbert, no assurance, but the contrary, an inexplicable coming and going. There is, in the Bible, no permanent reality of Grace within a permanent presence of the transcendent Mystery. But, at the same time, as the real word of God, if not the Mystery of the Word himself, the Bible carries within it not only a persisting value, but the potentiality of being the receptacle of Grace, which it can transfer.

It has already been seen how Herbert intends to produce *the book,* the word and history of the Son, in place of his own book, at the Day of Judgment (*Judgement*) and, again, in *The Thanksgiving,* how in *thy book,* he will read of the love of God, and train himself in *thy art of love*. But, on this point, Herbert is even more explicit in two sonnets: *The H. Scriptures*. I. and II.

The *H. Scriptures*. I. might well seem a puzzling mixture of true adoration and conventional morality if not for the clue already suggested. The explanation of what could be the puzzle seems to lie again in the unexpressed uneasiness of a non-explicit theology: in the reflection of this ambiguous stand-point which can hardly be expressed without the repetitive prefix, *un*. And, yet, the whole-hearted love is equally there, a love which can not be dismissed as morality or convention.

The Bible is seen as the source of comfort: the words of the Bible can smooth and illumine problems and anxieties; and the words of the Bible are not mere human words to be apprehended by the reasoning faculties, but they are the words of the Spirit, to be received into the heart, the container of man's spirit. Sweet and sweetness are ever associated, for Herbert, with his Saviour, Christ, and, if, therefore, he ascribes sweetness to the Bible, he must be identifying the words with the Word, even though he would withdraw, as he would from the Saints, from any conclusion of the Mystery of the realism of the Bible's objective Truth:

> Oh Book! infinite sweetnesse! let my heart
>   Suck ev'ry letter, and a hony gain,
>   Precious for any grief in any part;
> To cleare the breast, to mollifie all pain.

The use of the *suck-honey* image seems revealing here. It is as if Herbert is identifying himself with the bee in its work. But, the bee, for Herbert, is the envied creature in the World of Nature, which retains a constancy, unlike Man depending upon the arbitrary irruption of Grace. Thus, it is, as if he is hoping that perhaps the Bible, somehow, could be the alternative guarantee of salvation, a constant receptacle and, therefore, fount of Grace. But, for an avowed member of the Church of England, this solution would not hold. Such a solution would have meant an exclusive dogmatic assertion, which the Church would not give. Yet, for the moment, Herbert concentrates on the vital quality of the Bible. It is *all health*. Only life springs from the Bible, and the life gives life to more life, leading to *a full eternitie*, a life beyond life. And, in the mean-time, the Bible holds within itself mystery upon mystery, to heal, to teach, to please, to edify all who seek within it. Nothing lacks. Does Herbert feel himself too carried away, and approaching controversial ground when he suddenly stops in his direct praise, to turn aside to conventional morality which strikes a most unusual and discordant tone? Is this really the moment for pointing out to fashionable ladies that the Bible is the better mirror, correcting and teaching and cleansing, not, presumably, leading into further vanity? This retreat into morality, in effect, is very close to the brusque denial of the Saints. He can not allow himself the further step which, theologically, would topple him over into the chasm of the undefined. So, he draws back, breaks the tension of love by means of morality, and then resumes on a more formal note. The personal contact with the Bible, the mutual flow of love, is replaced by the image of the dignity of the Bible, not as itself, again the echo of Herbert's attitude to the Saints, but as the formally acknowledged representative of God. The World of Grace has sent its Ambassador into this world of sin, and the Ambassador remains an Ambassador, his credit in the commission, which, of course, can be withdrawn and renewed by the will of the King. But, as Ambassador, the Bible can not be equalled or over-valued:

> Who can indeare
> Thy praise too much? thou art heav'ns Lidger here,
> Working against the states of death and hell.

The Bible is the pledge of the joy to come. In the Bible, heaven becomes available in as far as the words of the Bible tell us of heaven and speak to us of heaven. If we aspire to heaven, climbing and toiling up towards heaven, in prayer and adoration, we can at least meet heaven, on our journey, in the Bible. The Bible is in no wise the end of the journey, for the mountaineer is on his laborious way, his knees bent for the next step up, but the Bible is an open map spread out for him to read and to help him thence to find his way, his knees bent as he climbs, and his knees bent as he prays. There is no assurance of salvation in the words of the Bible, nor is there the Mystery of immutable presence, but there is an inalienable source of help, a direct connection with the longed-for God:

> Thou art joyes handsell: heav'n lies flat in thee,
> Subject to ev'ry mounters bended knee.

The second sonnet, *The H. Scriptures.* II., goes, imperceptibly, even nearer to some identification with Christ, or at least to his effulgence of Grace, for here Herbert takes the *Light-Star* image, which is ever connected for him with Grace, and with Christ, the Son and the Sun. Herbert loves the intricacy of the Bible, the apprehension of separate themes, somewhere merging, somehow connected into one theme outside his grasp, or again breaking up, and joining in yet another way. He gives the impression of seeing the Bible as light broken up in a prism, dividing, and re-grouping with a consequent infinity of variations of meaning and interpretation. It is not possible to understand the Bible directly, as one might expect to understand some other book:

> Oh that I knew how all thy lights combine,
>   And the configurations of their glorie!
>   Seeing not onely how each verse doth shine,
> But all the constellations of the storie.
> This verse marks that, and both do make a motion
>   Unto a third, that ten leaves off doth lie . . .

But, Herbert goes strangely forward, or is it yet another deviation? Instead of keeping to the single theme of homage to the incomprehensible yet ever revealing truth of the Bible, he turns to the prophetic or pastoral quality. It is a side-ways jerk, again into a form of morality, in the speculation on the hidden personal significance that the Bible may hold for each one of us. The thread of direct homage to the Bible, as light, is lost:

> Then as dispersed herbs do watch a potion,
> These three make up some Christians destinie . . .

Apparently unconnected, as the ingredients of a drug or medicine, the verses, as the herbs, contain within themselves the potentiality of uniting into the drug or medicine. Superficially, the herbs remain disconnected from the drug, only regarding it from afar, and, yet, while retaining their particularity, they are the constituent parts. So, the verses of the Bible remain separate, but, at the same time, are connected in relation to a particular man's fate. The thought becomes even more involved. The theme has discarded the homage of the wonder at the Mystery, and turned the Mystery into an immanent secret, confirmed in every-day life. The Bible is now seen as a vehicle of moral reflection. In the story of the Bible, Herbert can trace his own sins and lapses, in the life of another, he can discover himself:

>   for in ev'ry thing
> Thy words do finde me out, & parallels bring,
> And in another make me understood.

The concept of the Bible, as a prophetic Book, or as a means for interpreting and directing one's life, comes to its fullness of image, in the final couplet. In the analogy with Astrology, the Bible seems finally removed from the realm of objective Mystery. But, it is left explicitly with the highest prerogative of instruction, and, implicitly, perhaps, with something more. The light image is not abandoned:

> Starres are poore books, & oftentimes do misse:
> This book of starres lights to eternall blisse.

iii. *The Eucharist*

Herbert could hardly avoid a confrontation with the most vital issue in the theology of the Church. Where did he take up his position in the dogmatic counter-assertions open to him? On the question of the Eucharist he remained strictly faithful to his Church, as indeed on all questions. He would not, in assertion, go further than in seeing the measure of the reality of Grace conferred in the Sacrament, as in accordance with the measure of Grace in the recipient. Thus, again, he is within the realm of the arbitrary, for how can he be sure that he carries within himself the Grace at the instant of reception? The Sacrifice of Christ, through Imputation, can only alone, even in the Eucharist, be relied upon to provide for the deficit in Man, either because of his impeding sin, or his lack of Grace. Thus, again, Christ is called upon, in Imputation, to enter within and, in effect, be the Inner Grace for which, otherwise, there is no criterion, and, hence, the questioning of the efficacy of the Eucharistic Grace. Herbert submits himself to the full impact of the non-assertiveness of his Church, and his poems, which bear directly upon the Eucharist, reflect the theological premise, and thence the spiritual condition at its most sensitive and pure, arising, as it does, from the full acceptance of such a premise.

Faith has already been discussed in another connection, but it may be helpful here to repeat, as a starting-point, the following lines:

> Hungrie I was, and had no meat:
> I did conceit a most delicious feast;
> I had it straight and did as truly eat,
>   As ever did a welcome guest.

The theological premise is laid of the personal responsibility, without the criterion for exercising the responsibility. By faith, Herbert can receive the bread and wine as the Eucharistic feast. But neither the measure of the faith required, nor the means either of experiencing the faith for certain as faith, or for being sure of evoking this particular necessary faith, is given to him. The Mystery becomes, in this connection, an immanent one, brought down to him into the Mystery of his reception, from out of the transcendent Mystery of the objective validity of the Mystery of the reality of the bread and wine as the body and blood of Christ. The Mystery remains transcendent only in as far as it is the transcendent Grace, outside his human volition, which alone can awaken his spirit to receive Christ as Christ within him. For, the reception is a true one, in the Mystery, through Grace, it is not a memory nor a symbol. The pain of the Eucharistic conflict thus becomes apparent in Herbert. And, I would suggest that this conflict, in Herbert, is not, as it might appear, the conflict between the Roman Catholic and Protestant stand-points. If this were so, Herbert would have been a reluctant Anglican, and there is no evidence of this. On the contrary, the evidence points directly to his allegiance to his Church. It would seem therefore far more to be the conflict, one might almost say the deliberate conflict, to which the Church of England submits each one of her faithful, the direct outcome of the positive acceptance of the non-assertion and thence the submission to the daily doubt, which could only be allayed from time to time by the inexplicable joy of the experience of the in-flow of Grace, giving rise to unspeakable love and trust. I am speaking here of course of the broad middle way of the Established Church, as it was envisaged and inaugurated.

The vital importance of love in the real experience of the Mystery of the Eucharist comes out very strongly in *The Agonie*. And, again, the elusive quality of the love which can realise the Eucharist within us is only to be explained by the fact that even our capacity of love, as of faith, emanates solely from Love, that is, through the inexplicable infusion of Grace. Once more, Herbert is within the circle, but, at these moments when the supreme joy of love is most prominent, he seems even oblivious of what otherwise comes with the pain of the imprisonment.

Herbert is spell-bound before the vast dimensions of two opposing energies, wholly beyond the comprehension of Science. Mountains can be measured, seas plumbed, politics disclosed, stars located and water divined. But, *two vast, spacious things* remain: *Sinne and Love*. Man and Christ confront each other. No sin that Man can devise against Man can compare with sin against God, and so, personified sin can at its most precise delineation be seen reflected in the agony of the Son of God.

> Who would know Sinne, let him repair
> Unto Mount Olivet; there shall he see
> A man so wrung with pains, that all his hair,
> His skinne, his garments bloudie be.

Sin is the instrument, forged by man, which lies behind the impetus of suffering enforced upon another. The pain seeks its nourishment from every motion of agony in the body, but, the pain is driven on to its chase by sin. Then, in direct contradiction:

> Who knows not Love . . .

Love is the victim of the Sin, and, at the instant of defeat, Love gives forth the immortal nourishment to Man, engendered of sin and pain. The agony is sacrifice, and the sacrifice is the sacrifice of Love which turns the pain to joy, and redeems the sin through love:

> Who knows not Love, let him assay
> And taste that juice, which on the crosse a pike
> Did set again abroach . . .

The sword pierced His side, and the blood ran out, the stream of pain to wash away sin. It is of the greatest interest that Herbert here uses the term for piercing a cask of wine, once more the image of the container, now referring to the life-giving blood of Christ, which in a variety of forms is destined to enter the human container of the heart. The *juice,* squeezed out by the wine-press of sin, is a juice which must be unique, for it is the drops of agony not wrung out of a human frame by Sin and Death, but, by Sin and Love. Sin would have been powerless if Love had willed it otherwise:

> . . . then let him say
> If ever he did taste the like.

The concluding two lines of *The Agonie* would seem to put Herbert's position precisely within the Eucharistic conflict. He does not deny, nor does he seem perturbed, by the fact that what he drinks, he is sensible of as wine. But, at the same time, his God feels it as blood, now, at the moment of the Eucharist, the sacrifice is not only unrepeatable in history except in commemoration, but it is present in the actual Eucharist. Love is the wine. It is sweet, the identification with Christ, and it is divine. Here, then, is the Mystery. In human terms, the wine, objectively, remains wine. But, in divine terms, it is blood. Within the Mystery of the divine Love, Christ, the wine is blood in the Grace of the receiving:

> Love is that liquour sweet and most divine,
> Which my God feels as bloud; but I, as wine.

The Bunch of Grapes leads into the same position, by a different route. At first comes the wretchedness for the *joy* has left him, that is, he lacks the condition which assures him, outside reason, of the essential presence of the Mystery of Grace. So Herbert seeks to recapture the joy by tracing the Christian way parallel to the way of the Jews, in allegory. He had felt himself drawing near to the Promised Land, somewhere salvation was in his grasp, and suddenly it was gone:

>   And now, me thinks, I am where I began
>   Sev'n yeares ago . . .

He has not reached Canaan, but instead he feels that he has been drawn back to the Red Sea, *the sea of shame*. The Jews had an actual journey, and each Christian also has a journey carefully allotted to him. We hardly emerge in a favourable light if we compare ourselves with the Jews, but there is the conviction to offset this:

>   Gods works are wide, and let in future times;
>   His ancient justice overflows our crimes.

Divine Providence has not left us to struggle on alone; in whatever form they may be, the gifts and favours God showered on Israel, He still bestows on us:

>   Then have we too our guardian fires and clouds;
>   Our Scripture-dew drops fast:
>   We have our sands and serpents, tents and shrowds . . .

And, Herbert adds, we follow the Jews equally in their less laudable behaviour:

>   Alas! our murmurings come not last.

Thus the crux of the conflict, through the allegorical preamble, is reached. Joy has escaped, and with the absence of the inner conviction of Grace within himself, the validity of the Eucharist seems to elude him:

>   But where's the cluster?

The Promised Land provided the grapes, where, then, is the wine of the Promise? Where the sensation of Presence?

>   . . . where's the taste
>   Of mine inheritance?

The Jews had the actual presence, hence their joy, if he is to share, in parallel, their laborious journey, should he not be allowed to share in the joy of presence?

> Lord, if I must borrow,
> Let me as well take up their joy, as sorrow.

And, then, comes the urgent question of the possibility of not doubting the Presence in his reception of the Eucharist. Could he not be worthy to receive without his cognizance, by the very fact of participation?

> But can he want the grape, who hath the wine?

If wine without the grapes is an impossibility, then, if he does drink wine, surely he can argue that the Presence is implied? The Old Law is fulfilled in the New. God gave the grapes to the Jews, but Christ gave us the New Testament, turning *the Laws sowre juice* into *sweet wine*. The wine is *sweet*, fragrant with the presence of Christ himself, and the presence is even further re-confirmed, once again, in the image of the wine-press. For his sake, for Herbert's sake as a person, Christ God gave himself to the wine-press of torment. The grape turned to wine. Surely the Presence can not be doubted? But, for Herbert, it still remains a question. He will not go further than the question:

> But can he want the grape, who hath the wine?

Yet, Herbert holds to the inherent hope:

> Ev'n God himself being pressed for my sake.

The doubt of the Eucharistic presence can only find its partial solution in a form of imputation. Somehow, Christ himself, in his sacrifice, imputes the Righteousness of Grace, to allow for the reception of his Blood, through the sweetness of his Grace.

The suggestion in *The Bunch of Grapes* of the transference of the notion of imputation into the Eucharist, that is, that Christ himself, in the Communion, bestows the worthiness to receive the Communion as his Body and Blood, comes out more explicitly and, therefore, more serenely, in *The Banquet*. Here is an alternative to subjective faith which can go further without despair or doubt, before it also meets the wall erected by the denial of the wholly objective reality of the Sacraments.

The Eucharistic feast is welcomed as something uniquely rare and precious. It is *sweet,* again the suggestion immediately of the presence of the Saviour, it is pure, beyond anything which the eyes can discern, and the pleasure it imparts no man can describe. In other words, the Eucharistic feast is joyously acclaimed as a superhuman Mystery. The *sweetnesse* is emphasised. The taste of the Presence of the Saviour totally fills his soul and infuses Herbert's soul with the Grace of Christ:

> O what sweetnesse from the bowl
> Fills my soul,
> Such as is, and makes divine!

In Christ, his lack is repaired. The sweetness of the bread ousts the smell of rotting, of sin. Death, the stench of corruption, is defeated in the sweetness of the Body of Christ, the incorruptible. It is as if all natural things that have a fragrant smell contribute to this defeat of death by death:

> Flowers, and gummes, and powders giving
> All their living,
> Lest the Enemy should winne?

But, it can not be a natural source for the fragrance. Nothing created could produce the scent to overcome the mortality of creation. The Creator, alone, can have the power, in taking a body upon himself, to give the fragrance of life into the heart of man:

> Doubtlesse, neither starre nor flower
> Hath the power
> Such a sweetnesse to impart:
> Onely God, who gives perfumes,
> Flesh assumes,
> And with it perfumes my heart.

The Sacrifice of God, the ransom of his agony, is paid for us. He is bruised that we may benefit by his Incarnation and crucifixion. It is his real body which suffered, that the Eucharist may have its final value. The breaking of the bread is the sacrifice of his body for love of us, and the love alone can make the validity of the Eucharistic bread:

> God, to show how farre his love
> Could improve,
> Here, as broken, is presented.

Again, there is no question of an objective sacramental change, the body is present in the love of God, and in the recipient's trust that the love of God is there to make the body present. This position would appear tenable until the trust also, as the faith previously, is queried as the gift of Grace. Then the joy, once again, turns to despair.

The H. Communion

> Not in rich furniture, or fine array,
>   Nor in a wedge of gold,
>   Thou, who for me wast sold,
>   To me dost now thy self convey;
> For so thou should'st without me still have been,
>   Leaving within me sinne . . .

This is indeed an introductory trumpet-call for the Church of England! In the images of wealth, ritual, gaudiness, Herbert addresses the Roman Catholic Church. He is very far from being in any way on the defensive for his Church, theologically or otherwise, and, in fact, he goes into the attack without too much apparent consideration for his antagonist's possible justification. He is only concerned with his case against the Catholics, and his contention is that the objective reality of the Sacrament, as claimed by the Catholics, would detract from the redeeming validity of the Eucharist. If the Communion is objective, then the recipient of the Communion may be left with the sin within him. In effect, Herbert is reversing the condition of doubt. He claims that the doubt arising out of the non-objectivity allows for the personal salvation, which would not be assured by the objective reality of the Sacrament working from outside. Such an objective reality from outside would be impersonal, in as far as its validity would not depend upon the direct pre-reception of Grace by the communicant, and would not, therefore, affect his personal sin directly. The making worthy to receive the Sacrament, the preliminary freeing from sin, would remain in the hands of the owners of the *rich furniture,* that is, the Church.

So, in this opening stanza, Herbert defies the Authority of the Church in as far as the Church holds the power of granting the absolution which makes the recipient worthy of receiving Communion. He insists on the Communion, in contradiction to the Roman Catholic Church, as a personal means of purification, solely founded on the personal accompanying Grace. The image of the Sacrament is of battle.

The assailant is the Communion, disguised as *nourishment;* and, almost unnoticed in its humble appearance, it creeps into his breast, that is, directly into his heart: the container of his soul, sometimes tender, and sometimes hard, but ever made of flesh and the seat of sin. Good and Evil continually fight out their battle in his heart. Now, the Communion, which is the source of his deliverance from spiritual turmoil, his *rest,* and which is the source for expanding and fulfilling the lapses and gaps in him, the *small quantities* his *length,* secretly deploys its army, to out-wit the strength and cunning of the opposing forces of sin.

But, immediately Herbert withdraws from the full implication of the assertion. He has, for the moment, ventured to claim the immediate and indubitable reality of the saving virtue of the sacrament. If he persists in this, he will find himself allowing space for some objective reality in the Mystery of the Sacrament. So, at once, he disclaims the efficacy of the Sacrament, as Sacrament, in itself. The work of the Sacrament, on its own, can not go beyond a certain strengthening quality. It can not penetrate beyond the outer fabric of the heart, and can only control the *rebel-flesh* to some extent and in the *name* of Christ cause consternation to the sin within him.

The Sacrament, in itself, can not be identified with Christ but has some power, or virtue as it were as his representative. The Mystery of the consecrated Sacrament bears within it already some strength, but the final virtue, of Christ himself, is not at the disposal of the Church. This stage is again clearly and emphatically reserved for the descent of Grace, outside the act of consecration, at the will of God, upon the person receiving the Sacrament:

> Onely thy grace, which with these elements comes,
> Knoweth the ready way,
> And hath the privie key,
> Op'ning the souls most subtile rooms . . .

It is the accompanying Grace which alone can penetrate into the innermost recesses of the heart. The elements are powerless in themselves to enter, but where they find spirits purified and fit to receive the Spirit of Grace, they wait at the entrance to the impenetrable room of the heart, until the friend, the Spirit of Grace, sends them the documents with the right of entry. The *dispatches*: again as in *H. Scriptures.* I, the image of the Ambassador of Christ:

> While those to spirits refin'd, at doore attend
> Dispatches from their friend.

The second half of the poem gives a sudden jerk into a totally different, even facile and light rhythm. It is as if a simple, if temporary, solution suddenly opens out before Herbert, as he expresses the experience of dichotomy between his soul, which belongs to heaven, and which he sees therefore as *captive,* and his body which is of the earth. Herbert feels death near, and wishes for it, if unity can not be gained otherwise. Before the Fall, the passage from earth to heaven was not difficult; death did not stand between, but even:

> A fervent sigh might well have blown
> Our innocent earth to heaven.

For Adam, it was only a question of going from one room to another, to pass from Paradise to heaven. The many chambers were open to him. But, Christ has restored the passage to heaven for us by the shedding of actual blood, of divine origin, Christ, God and Man, who suffered in reality for us. Thus, suddenly, Herbert seems to fling aside the whole conflict of the Eucharist as something negligible. Communion remains the food of the world, however understood, whereas the blood of Christ in fact has opened the way to heaven. Death is his way, and it is a way entirely unconnected with theology. Imputation, the redeeming blood of Christ, can, for Herbert, not be denied:

> Thou hast restor'd us to this ease
> By this thy heav'nly bloud;
> Which I can go to, when I please,
> And leave th' earth to their food.

These last lines seem to take on even a note of pitying scorn for all the troubles of theological dispute. Death, in the transient certainty of salvation through imputed Righteousness, is the relief.

In *Peace,* a strangely serene poem with no apparent self-contradiction, Herbert reiterates his contention of the healing quality of the Eucharist in itself. He does not assign to the Eucharist the independent reality of Presence, but, as in *The H. Communion,* he allows the Eucharist a sanctifying Mystery of its own. The Eucharist, again, can reach the *outworks,* what to-day we might even regard as the psychological sphere of morality, and, hence, the most disturbed and disturbing sphere, but, further, Herbert will not go. It is, perhaps, as if, seeing the Mystery of the Consecration of the Eucharist as in the Mystery of the hands of a man, he will not ascribe to it more potency, in itself, than the Mystery affecting the human level. But, as far as he goes, Herbert is deeply conscious of this free gift of healing, open to all.

The search for peace begins in the world, in what seem the remote distances first, under the earth:

> I sought thee in a secret cave,
> And ask'd, if Peace were there.
> A hollow winde did seem to answer, No:
> Go seek elsewhere.

Then, above the earth, stretching into the sky as far as Man can see, hoping that this is the actual border of heaven:

> I did; and going did a rainbow note:
> Surely, thought I,
> This is the lace of Peaces coat . . .

But, it was not: even in the act of thinking, the serenity was dispersed, the rainbow was obscured, clouds broke up and scattered. Perhaps peace was to be found on the earth, as beauty, in the guise of a flower. Could he feast his eyes on the charm of the Crown Imperiall and find his peace there? But, apparently, least of all, for such beauty is most mortal, death ever at its root:

> But when I digg'd, I saw a worm devoure
> What show'd so well.

Where is the peace then to be found? The answer came to him from a *rev'rend good old man*, perhaps the Holy Scriptures in person, for the story in the first place can only be found there. But, now, it has become the ancient tradition of the merging, allegorically, of the figure of Melchizedek, King of Salem, into the figure of Christ. Melchizedek met Abraham with his gifts of bread and wine: *And Melchizedek King of Salem brought forth bread and wine: and he was the priest of the most high God. And he blessed him, and said, Blessed be Abram of the most high God, possessor of heaven and earth* (Gen. 14, 18-19). Subsequently, Abraham was blessed with the promise of begetting the tribes of the House of Israel. Twelve tribes of Israel and twelve Apostles of Christ, who:

> . . . sweetly liv'd; yet sweetnesse did not save
> His life from foes.

The sweetness of the life of Christ inspired his death with the sweetness of life which sprang into the good seed, the *twelve stalks of wheat*. They, who were told by their Master to preach his word throughout the world, performed their mission, and this sweet, new bread, blessed in death, was infused with divine Mystery so that:

> It prosper'd strangely, and did soon disperse
> Through all the earth . . .

This is what their Lord had commanded. And, because the dispersal of the Eucharistic bread was a divine command, it must needs bring strength with it, and even more, the peace which their Lord brought, the peace which is not of this world. Those, who taste the bread, know by experience, and repeat to others, its strange efficacy:

> That vertue lies therein,
> A secret vertue bringing peace and mirth
> By flight of sinne.

Once the disturbing turmoil of warring sin is put to rout, there is space for the peace of the Lord, and there is rest for the troubled prodigal. Christ, himself, offers the bread to those who wish to taste of it, he gives it generously, freely, with his promise of release, for did not the grain grow in the garden of his Agony? Under the earth, above the earth, and the flowers of the earth, unite:

> Take of this grain, which in my garden grows,
> And grows for you;
> Make bread of it: and that repose
> And peace, which ev'ry where
> With so much earnestnesse you do pursue,
> Is onely there.

iv. *Suffering*

Perhaps, in the daily life, the acceptance of the World of Nature as cut off from the World of Grace, and, thus, the acceptance of joy as the pre-eminent sign of the temporary irruption of Grace into this World of Nature, has the most unhappy consequence. Grief, dryness, physical and mental suffering, sadness at non-achievement, can all take on a distorted quality of doubt. Is this condition due to the absence of Grace and, if Grace has withdrawn, where does the guilt lie? Is God angry? The concept of suffering, in any form, as a work to be integrated into the whole scheme of living, can become unacceptable, if the premise is made that where Grace is, there can be no misery. Suffering can then be doubled, first the actual suffering in itself, and secondly in the doubt as to the cause of the suffering. The spirit may become perplexed before the assault of grief, resentful and frightened, of the grief and of the source.

Affliction (I) gives a very clear picture of such a condition of puzzled wretchedness, only to be answered by irrational love. What other answer could there be, where the reason may not be found?

Herbert remembers the early days of his first awareness of belonging to God. Then, he was happy, it pleased him to serve God freely, he felt himself active and accepted because joy was his constant inner companion. He knew himself, in those days, to be in Grace, because all went well, his own stock of delights, produced by his own person and character, but in addition:

>Augmented with thy gracious benefits.

He was joyous, and so he was assured of the pleasure of God in him, and of the presence of Grace. The glory of God was his constant source of happiness, and the more he realised the glory of God, the more he was drawn into the sole love and service of God. Heaven seemed within his grasp, and the Earth also yielded to his success:

> ... both heav'n and earth
> Payd me my wages in a world of mirth.

Again and again, Herbert speaks of these early *joys*. The *joys* meant that the road that he was taking must be right, and so engendered *hopes* in him. Here, once more, *hope* comes as a word of warning. *Hope* is ever the consummation in this world and *Hope* therefore misleads and deludes that the transcendent aim is attainable. So, filled with hope, the idea of affliction never entered his head:

> Thus argu'd into hopes, my thoughts reserved
> No place for grief or fear.

Impetuously, he flung his whole being into the search for God, a search which at first continued to be apparently rewarded:

> My dayes were straw'd with flow'rs and happinesse;
> There was no moneth but May.

Of course this easy path could not persist over the years. Inevitably, sorrow crept in, insisting on participating where grief came as something unexpected and alien:

> But with my yeares sorrow did twist and grow,
> And made a partie unawares for wo.

Pain, even physical pain, constantly gripped and tormented him, the music of merriment turned to groans of pain. He could hardly believe in this reversal, until his misery made it abundantly plain that he was still alive, and so was the misery. Even when his own health was restored, a worse death befell him in the death of friends. These blows were so great, that it was as if every movement of his mind lost its vitality, its alertness, its critical or analytical capacity. He felt himself boring to himself and to others. With the joy, even the knack of agility of invention had deserted him:

> My mirth and edge was lost; a blunted knife
>   Was of more use then I.

Still in pursuit of God, Herbert remembers how, although his inclination was for Society, he was led into the academic life, before he quite realised what was happening. Herbert puts the whole onus of his former life on the Will of God, the joy, in the first place, was the action of the Spirit on his actions, and so every subsequent motion continued to follow the leading of the Spirit. The sensation of pleasure was the constant accompaniment to the fulfilment of the Divine Will. Whenever he was dissatisfied with the academic life, not on infrequent occasions, some pleasant achievement immediately reassured him that he was working within the Will of God. The medicine, that is the denial of his own will, was there, but it was ever a *sweetned pill*: the Divine presence within the bitterness. And, so, finally he arrived at his last home as a Priest, no more London, and no more Cambridge. Here, he must stay. Here, there could be no tangible success for which to strive:

> ... till I came where
>   I could not go away, nor persevere.

Having, as far as he could see, only followed where God led, the whole force of his present affliction overcomes him, for the grief must have some significance to which he lacks the clue. He is not allowed to rest, one ill after the other assails him: it would seem that God's Will now is directly contrary to his life, yet his life is what God disposed:

> Thus doth thy power crosse-bias me, not making
> Thine own gift good, yet me from my wayes taking.

Intellectually, there can be no answer to the quandary:

> Now I am here, what thou wilt do with me
>   None of my books will show ...

Again, the terror of the chasm between the World of Grace and the World of Nature opens before him, with himself, as Man, somewhere suspended. The constancy of nature is not his, neither the continuity of Grace:

> I reade, and sigh, and wish I were a tree;
>   For sure then I should grow
> To fruit or shade . . .

He would have his work, his set order, and be justified in it. Now he is non-plussed, perplexed, disorientated. For him, there can only be one answer, which is no solution to his agony of doubt, but which is a practical solution of survival:

> Yet, though thou troublest me, I must be meek;
>   In weaknesse must be stout.

One final moment of indecision, of revolt against the uncertainty:

> Well, I will change the service, and go seek
>   Some other master out,

And then the decision:

> Ah my deare God! though I am clean forgot,
> Let me not love thee, if I love thee not.

This is no paradox, but a climax of potential despair integrated into love. Even if Grace has deserted him, as by his grief it would seem to have done, even though he feels himself utterly forsaken, yet, Herbert insists on the necessity to persist in the work of loving God. If, however, this power of loving is in itself only possible through Grace, then he can only pray to God not to take away from him this last sign of Grace, to leave him with the power of loving, even if he appears to slacken in his love. For this interpretation, I am assuming that Herbert is using *let* in the sense of *prevent* or *hinder*, not in the sense of *permit*. However, the alternative interpretation, with the meaning of permitting or allowing would, in a contrary movement, retain in effect the same significance. Herbert would then be praying God to take away his last sign of Grace if he should slacken in his love. But, I prefer the first interpretation as more in keeping with the yearning pursuit.

Bitter-sweet is perhaps even more emphatically expressive of the condition of inexplicable suffering, by means of its very brevity. It is as if there is no space left for discussion. God is Lord, dear and angry at the same time. Of his love there is no doubt, and equally there is no doubt of the pain which he inflicts. God casts down and God raises up. Explanation is impossible. Only active response, within the bewilderment, appears at least the partial solution:

> I will complain, yet praise;
> I will bewail, approve:
> And all my sowre-sweet dayes
> I will lament and love.

Whatever else, the *sweetness*, the presence of his dear Lord, Herbert will not deny.

In *Paradise*, Herbert goes further, and in the image of the pruned trees, sees the necessity for pain. He also, thereby, tentatively would seem to approach the problematic ground of the benefit arising from the Fall, but hardly seriously. The Paradise he sees is perhaps more the new Paradise, where Grace can inspire, subsequent to the Sacrifice of Christ. Once more *sweet* and *Friend* in juxtaposition suggest the presence of Christ, and of the Holy Spirit, the down-thrust of the Comforter through the self-immolation of the Son of God. Imputation remains the only safe-guard in the confusion of suffering, cutting through to the heart with the sword of Grace:

> Such sharpnes shows the sweetest F R E N D :
> Such cuttings rather heal then R E N D :
> And such beginnings touch their E N D .

Complaining, still in the same realm of unexplained suffering, with the puzzled pre-supposition that somewhere and somehow an answer should be available, has yet an unexpected level of approach to the problem. There comes the hint, however reluctant, of the possible joy of participation. Can the answer to suffering lie in, however inglorious, but yet a participating in the suffering of Christ? Nothing explicit is said, but the hint may be found in the imagery.

The opening lines are concerned with the plea that the Almighty would spare his creature: God, who *is* Power and Wisdom is begged to show some leniency to the poor thing, which is Man, simply because of the fact of having been made by God:

> Because I am
> Thy clay that weeps, thy dust that calls.

Creator and created stand with a gulf between. The gulf persists:

> Thou art the Lord of glorie;
> The deed and storie
> Are both thy due . . .

The Lord of Glory on the one side, in whom lies all permanence, who has in his power and at his disposal everything, and to whom all must answer; whatever happens, whatever is enacted, relies on the Creator, whereas:

> . . . but I a silly flie,
> That live or die
> According as the weather falls.

God everlasting and mortal Man would seem to have no meeting-point. So, comes the next question. Can God really be an Absolute, Non-Personal Administrator of Judgment?

> Art thou all justice, Lord?
> Shows not thy word
> More attributes?

And on his side: Man

> . . . all throat or eye,
> To weep or crie?
> Have I no parts but those of grief?

The chasm is wide between them: God, All-Judge, and Man, distraught in meaningless grief. Yet, it seems, as if the first hint of a bridge has been made, already in the words:

> Shows not thy *word*
> More attributes?

This might well be the first suggestion of the redeeming Christ, who constrained his Absolute self, his One-ness, into the Incarnation of true Man. And this hint of participation comes out more strongly in the last lines, with Man's personal grief possibly entering into the grief of the Crucified Christ: Herbert speaks of his period of affliction as his *hour,* and this image surely can not lack the connection with the *hour* of Christ, the Passion. And, even more, Herbert seems to enter into the last prayer of Christ, who, as Man, longed for reprieve, in begging that his hour might be shortened. Would not God send his Grace upon him that relief might come, as he rises in spirit with the Risen Christ?

> Let not thy wrathfull power
> Afflict my houre,
> My inch of life: or let thy gracious power
> Contract my houre,
> That I may climbe and finde relief.

Thus, the risen Christ at the end of the poem would seem to become identified with the Lord of Glory, and so the sting of grief is drawn, in such participation. This overcoming of grief might well be seen as yet another form of Imputation, now giving meaning to suffering, imputed to Man, by means of divine suffering.

> O Who will give me tears? Come all ye springs,
> Dwell in my head & eyes: come, clouds, & rain:
> My grief hath need of all the watry things,
> That nature hath produc'd.

So *Grief* opens, in heroic style, which, in its artificiality, would seem to try and push away the grief, which one man actually experiences, and which is the source of the poem. The assertion of the inability for the human frame to demonstrate the extent of the grief to which he is subjected, continues, more and more emphatically:

> Let ev'ry vein
> Suck up a river to supply mine eyes . . .

And, then:

> What are two shallow foords, two little spouts
> Of a lesse world?

Nothing in this world, however big it may seem, is yet sufficient. His *griefs and doubts* find their root in the old quandary of Man's isolated position within the World of Nature, when he is bereft of Grace. The world around him feels no lack, while he feels himself constricted and desolate:

> . . . the greater is but small,
> A narrow cupboard for my griefs and doubts,
> Which want provision in the midst of all.

Herbert's poetry is not great enough to carry his sorrow. And, here, again, perhaps there comes the same hint as in *Complaining*. Does not Herbert in effect reverse the situation and see, for the instant at any rate, the possibility of the suffering as a participation in something beyond human experience, and thus in itself a sign of Grace, of direct Imputation from the suffering Christ? While he appears to deplore his condition, and in fact on one level does no doubt deplore it, somewhere, at the same time, Herbert be-littles not the grief, but the vehicle of poetry for the grief. Grief is beyond expression. Let poetry cease from seeking in its material verses to come to his aid, to express the inexpressible:

> And keep your measures for some lovers lute,
> Whose grief allows him musick and a ryme . . .

This surely suggests even a sharp differentiation between the grief of the flesh and the grief of the spirit. Poetry can still soothe the lover's woe, and poetry can contain the expression for his woe, but poetry, for this grief of the spirit, is finite, bounded and narrow:

> For mine excludes both measure, tune, and time,
>   Alas, my God!

This grief of the spirit stretches beyond place and time, and holds out imploring hands to God, who alone may understand his suffering. But, because Herbert can not understand the suffering, not even sufficiently to express it in his own verse, the grief must somewhere already be participating in the transcendent and, thence, a Grace. Such a consideration of suffering would remain consistent to Herbert's theological confession.

Affliction (II) seems to me the most beautiful of Herbert's poems of inexpressible suffering. I would suggest, moreover, that here, the previous hints that the only means for bearing suffering, although not explaining it, lies in the acceptance of the Imputation of the participation, become most convincing.

Herbert's desire naturally is to escape from the pain of grief, which he sees as directly descending upon him from his Creator:

>   Kill me not ev'ry day,
> Thou Lord of life . . .

And, Herbert gives his reason for the inefficacy of submitting him to this passion. He could not repay, as a man, God's one death for his sake, even if he repeated his own death over and over again.

His repeated non-voluntary effort of retribution, Herbert sees in the image of *broken pay,* and dying *over each houre.* The *broken pay,* as well as suggesting the payment in instalments, surely also suggests some connotation of the Eucharist, of the broken body of Christ, and the *houre* once again brings in the full echo of the Passion, of the Crucifixion, and hence the bread of the body. Thus, there is some indication of repaying Sacrifice by sacrifice, and this forthwith forcefully brings the immediate impression of a mutual confrontation, God and Man, some form of human participation, however inadequate, in the Sacrifice.

The subsequent lines bring out the inadequacy. No grief can compare with the grief of Christ. Man's tears are salt water, but the tears of Christ are the bloody sweat of redemption, the divine agony of bearing the full burden of the sin of the world. Man's tears, if allowed to mingle with the tears of Christ, could only weaken the force of the blood:

> If all mens tears were let
> Into one common sewer, sea, and brine;
> What were they all, compar'd to thine?
> Wherein if they were set,
> They would discolour thy most bloudy sweat.

The truth must be disclosed, that no suffering can be, unless it exists within the divine suffering of Christ: a separate existence of suffering is impossible because Christ included all suffering into himself:

> Thou art my grief alone,
> Thou Lord conceal it not . . .

In this context, God *is* the Grief, even as he *is* the Joy:

> . . . and as thou art
> All my delight, so all my smart . . .

The imputed Righteousness, which bestows the joy of Grace, of Christ on the Cross, would now seem equally to include Man, within his limited measure, into the active participation of the Divine Grief. God's Grief on the Cross took up Man's grief into his own as a promise, a pledge, of the future grief of Man, which Man himself had not yet experienced, but would share with his Lord, when he would come to experience it:

> Thy crosse took up in one,
> By way of imprest, all my future mone.

By a twist of challenging love, the extreme condition of no-Grace, the periods of dark suffering when no light shows the way, nor gives any assurance that the way is even there, suddenly turns to the highest point of Grace. How can the grief, anticipated by Christ, deny or exclude the presence of Grace? The absence is the presence. Grief is Joy. What might well be the deepest abyss of despair inside a theology, which allows for the arbitrary descent of Grace, is thus suddenly transformed out of dark negativity into potential activity. Yet, even so, one chasm of despair is still to be faced.

CHAPTER IV

The Angry God

I have suggested, at the end of the last chapter, how it seems that Herbert turned passive defeat in affliction and suffering into active victory by the thrust of love which identified, to the measure of his capacity, his grief with that of Christ. But, this would still seem to leave the final and most potent cause of despair. How, in the face of Christ the Redeemer, could Herbert overcome the division between himself and God? Did he really overcome it by submission, as would appear in so many of his poems with the images of conflict and surrender, or did he again manage a further twist of love out of the impasse of the two pressures, the arbitrary World of Grace, and the Imputation of Righteousness?

However much the Church did not question the Trinity dogmatically, and, in fact, asserted the Trinity, yet, once the concept of the humiliated, redeeming, sacrificed Christ was allowed, then the Mystery of the One-ness could not remain unaffected. Whether or not dogmatically denied, some split inevitably was implied in living theology between the Persons of the Father and of the Son. Repeatedly, in Herbert's poems, there is found the actual redemption, payment by the Son to the Father, in lieu of our sins. Father and Son confront each other, and, hence, we, in turn, can not help but confront the Father, as One in need of placating. This confrontation between God and Man, sometimes more explicitly defined by Herbert as the Father and Man, often appears as a meeting of inherent antagonism and love. God, the just God, demands payment from Man. In himself, Man has not the means of payment. Christ pays. That is one level of the conflict. The other level is the constant inadequacy of Man before God. It is here that the question of submission arises, with the many instances of temporary peace, of rebellion, and, then again, of surrender. All revolves round the split between Man and God, a split between God and the redeeming Christ, and, even in some measure, a split of Man away from Christ, because, with the admission of Imputation, the Church, as illustrated in Herbert's attitude to the Saints, must somewhere be denied its one-ness with Christ.

How then can conflict and submission be traced in Herbert, and does he leave submission as simple submission? Can love still achieve the miracle?

H. Baptisme (II) seems to indicate the essential way of submission. A child is innocent, and a child has, as yet, developed no independent life. He is wholly attached to his father, indebted to him, not only for his actual birth, but subsequently for the possibility of continued life, for nourishment and protection, for the means of remaining alive. And did not Christ himself reserve entrance into the Kingdom of Heaven for little children?

> Since, Lord, to thee
> A narrow way and little gate
> Is all the passage . . .

Childhood, therefore, is synonymous, in image, with a condition of Grace, with awareness of the Spirit, alertness to the Word. As a baby, Man can have no conscious faith, but he can receive, most fully and profitably, the gift of potential faith, and so:

> . . . on my infancie
> Thou didst lay hold, and antedate
> My faith in me.

Now the plea: can he not, *in spirit,* retain his childhood, so that he is still near to the Kingdom of Heaven? So, that he may enter in? Can not the relationship persist now in his desired open-ness to God?

> O let me still
> Write thee great God, and me a childe . . .

He wants to be malleable, pliant to God, still unformed. For, with form and shape, must come hardness, the hardness of the Fall, of the rejection of God.

> Let me be soft and supple to thy will,
> Small to my self, to others milde
> Behither ill.

As Man, Herbert has no option but to grow in body, but

spiritually he denies the growth as a delusion. The richness lies in the seeming-poverty of childhood, that is in the spontaneous humility before God. Self-will, the flesh, is an excrescence, a seeming acquisition of wealth, that, at a touch, disintegrates to nothing. Man's autonomy is spurious, not even a genuine part of himself, but an outer symptom of sickness within:

> Although by stealth
> My flesh get on, yet let her sister
> My soul bid nothing, but preserve her wealth:
> The growth of flesh is but a blister;
> Childhood is health.

In *Man,* the apparent necessity of service comes out very clearly, if only as the interim stage before the Kingdom of Heaven is realised upon earth. Until such time as God returns, it would seem that the only possible relationship on Man's part can be of active service. The division between Man and God is stressed, God, as it were, removed into a realm where He reigns aloof and must be placated.

Herbert sees the future return of God to earth as at one with an inner regeneration of Man. God created Man, and no-one builds a *stately habitation* without intending to live in it. And what can be more stately than Man? Man out-does all created nature:

> He is a tree, yet bears more fruit;
> A beast, yet is, or should be more . . .
> . . .
> Man is all symmetrie
> . . .
> He is in little all the sphere.

All nature and nature's resources are at the command of Man, for the comfort of Man:

> More servants wait on Man,
> Then he'l take notice of . . .

Man, in himself, is indeed a microcosmography, and, a world in himself, he has a world to serve him. And, so, the prayer: if God has made this wonderful world of Man, and world for Man, then, will he not enter into the world, and *remain* within it, that Man may be finally redeemed? Herbert is again faced with the dread of the lack of continuity. At present, for Man, he can only see the descent of Grace, to be renewed from instant to instant, never constant. Man is depraved, cut off from the World of Grace, other than by Imputation. Thus, it would seem that he can only implore for the nearest condition in which he can envisage any serenity, that of constant service which would at least connect him to God, somehow, without repeated breaks in the withdrawal of Grace, and with the hope of permanency. Herbert makes the link on the side of Man, by denying passivity, and substituting active service, in total submission:

>Since then, my God, thou hast
> So brave a Palace built; O dwell in it,
> That it may dwell with thee at last!
> Till then, afford us so much wit;
> That, as the world serves us, we may serve thee,
>   And both thy servants be.

Submission is a strange poem, somewhere even cruel in the distorted image of blindness. Did not Christ stretch out his hand that we might see? How can it be possible to think of blindness, in any context, as the means of serving God, or of seeing and following the Truth? In *Submission*, Herbert would seem to deny that the God, who gave Man a mind, might expect Man to serve him with the gift. He insists on jealously guarding his right to serve God, blindly, in total subjugation, leaving no room for the work of the Spirit.

In *Submission*, Herbert cramps himself, in all his stature, into the dwarf dimensions of an ideal child. And the distortion of such an inadequate solution comes out in the repugnant image of the sight-less man, his eyes in the grasp of his Lord. The latent disgust is intensified by the simplicity of the rhythm and of the rhyme. The situation would appear grotesquely commonplace:

>But that thou art my wisdome, Lord,
> And both mine eyes are thine,
> My minde would be extreamly stirr'd
> For missing my designe.

Herbert thanks his God for maiming him to ensure his servitude. A passing thought that he might serve God better in his full strength is brushed aside:

>How know I, if thou shouldst me raise,
> That I should then raise thee?
> Perhaps great places and thy praise
> Do not so well agree.

No, there would appear only to be the one solution: this simple one of nightmare quality:

> Wherefore unto my gift I stand;
> I will no more advise:
> Onely do thou lend me a hand,
> Since thou hast both mine eyes.

To such depths can rational disorientation lead, but, equally, the balance is retained. The continuity, from Herbert's side, whatever the cost, is preserved. The submission has a purpose, in the first place of substituting personal service, as the alternative, to the lack of guarantee for the continued presence of Grace. If God alienates himself, if Grace comes and goes, Man can yet, on his part, refuse to withdraw from God.

Affliction (v) is again concerned with this problem of submission, with assured captivity so that the presence of God remains constant. Grief is the possible solution. And, thus, the Church of Christ may be seen as more stable than Paradise, in as much as Christ has participated in our wretchedness:

> As we at first did board with thee,
> Now thou wouldst taste our miserie.

God is the hunter and his means of trapping are two-fold: through Joy and through Grief. And God has more than one possibility in both kinds of allurement for his satisfaction:

> ... then thy double line
> And sev'rall baits in either kinde
> Furnish thy table to thy minde.

For the Angels there is Joy, but, for Man, the most persuasive means is Grief. As trees, we strengthen through rough buffeting of the gales of affliction. Fancy gardens, with frivolous, pretty designs to catch the eye with superficial charm of the unexpected and unusual, can not withstand assault. And, yet, the prayer is not for Grief alone, however much it might strengthen us. How can we tell how much we can bear without denying our submission? It is better, in all humility, to pray to God that he may mingle the Joy and the Grief, with the precise balance of ingredients to allow us to continue in our work of submission without despair:

> My God, so temper joy and wo,
> That thy bright beams may tame thy bow.

From God, alone, will come the balance; He is the Sun, and He can bring down upon us the light of the sun-shine of joy, and the darkness of the storm of grief. But, the rainbow is already the signal of the victory of sun over storm. Yet, as the rays increase in brightness, the bow becomes less distinct. The serenity of the tempered joy and grief prevails, and affliction and happiness are equally brought into the one peace of the acceptance of God's Will: *We are thine:* the repetition of the demand on God: the contract is being pushed from the side of Man.

In *Obedience*, the insistence, that God will accept our full, voluntary, and unequivocal servitude, persists more emphatically, and the formal movement of the poem, the conventional tone, the legal image of every-day commerce, emphasise the natural relationship which God can hardly refuse.

In commercial transactions, a deed is drawn up which transfers ownership according to the wish of the seller and of the buyer. Why can not this poem, therefore, serve the same purpose of self-transaction:

> My God, if writings may
> Convey a Lordship any way
> Whither the buyer and the seller please;
> Let it not thee displease,
> If this poore paper do as much as they.

The ink is the very blood of his heart. And, with his very life, body and soul, Herbert conveys himself legally to God. He adds, moreover, that if later he should have some qualms, if worldly desires, in the person of pleasure, should at any time wake up in him again, demanding their share of his life, as if he had given himself to God with some clause refuting God's absolute ownership, then, here and now, he leaves no space for the possibility of any heckling rebel within the precious compass of God:

> I here exclude the wrangler from thy treasure.

Nothing will be allowed to take a fraction of the room dedicated to God, and, on his part, God must then take total possession of his property. With this total and legal self-conveyance to God, God has no right to go. He must stay. This will put an end to the despair of the gaps in the lapses of Presence. Is this not an incontrovertible legal agreement?

> O let thy sacred will
> All thy delight in me fulfil!
> Let me not think an action mine own way,
> But as thy love shall sway,
> Resigning up the rudder to thy skill.

Debarred from the continuity of inner Grace, no longer assured of salvation within the guarantee of the Church, Herbert demands, in his total surrender, that God can not abandon him. God, himself, must be his assurance of salvation, ruling him from within. The submission becomes the capturing of God. God is perfect, and, so, if God sees his sins, why can not God direct him?

> So great are thy perfections,
> Thou mayst as well my actions guide, as see.

Then, Herbert produces, as it were, his trump card in this contest with God. Whatever else, the Crucifixion can not be denied. God, as Christ, demonstrated his love for Man. The image of commerce persists:

> Thy sorrows were in earnest; no faint proffer,
> Or superficiall offer
> Of what we might not take, or be withstood.

In earnest: the Crucifixion was a promise, a token, of a subsequent full settlement. The Crucifixion was no casual, no half-meant overture of sale. Nor was it an offer which we could refuse. It was the promise of our redemption, nothing less:

> Wherefore I all forgo . . .

But, Herbert makes one stipulation. In the Crucifixion, there was the suggestion of a free gift. Christ died for us. He was our ransom. He asked for no payment in return. Yet, Herbert insists. This deed, which he is now presenting:

> Lord, let it now by way of purchase go.

His answer to God's love is a submission on legal terms. He will pay. And his payment is the obedience.

The end of *Obedience* is a little puzzling. Why does Herbert suddenly, at this point, refer to someone else? It appears that he would wish some other person also to sign the deed, and he would rejoice if the contract, thus made for both himself and the other person, would be recorded in the heavenly Court of Rolls. The apparent digression in so compact and intimate a poem suggests the possibility that the personal intimacy is not as explicit as it may appear, but that there is some measure of objectivity, of formality, in what Herbert argues with such intensity of feeling. He discloses the secret clue of submission as an active means of survival:

> How happie were my part,
> If some kinde man would thrust his heart
> Into these lines; till in heav'ns Court of Rolls
> They were by winged souls
> Entred for both, farre above their desert!

Giddinesse goes a further step in the contract. Herbert does not only submit in order that God should enter into contract with him, but he exceeds the submission. Herbert dares to demand what he most dreads. The daily terror is of the arbitrary coming and withdrawal of Grace. So, he openly claims the continuity of renewal as his sovereign right. God must grant it, as his part of the bargain, for the willing submission on Herbert's part.

Man is a creature of restlessness, of uncertain desires, of shifting values and aims:

> He is some twentie sev'rall men at least
> Each sev'rall houre.

It is the usual repetitive quarrel between the one inner self, straining to heaven, and the other, longing after immanent satisfaction:

> One while he counts of heav'n, as of his treasure:
> But then a thought creeps in,
> And calls him coward, who for fear of sinne
> Will lose a pleasure.

Full of contrary ambition, Man is blown from side to side. His imagination builds up dreams, only to be swept aside by fresh fantasies. Such is Man's inconstancy, that if his appearance reflected his mind, he would indeed be a grotesque picture of shifting colours! Even more, if we could see into each other's heart, we would certainly not dare to enter into any transaction in the face of such potential deception. This time, the legal contract is between man and man, and the contract is seen as probably invalid:

> Surely if each one saw anothers heart,
>   There would be no commerce,
> No sale or bargain passe: all would disperse,
>   And live apart.

Nor is it the single occasion for a bargain or contract with God. The contract is surpassed into the demand for renewal: the purchase is not of what is, but what will be, repetitively, pure and fresh, re-fashioned by God himself, for God himself. The renewal is a triumph of unity with God, no source for dread of exclusion:

> Lord, mend or rather make us: one creation
>   Will not suffice our turn:
> Except thou make us dayly, we shall spurn
>   Our own salvation.

We shall spurn our own salvation: we should not only be incapable of benefiting from the imputed Righteousness of Christ, but we should reject it. Only God can give us, from one day to the next, the capacity and the will to be the recipients of his Grace. Even to wish to receive the salvation, however passively, is outside our field of willed action. So, we must bind God to us, or we are lost.

> As I one ev'ning sat before my cell,
> Me thoughts a starre did shoot into my lap.
> I rose, and shook my clothes, as knowing well,
> That from small fires comes oft no small mishap.

Once more, the strangely conversational opening tone of *Artillerie* makes whatever follows natural and recognisable. So might anyone sit quietly on a star-lit night, immersed in his own thoughts, glad of the quiet beauty around him. But, into this self-centred peace, comes the attack, sharply, unexpectedly descending from heaven, brought down by no human volition. The missile is fire. The re-action, the normal, worldly self-protection, is to shake off the danger as quickly as possible. The demand of the Spirit is not comfortable and will never stay small, one chink in our hardened armour of pleasure, and we are caught up in the flame of Love. Herbert tries to preserve his aloofness, and he hears the voice, even contemptuous of his customary and trivial denial:

> *Do as thou usest, disobey,*
> *Expell good motions from thy breast,*
> *Which have the face of fire, but end in rest.*

The trial must be by fire, the fire of the Spirit, the fire of martyrdom.

Conscious that the fire can only come from God, an attack from God, Herbert denies that he can be held responsible for any disobedience; even if he has refused the summons of his *dread Lord*, yet his refusal is covered, and his fault cleansed with blood; once more Herbert claims forgiveness as his right, paid for in the self-sacrifice of Christ. Yet, again, he will not rest in the negativity of imputed Righteousness. For him, this is too passive a condition. The tables, as it were, are turned on God. Now he, on his part, attacks God so that their relationship be secure and mutual, that God may not escape him, even as he may not escape God. Herbert attacks God with his double weapon of tears and prayers. And, the implicit fact that this is not essentially a battle of conflict, and that Herbert has, in fact, far surpassed the unbalanced concept of a God to be placated, is strongly suggested in the image of courtship. This is a battle not of conflict, but of love:

> My tears and prayers night and day do wooe,
> And work up to thee . . .

For Herbert, God is constrained to accept his demands because of the Promise, not because of any intrinsic value in Man himself. And, God, the Almighty Creator, in his love, allows the assault. He condescends to let his own creature assail him with his demands of love, in return for God's demand on his creature. And, what is more, God condescends to make the demand of love on his own creature. What can be the solution of this contest?

> Then we are shooters both, and thou dost deigne
> To enter combate with us, and contest
> With thine own clay.

Dexterously, Herbert turns the situation round into the balance. With God, he can not contend, so, he will make the treaty: and the treaty is one of total submission, on condition that God will accept his tears and prayers, that is, that God will keep him in Grace:

> Shunne not my arrows, and behold my breast.
> Yet if thou shunnest . . .

God is caught in Herbert's love. How can He escape? In submission, Herbert pronounces himself totally God's. He rejects even the need of any form of legal negotiation. God and he are unequal partners. Herbert is the finite creature, but his love for God draws him into God, into the transcendent. And, there, beyond the immanent, they can not be parted. The fire which descended from heaven into Herbert, he returns to God, as love, and because it is the fire of God, Himself, it can not burn to ashes:

>There is no articling with thee:
>I am but finite, yet thine infinitely.

Occasionally, the underlying joy of the solution of the submission, which results in the abiding presence of God, comes out more explicitly. This happens in *The Glance*, which recalls the first demand of subjugation, even by one look, one breath of Grace. The unemphatic call of God was sufficient to fill Herbert with inexplicable bliss, of a gladness beyond the power of any immanent pleasure to evoke:

>I felt a sugred strange delight,
>Passing all cordials made by any art,
>Bedew, embalme, and overrunne my heart,
>And take it in.

Herbert was captured. Subsequently, the world re-asserted itself in him, yet, nothing could destroy that first impact, which persisted in its underground activity within him. And, suddenly, the glorious excitement bursts out of the hope of the future:

>What wonders shall we feel, when we shall see
>Thy full-ey'd love!

Now, indeed, we see the love, as in a glass, darkly, as some passing glance, obscured by all around, but, then, there will be nothing to separate, blind submission will be raised into radiance of Presence:

>And one aspect of thine spend in delight
>More then a thousand sunnes disburse in light,
>In heav'n above.

Sometimes, the theme of the relationship, as it were, turns upside down. The inherent demand is to install himself so incontrovertibly as the Servant of the Master that the Master can not evade him. The longing is ever for the continuity, and, yet, Herbert even on his side can not always retain the continuity. How then will God? And, if, in spite of the apparent failure in himself, Herbert still knows that the continuity *is* retained, then surely he can assume that the continuity is also retained in God?

In *Justice* (I), Herbert begins by declaring that he can not understand the apparent contradiction in the way God treats him. He is God's creature, yet God mars and spoils, disfigures what he himself has made, destroying his own possession. Yet, even as God hurts and afflicts, he provides the necessary and only means of relieving the pain. And, again, even as God relieves, through him comes death. And, lastly, God kills, and God reprieves. It would seem an unanswerable riddle. But can there be a parallel? Herbert finds the parallel in himself, and in his attitude to God:

> But when I mark my life and praise,
> Thy justice me most fitly payes . . .

Herbert knows that he praises God constantly, yet, *I praise thee not*. He knows that his prayers are directed solely on God, *yet my prayers stray*. He knows that his intention is good, but, *sinne the hand hath got*. And, above all, and most indicative of the inherent longing:

> My soul doth love thee, yet it loves delay.

If he can not understand his own human ways, how can he understand the working of God? All that he knows is, that in the seeming *in*attention, the attention is always there. In the unceasing love, there would appear procrastination. If his love for God, and he knows without doubt that he loves God, can therefore seem to himself as irregular, is it not only just that God's love for him, so far beyond human comprehension, might also appear erratic? So, once more, God and he are forcibly connected, into a relationship which can even mutually explain itself.

The demand is more straightforward in *Nature*. Herbert cries to God to ignore his side of the relationship. At the moment, he is *full of rebellion*, he would go to the uttermost limit of violence to deny God. So, God must make a more determined attack to counter-balance Herbert's passivity:

> O tame my heart;
> It is thy highest art
> To captivate strong holds to thee.

If God does not over-come him, he is lost, for he can not then retain God. And, if he can not retain God, he will disintegrate into the nothing of evil, and, an impassioned plea to God, make nonsense of his divine creation:

>   And thence by kinde
>   Vanish into a winde,
>   Making thy workmanship deceit.

Herbert begs to God to level the rough surface of his heart, convulsed by passion, to a serenity in which can be inscribed:

> . . . thy rev'rend Law and fear . . .

It would not be outside God's power to re-make his sterile heart, to pour the water of renewal of Grace into his *saplesse* heart. His heart is dry and barren, so hard that it is much more fitting to be its own sepulchre than to contain God. God must, from outside, make his heart fit to receive God. The living, creative Grace inside his heart is not in Herbert's power to stimulate, nor to foster. It must be re-newed. And, for the renewal to be possible, the continuity of unsevered relationship must be presumed. Only if Herbert insists on submitting, can he be sure of retaining God inalienably.

It would seem that in this complicated relationship with God, in the appearance of conflict, the assaults, the rebellion and the taming, mastery and subjection, three poems are particularly revealing in three aspects: *The Odour, Discipline,* and *The Crosse.*

i. *The Odour. 2 Cor. 2, 15*

> For we are unto God, a sweet savour of Christ, in them that are saved, and in them that perish.

In this verse to which Herbert refers, St. Paul has written that *we* are *the sweet savour of Christ.* Yet, Herbert opens *The Odour:*

> How sweetly doth *My Master* sound! *My Master!*

The sweetness has been transferred from servant to Master. This would seem to have been possible only by the interceding figure of Christ. If Righteousness is imputed to us by Christ so that we are received into the forgiving love of God, who otherwise would remain the alienated God of the Fall, then, in the same movement, the love of God must reach us, through the link of Christ's ransom. It is the legal, or commercial image now taken to its limit of mutual acknowledgment. The joy of the *Master* relationship is the highest joy of the immutable love of Christ.

My Master is permeated with the rich delight of *an orientall fragrancie.* The scent of the Grace, which has come through Christ, and which, because of our imputed Righteousness, through Christ, is legally indissoluble from us, is Herbert's constant companion and puzzle. He longs to know precisely, perhaps so as to make even more sure that he can not lose it, with his reason, not emotion, how this Grace comes, and stays, and strengthens him:

> With these all day I do perfume my minde,
>   My minde ev'n thrust into them both:
>   That I might finde
>   What cordials make this curious broth,
> This broth of smells, that feeds and fats my minde.

Both words exercise his mind: it is the dialectic of his triumph: *My* Master. God, his Master, is *his*. Through Christ, the other-ness of the Almighty is overcome.

Now Herbert prays that perhaps, he, as himself, not only in Christ, sacrificed, outside him, may also be received into the love of God. Can not the *My* of *My servant,* take on the same unifying significance? Even with the limitation of the man that he is?

> *My Master,* shall I speak? O that to thee
>   *My servant* were a little so,
>   As flesh may be;
>   That these two words might creep & grow
> To some degree of spicinesse to thee!

The Spirit, within Herbert, should perhaps return, insidiously, whence He came. If the Spirit would be as an intermediary, passing from Herbert to God, from God to Herbert, in the uniting of the possessive Master and servant, then, the Spirit would increase within him, and, in increasing, in the light of the clarity of Reason, would gain the power to increase even more:

> Then should the Pomander, which was before
>   A speaking sweet, mend by reflection,
>   And tell me more . . .

What was, at first, even an instinctive expression of the Grace within, would, in the light of thought, grow and strengthen and become more explicit.

The fullness of the joy would come in this new total mutual inter-play. With the Spirit within him, Herbert can reply to God inversely, that is, where previously he was satisfied with owning God as his master, now, the trade can be plied the other way, not without God's pleasure, with God owning him as his servant. For each the sovereignty lies in the seeming opposite, for neither is it my *Master,* nor my *servant,* but, it is *my* Master, and *my* servant:

> For when *My Master,* which alone is sweet,
> And ev'n in my unworthinesse pleasing,
> Shall call and meet,
> *My servant,* as thee not displeasing,
> That call is but the breathing of the sweet.

Without Christ, it is not possible because of the initial unworthiness, but Christ is the synthesis which allows for the meeting. And, the Grace, poured down upon Man, can, in the reversal of the imputed Righteousness, return up to God, claiming God, as God claims Man. God allows Man to be equal to him in the *my* and permits the contract of constant trade. This is the victory over the terror of the demand of the minute-to-minute renewal of Grace, which would seem inevitable with the rational denial of the Church as the custodian of Grace. If the permanence can not be assured by the Church, then it will be assumed by the personal effort of the triumph of possessive submission. The trade of Grace, and the fruits of Grace which call forth yet more Grace, flows uninterrupted, so that renewal, if renewal there is, in the breath of the Spirit, may become imperceptible in the impetus of love, which never slackens, but gladly toils for unspeakable profits:

> This breathing would with gains by sweetning me
> (As sweet things traffick when they meet)
> Return to thee.
> And so this new commerce and sweet
> Should all my life employ and busie me.

ii. *Discipline*

There is no assurance in the Church that we are in Grace. So, in *The Odour,* in a revelation of delight, the only assurance had been as the love which God can not deny. The love, inspired by the Spirit of God, breaks down all barriers. And, so, how can there be an alien God of wrath? A God to be placated?

The foundation of Christ, again as the synthesis, is implied. How could God and Man meet on common ground without Christ, who gave Man the open door for participating in Love?

In *Discipline,* Herbert does not plead. He claims as his right:

> Throw away thy rod,
> Throw away thy wrath:
> O my God,
> Take the gentle path.

It is the unity of the double submission which Herbert is seeking, the Master-servant reciprocal relationship. In such a relationship, it is not enough for the man to yield, that would be the action of alienated Man, afraid for himself, surrendering in terror to the God of Wrath. The consent must be given on both sides, from God as well as Man. Man submits. But, God agrees to receive the submission. Imputed Righteousness would once again seem diverted through the redeeming Christ into Man himself:

> For my hearts desire
> Unto thine is bent:
>   I aspire
> To a full consent.

It becomes more emphatic that the claim of mutual agreement is through the Word of God, the justification from outside coming within:

> Not a word or look
> I affect to own,
>   But by book,
> And thy book alone.

Only God's *book*, but, nevertheless, Herbert claims his capacity to *own* it; it is *his*, growing from inside, not arbitrarily reaching him from outside. Herbert enlarges on this personal capacity and responsibility. The abhorred irregularity, outside his own volition, is losing its dread reality. He is no longer simply a passive instrument on which God sometimes plays. He is no longer the passive receptacle of a down-striking of Grace. The Grace is within him, and he is free to work inside a continuity assured by the personal relationship of love with God. He may fail, he will fail in his journey to salvation, but he is himself, not tossed about helplessly, not left wondering whether he is chosen, not powerless to assail the Kingdom of Heaven:

> Though I fail, I weep:
> Though I halt in pace,
>   Yet I creep
> To the throne of grace.

The God of Wrath is thrust aside triumphantly. Christ has won the victory of love. And, through Christ, the impossible has become possible. He can establish a treaty of love with God. The blood of Christ washes away the sin. Hard hearts of stone become new and tender and shed their drops of blood of repentance. Sin alienated

Man from God. But, in Christ, Man, on his own, dare again approach God without any other intermediary but the crucified Christ:

>   Then let wrath remove;
>   Love will do the deed:
>   For with love
>   Stonie hearts will bleed.

The answer to the solitude arising from the denial of the absolute Church on the one hand, and the distaste for any final teaching of imputed Righteousness on the other, is found in personal love. Love is seen as the unconquerable force. God, himself, can not withstand love, however weak and mean it may be:

>   Love is swift of foot;
>   Love's a man of warre,
>   And can shoot,
>   And can hit from farre.

Was not the Incarnation, the highest manifestation of love? And is not this Divine Love of self-limitation the same love which Herbert carries in his heart?

>   Who can scape his bow?
>   That which wrought on thee,
>   Brought thee low,
>   Needs must work on me.

There is no option for God, but to submit to the love, which He, himself, *is*, to the love, of Christ, who *is*, himself, Love, and to the love of Man, which He, himself, created in all its inadequacy. Weak as Man's love is, it *is* love within human measure, and Love can not answer love with condemnation:

>   Throw away thy rod;
>   Though man frailties hath,
>   Thou art God:
>   Throw away thy wrath.

iii. *The Crosse*

The Odour and *Discipline* are at the peak of convicton that, through love, the joy of consistent Grace can be experienced. Both poems defy the torment of the arbitrary descent of Grace into helpless Man. Submission in both is the victorious weapon turned back on God. *The Crosse* carries the same theme, but more strongly, for the theme is upheld within the doubt and not in the rare moment of assured tranquillity. *The Crosse* is explicitly the expression of a split, which, in this mood, Herbert can not deny. Yet, inside the tossing of the inescapable encounter, the answer of submission, of the supreme artillery of love, remains obstinately steadfast.

Herbert faces the dreaded anomaly. With all his being, mind, heart, will, he would serve God. He longs only to worship God, to dedicate himself, his family, all and everything in his seeming control to the profession of God. He yearns, he longs for this possibility to the point of sickness:

> To make me sigh, and seek, and faint, and die,
> Untill I had some place, where I might sing,
>   And serve thee; and not onely I,
> But all my wealth and familie might combine
> To set thy honour up, as our designe.

And, yet:

> What is this strange and uncouth thing?

thing: an actual presence of an unknown, unaccountable, and thus somehow menacing obstruction to his deepest intention. Even as he seems to have reached the longed-for point, the achievement is snatched from him. He finds himself powerless.

Of course Herbert may have been referring here, on one level, to his health, to the deterioration so soon after he became a Priest. But, equally, such an explanation, in the full context of his theology, does not seem adequate. The other level surely may not be ignored. The suggestion of conflict is too great. Herbert has fought, on his part, and it is his menaces and efforts which are overcome, and they lie bleeding. Somehow, Grace is withheld. He wants to love, and the inspiration is not granted. But, if his longing lies bleeding, then already, there is the hint of the final solution, once again, through Love. Did not Christ bleed for us? Suffering, in whatever form, can not remain undivorced from Christ and thus the way is already implicitly open, in the defeat, to overcoming the alienation of absence of Grace:

> And then when after much delay,
> Much wrastling, many a combate, this deare end,
> So much desir'd, is giv'n, to take away
>   My power to serve thee; to unbend
> All my abilities, my designes confound,
> And lay my threatnings bleeding on the ground.

Now comes the assertion, and the counter-demand on God. Physically and spiritually Herbert is in a distracting fever. Tossed and turned, he is only sure that the passivity might be allowed to turn into activity: the suffering must be creative; his agony must, in his measure, be the redemptive agony. The discordance and multiplicity of meaningless, that is, love-less, misery can yet be turned, if God submits to the contract, to the unity of the positive symphony:

>One ague dwelleth in my bones,
>Another in my soul (the memorie
>What I would do for thee, if once my grones
>   Could be allow'd for harmonie) . . .

The broken weakness, which he finds in himself, would indeed seem the final impotence. But, immediately, the reminder: how can weakness be impotent when submission can be the only solution? When the appearance of freedom, of power, can be the only real source of harm and pain?

>I am in all a weak disabled thing,
>Save in the sight thereof, where strength doth sting.

Herbert is fully prepared to accept the paradox of his strength in his weakness, physical and spiritual, and yet he sees the stumbling-block. It would seem that even his weakness is not permissible. Where can his success be? When he subjects his will entirely to God, still he achieves nothing:

>Besides, things sort not to my will,
>Ev'n when my will doth studie thy renown . . .

Everything he does, or tries to do, in submission to the Will of God, as he believes, turns round on him, as his own sword reverting on him, ruthlessly and sharply to cut his success to nothing. He may *seem* to be successful, but the assurance is not only missing, but unmistakably severed from him:

>Thou turnest th' edge of all things on me still,
>Taking me up to throw me down . . .

The assurance is taken from him by God alone. God turns the edge. God gives him the practical appearance of success, raising him out of the slough of non-assurance and God casts him down again in the spirit at the very instant of actual achievement, to remind him that he can not know of success, nor even experience success *as* success:

> So that, ev'n when my hopes seem to be sped,
> I am to grief alive, to them as dead.

The image of conflict once again is foremost. Herbert has shot his arrow to defeat God, to know for certain that he was doing the Will of God, that he was on the way to salvation: the arrow has landed. And, he is further from his target than at the first movement of taking aim:

> To have my aim, and yet to be
> Further from it then when I bent my bow . . .

He can hardly contain his cry of despair, at the tormenting nonsense of the situation; everything turned back on him: his *hopes*, his torture: once again, the seductive delusion of *hope:* the sum-total and reward of his grieved efforts, more grief. He feels himself tormented to the uttermost by the reversal and the contrast. His pain is not single, but double, because it stands out in relief to freedom from affliction. His is the poverty amidst the possibility of plenty, and his is the un-blossoming in the Garden of Delight:

> Is in the midst of delicates to need,
> And ev'n in Paradise to be a weed.

He cries to God, demanding his attention, not as *Lord*, but as *Father*. Could this perhaps be a preliminary self-identification with the tormented Christ, on whom, alone, he relies for God's condescension? God is his *deare Father*, and he begs:

> Ah my deare Father, ease my smart!

He implores that he may be spared from these contradictory movements, which are imprisoning and destroying him. These movements, which would appear to be antithetical, denying each other, he sees in the image of *crosse actions:* actions, opposite to each other, and apparently mutually exclusive and destructive:

> These contrarieties crush me: these crosse actions
> Doe winde a rope about, and cut my heart . . .

And, at this last moment, victory is won, his victory, in the triumph of the Cross. These same contradictions, this cross, are true to the Person of His Son. The synthesis is perfect in the Incarnate Son on the Cross, his arms stretched out in apparent contradiction, by death, of His eternity, by the abandonment of him by God. The contract is re-asserted in the Glory of Christ, crucified:

> And yet since these thy contradictions
> Are properly a crosse felt by thy Sonne,
> With but foure words, my words, *Thy will be done.*

So, I have attempted to trace through this chapter how, in the uncertainty of any assurance of continued Grace, in the no-knowledge of success, and, with a seemingly inherent distaste for an absolute doctrine of the imputation of Righteousness, Herbert found his own path by a creative submission to *the Angry God*. This submission, in fact, involved God, as it were, into a contract of love. But, such a contract would only seem possible on the premise of the synthesis of the One Person of Christ, true God and true Man. It would therefore seem of the greatest importance to enter into Herbert's personal relationship to Christ.

PART II

THE WORK OF LOVE

CHAPTER I

The Person of Christ

The direction would now seem to turn. Orientation on Christ, openly and singly, alone can dispel the fearful anticipation of the descent of arbitrary Grace. Passive reception of imputed Righteousness can turn, in the vision of Christ, to active participation in Love.

Already, in the preceding chapters, it has gradually become more and more clear, that whatever the theological position, somehow the Person of Christ is foremost. It has also been suggested how Herbert ever overcomes the rifts inherent in the broad theology of his Church by the sudden twist of love which over-rules the gap, giving meaning to grief and submission. How and where, then, does Herbert lay his emphasis on the Person of Christ, and how does this emphasis free him from any potential passivity of theological latitude?

i. *Christ: The Redeemer*

The conflict between Sin and Grace is directed to the Person of Christ in *L'Envoy*.

Salvation lies in the acknowledgment of Christ, the Redeemer, the actual Cross is the salvation. Grace lies in the confession of Christ, and in Christ alone lies the Mystery of the power to awaken the soul to this confession, so the prayer to the *King of Glorie, King of Peace* not to allow Sin to lead the people of Christ into the misapprehension that his *bloud is cold,* or that his *death is also dead,* or that his flesh has *lost his food,* or, finally, that his Cross is *common wood.* Herbert prays for the confirmation that from Christ alone, and unquestionably, comes the full sovereignty of redemption.

In the image of *Marie Magdalene,* the sinner, again comes the direct premise of Christ, alone, as the source of redemption:

> Deare soul, she knew who did vouchsafe and deigne
> To bear her filth . . .

But, here, there is the denial of passive redemption, that is the denial of the arbitrary imputation of Righteousness. There must be, apparently, the effort of love towards Christ, only of love. Love over-rides the theory of an inexplicable condition of faith. Mary came to wash His feet, moved by a real love, for a real person, and so:

> As she had brought wherewith to stain,
> So to bring in wherewith to wash:
> And yet in washing one, she washed both.

Grace, the Sacrament of Baptism, and the redemption of the Crucified Christ, the imputed Righteousness of Christ carried within his Sacrifice, become strongly inter-locked in *H. Baptisme* (1).

Man's life of sin, since baptism, is the *dark and shadie grove*, an unclear region of ground, over-grown with clinging and inter-lacing branches so that it is not easy to distinguish one act from another, nor see any one act in relation to God. The probing into this undergrowth means a condition of ever-increasing confusion. The only answer is not to dwell on personal sins, for which there can be no clarification within oneself, but to turn one's attention to the Sacrament of baptism:

> ... and to that water flie,
> Which is above the heav'ns, ...

The water of baptism, that is the Mystery of the Sacrament, derives only from God. It is an incomprehensible Sacrament. But, at one and the same time, its healing quality persists, for it is the Grace contained within the Sacrifice of Christ, and not dependent on human sin, nor on human virtue:

> ... whose spring and vent
> Is in my deare Redeemers pierced side.

The Sacifice of Christ not only provides the means for healing of the sin, but, also, has the power to make up divinely, what must be lacking humanly. Yet, this statement of imputation, through the connection with the Baptismal Grace, loses its absolute objectivity:

> In you Redemption measures all my time,
> And spreads the plaister equall to the crime.

The election becomes universal through baptism, and, even more, unfailing in its persisting quality of redemption:

> You taught the Book of Life my name, that so
> What ever future sinnes should me miscall,
> Your first acquaintance might discredit all.

In *Justice* (II) comes out the unrelieved terror of the encounter with the God of Wrath, on that last dreadful day, if not for the personal sacrifice, and, thereby, intervention of Christ. Herbert now sees that first picture as distorted, but it had been there, and could hardly avoid being somewhere there if, by human measures, we ascribe a relationship from God to Man:

> O Dreadfull Justice, what a fright and terrour
> Wast thou of old,
> When sinne and errour
> Did show and shape thy looks to me,
> And through their glasse discolour thee!
> He that did but look up, was proud and bold.

Although the picture of terror is a discoloured one, yet, without the knowledge of Christ, it would still be an act of the greatest arrogance to dare, on one's own, to look upon the Day of Judgment. Human courage and human intellect, both shrink to nothing in the face of this gruesome presence of accusation and condemnation:

> The dishes of thy ballance seem'd to gape,
> Like two great pits;
> The beam and scape
> Did like some torturing engine show;
> Thy hand above did burn and glow,
> Danting the stoutest hearts, the proudest wits.

It would have been, and, indeed, was, an impasse of sinful impotency on the one side, and righteous Omnipotence on the other. But, in Christ, the veil of the temple was rent in two, and a meeting-point established between human sin and divine Goodness. Through the sacrifice of the spotless Lamb, the *pure vail* of Christ, fear is dispelled. The scales of Judgment, within the redemption of Christ, are held and balance by his total purity. The scales are directed by his *white* hand, and the scales, because of his intervention, are no longer mutually exclusive. Bad is not irrevocably isolated from Good. The scales now alternately come down to earth to scoop up bad and good alike to heaven. There is no need to fear justice, when justice is embodied in Christ. When there was no redeeming Christ, then God called Man directly, and Man directly answered, and was directly responsible to God. But, now the responsibility is not in Man's hand. It is only for Man to call on the name of Christ, to present Christ at the Judgment. Christ answers for Man at the Judgment. What, then, is there to fear? Nothing can lack. There can only be an abundance:

>   Gods promises have made thee mine;
>   Why should I justice now decline?
> Against me there is none, but for me much.

In *The Discharge,* Herbert goes even further into the question of personal responsibility at death, and, hence, constant anxiety in life. It would seem that reasonably it is not possible even to conceive, within the mortal mind, the instant after death. Thus, Herbert relegates the inquisitive concern to the realm of the heart, the searching of the spirit where it may strive to reach; and the heart is the casket, the container, of unearthly Grace, as well as of Sin. It is the *busie enquiring* heart, which strains after what it can not reach, distending itself, as it were, out of its own shape, looking high and low for the answer which it can not obtain. And it is the heart, which, Herbert reminds, has totally submitted. Once again, the image of commerce: the heart has made its accounts, obtained the total, and given up *the whole.* And, in the yielding of the whole, it yielded its rights, both for the future, and for the past. In the yielding, Herbert sees the life of his heart now as God's, fully within God's dispensation and rule; it is not for the heart to choose when to act, or what to do. Time and achievement within time mean nothing. Human measures have yielded to heavenly measures in the submission. There is no autonomous future for his heart:

> Thy life is Gods, thy time to come is gone,
>   And is his right.
> He is thy night at noon: he is at night
>   Thy noon alone.
> The crop is his, for he hath sown.

The submission is the acknowledgment of God's prior claim. The soul's salvation lies in this act of God, of taking the human soul into his own scheme of Providence:

> And well it was for thee, when this befell,
>   That God did make
> Thy businesse his, and in thy life partake:
>   For thou canst tell,
>   If it be his once, all is well.

Herbert, hence, insists that, if the future is the monopoly of God, fully in his hands alone, then the soul is not only free to concentrate on the present, but, in fact, is in duty bound to do so. The suggestion of the image of commerce continues:

> Onely the present is thy part and fee.

The peering into the future and the dread of the outcome is not only vain in the circumstances but obscures the real work of the present:

> If, though thou didst not beat thy future brow,
> Thou couldst well see
> What present things requir'd of thee.

The servant of the contract between God and Man discharges himself finally from the onus of the future. The present things demand sufficiently. Searching vainly into the future is only as the stirring up of muddy water in a clear pool. The work is to drink of the manifest waters of what is known and evident. A seeking after the fear and grief of the future merely increases the inherent grief. The work is now:

> Man and the present fit: if he provide,
> He breaks the square.

There is, therefore, even a mathematical congruity between Man and the present time. If he seeks to look ahead, he disrupts the harmony of the diagram of human life. Now, there stands out strongly, challengingly:

> This houre is mine: if for the next I care,
> I grow too wide,
> And do encroach upon deaths side.

This houre is mine: It is hardly possible not to see in these words, somewhere, a connection with *the hour* of Christ, the Redeemer. *The hour* for Christ was the hour of his Passion, the hour of his Crucifixion, the hour of his taking upon himself our full humanity, our sin as one whole. In claiming the hour as his, Herbert, it would seem, openly states his one possibility of participation in the suffering of Christ, and, thereby, in his Glory. Herbert insists that he must accept the reality of the present time, as humanity comprehends it, and seek no escape, even under the disguise of fear and anxiety, into the future. Trespass on to the side of death goes beyond human capacity and, thereby, denies salvation in *the hour* of Christ. Christ redeemed Man *within* temporal time. Eternity is never lacking, but it encircles *the hour* of the present and may only be reached through death, not through any form of speculation as to what may or may not occur in the future:

> For death each houre environs and surrounds.
>   He that would know
> And care for future chances, cannot go
>   Unto those grounds,
>   But through a Church-yard which them bounds.

The present must wither and die, but, in the mean-time, absorption in the fear of the after-life only prolongs and extends the thread of fear unceasingly. In his compassion, God has chained up the hound of terror while it is yet day. Why should we let slip this dog of grief, and, thus, double the grief, bearing it now and after death? Or, perhaps, the grief will not ever come. This going out to meet the problematic terror of death is, in effect, a betrayal of Christ's Sacrifice, of Christ's redeeming act of ransom:

>   Away distrust:
> My God hath promis'd; he is just.

The Dawning demands the unequivocal acceptance of the redemptive act of Christ without the least weakness of dis-belief, and, thence, into despondency. It is not even a question of working in the present and postponing the future to the promise of Christ, but it is the more exacting demand of feeling happy and certain now, in the present, in the serene and joyous assurance of the salvation. Not a moment must ever be wasted in lingering on the suffering of Christ, for the suffering was a triumph not a defeat. Herbert rebukes his soul for obstinate lingering on the Cross, and with the Cross of Christ, the implication of our grief, rather than on the significance of the Cross in the scheme of salvation:

> But thou dost still lament, and pine, and crie;
> And feel his death, but not his victorie.

This obdurate denial of the salvation prevents the experience of Christ's Resurrection as the Resurrection of all. It is interesting that, once again, it would seem that Herbert denies any form of *passive* salvation. The Cross and the Resurrection have saved us. Yet, we must make the effort, some effort, as Mary Magdalene. Herbert seems to resent any suggestion that he can be saved without his volition, and so once more he denies any kind of absolute theology of imputation:

> Do not by hanging down break from the hand,
>   Which as it riseth, raiseth thee:
>   Arise, arise;
> And with his buriall-linen drie thine eyes . . .

As a poetic image the final couplet verges ridiculously on bathos, but, in content, it is far from foolish as Herbert brings the universal theology of redemption to the finest point of the single person:

> Christ left his grave-clothes, that we might, when grief
> Draws tears, or bloud, not want a handkerchief.

The theme of despair, approached from a different point, is taken up again in *The Bag,* and, once again, seen as resolved in the redemptive act of the Cross, an act which persists from minute to minute.

There is no condition of storm to which Christ can not bring peace: the boat of Herbert's life is as safe as the little boat tossing on the waters of the Sea of Galilee. It is safe because *my Lord Jesus di'd.* This is the story of Christ's self-limitation for the salvation of mankind. As he rode, the God of Power, in his majestic robes of Glory, he made the decision to descend to earth. Was this image of the riding already the pre-image of the Entry into Jerusalem? So, he shed the dazzling light of the Array of Heaven, the stars, the clouds, lightning, and the sky, for he knew what clothes he would wear. He, alone, God Incarnate, could not help but know all that awaited him. And, he took all upon himself:

> He smil'd and said as he did go,
> He had new clothes a making here below.

In the taking of all upon himself, only one last sacrifice remained. The full payment of our sins was yet to be made:

> And having giv'n the rest before,
> Here he gave up his life to pay our score.

Our score: our account within the world, the payment for our birth into sin, which he began with the payment of his birth at the Inn. He paid *our score,* as did the Good Samaritan in the same Inn for the Jew fallen by the assaults of the flesh. But, and this is a question which can not be avoided, *to whom* did he pay it? In this image still somewhere looms the possibility of a theological rift between God, the Father, and God, the Son, the division between God and the fallen world, which must be bought back into unity by means of sacrifice. At the moment of his returning to heaven, having paid our debt in full, Christ received the stroke of the spear in his side. The hole was rent in his side. He was no Judas, he was Christ, nor was he one of his own disciples, for he carried no bag for his journey. His journey was the return to his Father, and any message to his Father could be put within the hole in his side, and thus be assured of the safest delivery. In his death, Christ, in the most realistic way possible, opened himself to include us in our sin, and, in our repentance, takes us within himself, to present us, with the blessing of his suffering, to his Father for forgiveness. The door of his pierced side remains open. Christ is the door, and his blood continues to flow for all who drink to their redemption: *any of my friends.* As always, *friend* has the connotation of the Holy Spirit, and so the suggestion is of those who make their communion *in the Spirit,* in the Grace of the faith to experience the reality of the Mystery. True repentance, true seeking after Christ, will for ever retain its first validity of salvation. There can be no room for despondency:

Sighs will convey
Any thing to me. Harke, Despair away.

The doubt of despair comes again in *Assurance.* The doubt is the poison which creeps into Man, slily suggesting that he is resting in a false assurance of security. The Covenant, which he might have imagined between himself and God, was far more slender than he thought, and in fact already nearly dissolved, if not completely. This is insidious poison, suited for unlocking:

the doore
To cold despairs, and gnawing pensivenesse . . .

The poison of the thought could gnaw at Man's mind like rats at food, until nothing should remain. The answer can only again be one: the repentance and the full reliance on the mediation of Christ. First, the repentance of the Prodigal:

But I will to my Father,
Who heard thee say it.

Again, no passive redemption, but the active seeking out, the throwing-off of sinful apathy. And, then, the conviction that Man's faith in his salvation is not on himself. If his reliance were on himself, then the devil would indeed speak true in prophesying destruction. But, *in this league,* Christ again fills in the gaps:

> Thou art not onely to perform thy part,
> But also mine . . .

The contract was dictated by Christ, who guided Man's hand as he wrote, a suggestion here again of the validity of the Baptismal Sacrament. If Christ fails Man, then Christ is not Christ. But Christ is his rock, and Man therefore is invincible. When all else crumbles:

> Then shalt thou be my rock and tower,
> And make their ruine praise thy power.

It is the Person of Christ alone, who is the Rock of Salvation, the direct transference. Here, there is no space for the intervention of the Church. The thought of despair is the thought without Grace. It is the thought induced by fallen Man who has forgotten his original condition of Grace, and so Herbert taunts the thought with its nakedness:

> Now foolish thought go on,
> Spin out thy thread, and make thereof a coat
> To hide thy shame . . .

The fool's words of the enemy will stick in his own throat. The fall is not the end of Man. The Creation was a creation of love by God for himself, but the Redemption was an act of love for Man. Christ, who is Love and who is Truth, completes, in his act of redemption, the work begun by God in the creation:

> What for it self love once began,
> Now love and truth will end in man.

In *An Offering,* there comes out very fully this repeated contention in Herbert of Christ's act of redemption finding its expression in the over-flow of his Grace to compensate for our lack, hence allowing us to render back to him what is due. On each occasion, Herbert writes of this, he is extremely precise in his insistence on this point of redemptive theology. The righteousness of Christ does not merely cover our faults indiscriminately, but it becomes our own inner Grace that we may, as ourselves, work towards salvation.

The offering is our heart, that is ourselves. But can a human heart be pure? And how can it, at its purest, compare with Christ's self-limitation, as God, to save us?

> Yet one pure heart is nothing to bestow:
> In Christ two natures met to be thy cure.

Could we not offer more if we could feel that good begets good within us? Would it not be possible for one good part of our heart to represent the rest of it and win Grace in its single goodness, while the remainder were even unaware of what was happening? But, Herbert's fear is of the irreparable disunity in the heart induced by warring passions:

> These parcell out thy heart: recover these,
> And thou mayst offer many gifts in one.

The effort of unifying must be made. But, this is not possible on one's own. There is only one ointment which can repair the damage of disunity, of the warring of the Legion. This is:

> . . . . a balsome, or indeed a bloud,
> Dropping from heav'n, which doth both cleanse and close
> All sorts of wounds . . .

Christ's blood purifies and heals. Christ's blood alone brings unity into multiplicity. But, the burden is on us to find it, that is, not to imbibe it passively but with all the vigour of penitential love. The blood must be drunk to good and not to condemnation. And, strong, in the strength of Christ, only then, it becomes possible to bring the offering of the heart to him:

> Since my sadnesse
> Into gladnesse
> Lord thou dost convert,
> O accept
> What thou hast kept,
> As thy due desert.

The gift on its own lacks the relish of any sanctifying Grace, but:

> Yet thy favour
> May give savour
> To this poore oblation;
> And it raise
> To be thy praise,
> And be my salvation.

In *Longing,* the conviction of the redeeming Christ is there, but, the uncertainty of the actual realisation of the presence painfully pervades the trust. *Longing* is a cry of total trust, but, so too, the agony of maintaining such a trust unflinchingly in the face of persisting counter-suggestion.

Herbert's pleading for confirmation of his dependence rises in sick terror to what seems to him torturing impassivity. He must have a sign of re-action that his fear may even be slightly allayed. He can not believe that the presence of Christ's saving love can be there, if he can not experience any sign of it. And, so, he seeks and begs and implores, his condition growing worse and worse in the face of apparent silence:

>   With sick and famisht eyes,
> With doubling knees and weary bones,
>   To thee my cries,
>   To thee my grones,
> To thee my sighs, my tears ascend:
>   No end?

In his agony, he only knows that any goodness in us derives from Christ:

>   From thee all pitie flows.
> Mothers are kinde, because thou art,
>   And dost dispose
>   To them a part . . .

Christ is all for Herbert. Why does Christ then not listen? Why does Christ take no notice of his burning torment? Then Herbert pleads for Christ to remember his death on the Cross. He died on the Cross for our salvation. He bowed his head in death upon the Cross, that we might live, how can he then be more dead to the sound of Herbert's pleading now than when he was on the Cross? How can Christ, who created us, be deaf to our cries? God created us out of dust, and now the created dust is animated; and, animated, it becomes mobile, and directs all its motions towards Christ alone. How much longer can he delay to give the nourishment implored from him by the heap of living dust, a man?

>   Wilt thou deferre
>   To succour me,
> Thy pile of dust, wherein each crumme
>   Sayes, Come?

The image of bread at this point is strange and evocative. Bread can only signify the Eucharistic feast, the body of Christ. But, Herbert is speaking of himself. Thus, he seems to suggest that the living body of Christ is the whole Church, of which he, himself, is a particle. The particle of dust, his humanity, is also a crumb of bread, his redeemed humanity. The crumb, which he is, is the measure of his sanctity in Christ, which allows him to dare to call upon Christ.

Herbert will not accept a world let loose, outside the dispensation of Providence, to run its own course recklessly to final headlong destruction. He reasserts, in spite of his state of despair:

> Indeed the world's thy book,
> Where all things have their leafe assign'd . . .

Thus, he insists on a primary providential order, where Man receives his due reward or punishment, the scales of *Justice* (II). But he will not move from the obstinate conviction, that there is space between the lines of the Book of Judgment, and the space is within the sovereign power of *a meek look*. Christ is delivered up, the sacrificial lamb, and through his sacrifice, Man lives. The table is full, but still the side-roads can be searched and room found for the poorest and meanest guests at the banquet. And, the banquet is no mere passing meal, but a home, the first home, within the Grace of the Holy Spirit:

> Thy board is full, yet humble guests
> Finde nests.

Yet, now, the answer is still delayed. Herbert reproaches his Lord for the delay, he reminds his Lord that through the redeeming limitation he is now the son, and, thereby, he feels that he deserves some sign of recognition:

> Thou tarriest, while I die,
> And fall to nothing: thou dost reigne,
> And rule on high,
> While I remain
> In bitter grief: yet am I stil'd
> Thy childe.

And, again, he questions in reproach. If Christ left heaven to become Man, was it not that he might redeem Man? Then,

>   . . . how can it be,
>   That thou art grown
>   Thus hard to me?

hard: Herbert has transferred in his agony the adjective he normally reserves for his own heart, when it is not amenable to Grace, to Christ. But, with such a transference, comes of course the mute suggestion that fault somewhere must still rest in him. It is his own hardness which, in the last count, can only cause the seeming hardness in Christ. Christ has overcome death by death, his promise of redemption surely pleads for Man. And, equally, Herbert denies once more, any question of passive redemption. His pleading is active, his repentance, real, his heart broken in pieces in representative image of Christ himself:

>   Lord JESU, heare my heart,
> Which hath been broken now so long,
>   That ev'ry part
>   Hath got a tongue!
>   Thy beggars grow; rid them away
>   To day.

The pain becomes unbearable. The torment will destroy him. But, he clings to the feet of the crucified Christ, his Redeemer, from whom alone comes the sweet Grace of salvation, who alone can heal the contortions of sin:

>   My love, my sweetnesse, heare!
> By these thy feet, at which my heart
>   Lies all the yeare,
>   Pluck out thy dart,
> And heal my troubled breast which cryes,
>   Which dyes.

The *Clasping of hands* would seem the finest and most complete expression of Herbert's interpretation of the redeeming Christ. Here, he brings out most forcefully the non-passivity in Man, which alone can give energy to the act of redemption; in Man's activity, the redemption springs over from an objective, unpredictable force, from outside, into an objective, but comprehensible force from inside: the final inter-locking of Imputation and Inner Grace in the Mystery of the Person of Christ, and in the spiritual activity of Man.

> Lord, thou art mine, and I am thine,
> If mine I am: and thine much more,
> Then I or ought, or can be mine.

Christ is ours, in as much as he became Man, and, in becoming Man, he took us upon him. Creator and Redeemer, Christ owns us far more than we ourselves. And, what is more, being Christ's, we become far more ourselves, in as much as the disguise of sin falls off, leaving us as we really are:

> Yet to be thine, doth me restore . . .

Furthermore, receiving Christ, we receive Christ's strength, over and above the restoration of our own power in him:

> Since this being mine, brings with it thine,
> And thou with me dost thee restore.

Life without Christ would be a no-life:

> If I without thee would be mine,
> I neither should be mine nor thine.

Through his suffering for us, Christ would even seem more to belong to us than to himself. His giving of himself for us, brings his Person flowing into ours:

> Lord, I am thine, and thou art mine:
> So mine thou art, that something more
> I may presume thee mine, then thine.
> For thou didst suffer to restore
> Not thee, but me, and to be mine . . .

This contention, that Christ, in his redeeming sacrifice, is rather ours than his, grows even stronger, for in death he was Man, not God:

> And with advantage mine the more,
> Since thou in death wast none of thine,
> Yet then as mine didst me restore.

But, the lingering fear of the arbitrary removal of Grace is never fully absent from Herbert. So, the last plea is once again for the constancy, that Christ is ever his, and he Christ's, or, even more to be longed for, that the theological concept of the split may finally be overcome and the Grace from outside be at one with the Grace within:

> O be mine still! still make me thine!
> Or rather make no Thine and Mine!

ii. *Christ: the Beloved*

Christ, the Redeemer, does not stay in Herbert's theology in any sense as a mere idea. Christ is ever fully a Person, the Person of God, Incarnate. And, Herbert persists in emphasising the reality of the Person of Christ, as God, and as Man. The essence of the reality, for Herbert, lies in the motive for the Incarnation and the Redemption. He sees the motive, as far as can be comprehended in human terms, as nothing but love, Divine Love within human measures. Once the Love is seen, and recognised as Love, then the only answer to it can, in its turn, be love. The personal love of each one of us towards Christ and, since Herbert sometimes differentiates, for God, is, in the last count, the most effective statement of theology. Without love, theology is an empty word. Thus, Herbert re-enacts aspect after aspect of God's actual love for us, and our reciprocal obligation and yearning, and, thereby, lays the foundation and structure of any Christian theology.

However else one sees the suffering on the Cross, it can not ultimately be otherwise understood than as a manifest act of love. Christ suffered in reality, in the full awareness of pain. Herbert emphasises this basis of Christian theology. He pours his poetry into reminding us that the Crucifixion was not an idealism, but a reality. In *The Sacrifice*, the refrain is like the slow dropping of blood:

> Was ever grief like mine?

Verse by verse, the evidence builds up against our betrayal of Christ, our indifference, our blindness to the light of his love. They, who could not survive without him, wish him dead: they, who were weak, use the power given by him against him: his own Apostle sold him: He knew the agony before him, and prayed that the cup might yet pass from him: His blood, destined to heal all wounds, but his own, and the Disciples could not even keep awake to offer some comfort of love. Mean little men, with tiny flickering lights, dare to lay hands on the Sun. They lay their hands on him who is the Way and the Truth, and most true to his betrayers and murderers. He is alone in his grief, even deserted by those who recognised him as the Christ. All the accusations are brought against him, particularly of a variety of blasphemy. They accuse

Christ and condemn him to die, who gave them the breath to live. They accuse and mock him and his reply is: love. He sends out to them his Comforter of love, and their hearts, hard with sin, reject the Spirit. Theirs is an active, not passive denial of this offering of divine love:

> My silence rather doth augment their crie;
> My dove doth back into my bosome flie,
> Because the raging waters still are high . . .

The cry of his loved people is to crucify him. Contorted in their hatred, they only wish to destroy him, who loves them. Once God made water to spring from the rock for parched Israelites, but the rock of their hearts is closed for they deny Christ, and proclaim Caesar as their king. They deny Christ and torture him, and mock him. And give him to death. It is too late for the Disciples, who slept, to weep now. Christ's tears suffice for all. The scarlet robe proclaims that his blood alone can redeem us. On his head, thorns, in the place of the vine which he had planted. The curse of Adam is upon him, and they strike his head, the source of all blessings. And Love, Truth, turns all to love. Scourged and mocked, he is led out to be crucified, and first he, then Simon, bears the cross. He is led to be crucified on the tree to atone for Man's disobedience with the fruit of a tree. The grief he bears would be enough to melt the strongest armour of sinful indifference, but the climax of the grief comes with an overwhelming terror. The refrain changes from the bearable to the unbearable:

> But, *O my God, my God!* why leav'st thou me,
> The sonne, in whom thou dost delight to be?
> *My God, my God* ———
>   Never was grief like mine.

And, then, the grief returns again to the compass of human suffering. How can men ever compete in the grief of God refused of God? The mockery is picked up again, growing in intensity at the last minutes of human life. And, the answer of Love to the scornful reproach that he will not heal himself:

> In healing not my self, there doth consist
> All that salvation, which ye now resist;
> Your safetie in my sicknesse doth subsist . . .

The crucifixion is seen as the final humiliation, a King, put to death by his subjects, in the company of thieves, vinegar offered mingled with gall, his garments parted. And, in this humiliation, the final effort on the Redeemer's part of redemption:

> Nay, after death their spite shall further go;
> For they will pierce my side, I full well know;
> That as sinne came, so Sacraments might flow . . .

The climax of the unbearable grief is picked up in the final verses. The death is the salvation, but the cost remains beyond all measure:

> But now I die; now all is finished.
> My wo, mans weal: and now I bow my head.
> Onely let others say, when I am dead,
>   Never was grief like mine.

The sudden and horrified realisation of the real suffering, the real entombment, no mere legend, no discussion of theory, comes again in *Sepulchre*.

> O blessed bodie! Whither art thou thrown?
> No lodging for thee, but a cold hard stone?
> So many hearts on earth, and yet not one
>   Receive thee?

The *cold, hard stone* of the sepulchre is emphatically connected, by image, with the hardness of a heart impervious to Grace. Christ of the sepulchre is identified with Christ within us. In our hearts there is wide room for every conceivable nonsense, only there is no room for Christ. The rock of the sepulchre is pure, the stone of our hearts corrupt. The sepulchre had been used for no one previously, the stone of our hearts encloses sin after sin. Three forms of stone: the pure rock of the sepulchre, the rock which reminds us of the rock who is God himself, and the rock which is the first Covenant; then, the thick protection with which we enclose our hearts against Grace; and, finally, the actual missiles with which we try to destroy Love, coming to seek and save us. But, we can not stop Christ from loving us; try as we may, his love refuses to be rejected, and, in spite of ourselves, we are not allowed to destroy ourselves by the weight of the stones of our sin:

> Yet do we still persist as we began,
> And so should perish, but that nothing can,
> Though it be cold, hard, foul, from loving man
>   Withhold thee.

Sunday brings out another aspect. In the face of Christ's love, we can not help but re-act, somehow, in our own slight measure. Each Sunday seems an aid towards somehow returning the love, poured down upon us. Sunday heralds heaven, the promise of redemption written by a *friend,* and the ink is his *blood.* Sunday is therefore the light of the week, illuminating the way forward. Sunday is the face of the week lying behind it. Sunday is the weekly force to turn us round and re-orientate us to what lies beyond. Sundays are the pillars of the house of life, week-days the rooms filled with vanity. Sundays, threaded together, are the ornament of the Church, Brides of Christ, *the eternall glorious King.* Sundays provide the real blessings, far out-stepping *hope,* erroneous expectation. Sunday is the particular day chosen by Christ in which his people might feed, and Sunday is the day which replaces the last day of Creation because:

>Christs hands, though nail'd, wrought our salvation,
>And did unhinge that day.

The last day of Creation had been glorious, but in the Fall, we sullied our first robe. Only Christ could provide a new robe for us and this he did, but only with his own life. He paid to the last for our renewal:

>Wherefore that robe we cast away,
>Having a new at his expence,
>Whose drops of bloud paid the full price,
>That was requir'd to make us gay,
>And fit for Paradise.

Our new baptismal clothes are bought by his generosity alone and the gaiety of our salvation is at his expense. The only answer to such generosity can be a whole-hearted reception of the gift, and a full-loving and joyous re-orientation towards him who bestows the gift. Herbert enthusiastically longs to overtake the Sunday on its swift ascent to heaven, to leap up side by side with it, from one stretch of harmony to the next, rising gloriously together, until he and Sunday as one, he and the day of Christ, he and the day when by his blood Christ redeemed man, arrive to Christ in heaven:

>O let me take thee at the bound,
>Leaping with thee from sev'n to sev'n,
>Till that we both, being toss'd from earth,
>Flie hand in hand to heav'n!

Five poems seem particularly to emphasise Christ's actual comfort and love for us, strong and personal.

Antiphon (II) is a hymn of praise in which angels and men join together in singing of the God of Love: the angels and men are divided, one choir sings from above, and the other from below, one choir have proved the friends, the other the foes, one choir was made by God, for the other he was sold. But, the lyrical praise rises, higher and higher. Though one choir adores while the other may only crouch in shame, yet, such is the love of God that the hymn may still reach its joint crescendo:

> *Cho.*   Lord, thy praises should be more.
> *Men.*   We have none.
> *Ang.*   And we no store.
> *Cho.*   Praised be the God alone,
>   Who hath made of two folds one.

Prayer (II) takes up the song of gratitude for the immediate and generous divine response to human needs. It is a matter of immense wonder and joy how Christ, as a receptive Person, is available, he, the Lord, is yet of *an easie quick accesse*: the *quick* here surely carries with it not only the speed but so too the living response to the demand. The request *suddenly* seems to reach Christ: a suggestion again of speed, but, so too, of the unexpected working of Grace outside our power of dispensation. Christ, the Person of Love, can no more be deaf to our requests, than die. And, the implication stands out grimly, we should know that he can not die, for did we not try to kill him? And did he not die for us, in the first instance? All is within the compass and providence of divine power, there is nothing too mean to ask of Christ; all belongs to him. The world, which he created, has a measure of time and place, but his love has none. When there was no alternative, he took our flesh, to die as we do, to rid Man of the inescapable curse of sin, that he would be free to pour his gifts upon us. Such love surely can only be answered by worship; for Christ's attributes of *Ease, Power,* and *Love,* Herbert would gladly exchange any possible attributes of his own, to gain the capacity of worship, and to acquire thereby far more than he might seem to lose. Herbert sees the love within the act of redemption, and love can only be answered by love:

>   I value prayer so,
>   That were I to leave all but one,
> Wealth, fame, endowments, vertues, all should go;
> I and deare prayer would together dwell,
> And quickly gain, for each inch lost, an ell.

Jesu repeats the comfort theme of *Prayer* (II): in grief, Jesus alone can bring back wholeness and harmony:

> Jesu is in my heart, his sacred name
> Is deeply carved there . . .

And when a great sorrow seems to break the heart on which *Jesu* is carved, the letters appear disconnected; yet, in disunion, the sound of comfort remains, even in the dispersed letters, to meet again in the fullness of the Name:

> I sat me down to spell them, and perceived
> That to my broken heart he was *I ease you,*
> And to my whole is *J E S U* .

The same theme comes in *Love-joy* with the inscription *J* and *C* on a window. Herbert reads these two letters as representing *Joy* and *Charitie*. The reply is that he is entirely correct:

> Sir, you have not miss'd,
> The man reply'd; It figures *J E S U S   C H R I S T* .

Again, in *The Sonne,* Herbert delights in the accident of pronunciation:

> How neatly doe we give one onely name
> To parents issue and the sunnes bright starre!

He sees Christ, Son and Sun, enlightening the whole world in the West from the darkness of Adam's sin in the East; and he identifies the humiliated Christ with the glorified Christ, by the single use of Son and Sun; the Son of Man, crucified, is indeed the Sun of Man, in glory:

> For what Christ once in humblenesse began,
> We him in glorie call, *The Sonne of Man.*

In the face of such love, the desire to reciprocate, somehow, intensifies. In the first place, there comes the wish, however inadequately, to imitate Christ. *Lent* is indeed a fitting season to make the attempt. Herbert sees no difficulty in fully accepting the period of Lent as a time of fasting. The *deare feast of Lent* is welcomed by him, whatever the doctrinal divisions concerning it. He sees fasting not only as a spiritual but as a physical medicine, where the consequences of gluttony have exacted just punishment of pleasure:

> sluttish fumes,
> Sowre exhalations, and dishonest rheumes,
> Revenging the delight.

The seeds sown in the fasting of Lent undoubtedly bring better and more prolific fruit of Easter. It is no excuse to avoid the fast of Lent because other men abuse it:

> . . . lest by that argument
> We forfeit all our Creed.

And, then, Herbert gives his own real reason for loving Lent. It is not a question of Church Authority, nor of health, nor of doctrine, nor of reward, but:

> It's true we cannot reach Christs forti'th day;
> Yet to go part of that religious way,
> Is better then to rest:
> We cannot reach our Saviours puritie;
> Yet are we bid, *Be holy ev'n as he.*
> In both let's do our best.

The longing is to follow in the steps of Christ, step by step. Surely such labouring will save a little time of the journey? Will not Christ in his love perhaps even help a little?

> Perhaps my God, though he be farre before,
> May turn, and take me by the hand, and more
> May strengthen my decayes.

It is the desire to be with Christ, and nothing else, which can in the last count stimulate to fasting. The discipline of the Church, as discipline, means very little. But the love of Christ means a great deal. Discipline may lead to an aimless Lent, but the love of Christ leads to fasting which brings with it the love of Man. In his Name, the poor are then fed, and the food of their bodies is the feast of their benefactor's soul. The true Lent is the Lent not only of the body, but even more of the spirit:

> Yet Lord instruct us to improve our fast
> By starving sinne and taking such repast
> As may our faults controll:
> That ev'ry man may revell at his doore,
> Not in his parlour; banquetting the poore,
> And among those his soul.

The contradiction in the last two lines is most emphatic in the contrast between the benefactor's material wealth and the poverty of the poor, but at precisely the same time his identical poverty, though of the spirit. It is not easy for a rich man to enter into the Kingdom of Heaven, or, again, the story of Lazarus and the great gulf. Lazarus lay at the very gate at which Herbert suggests that the poor should be fed.

Mattens fully expresses this sense of reciprocal love. At the very minute of his awakening in the morning, Herbert is aware of Christ's waiting presence, his loving demand that the whole day, not merely a Morning Service, should be offered to him as his due sacrifice:

> I cannot ope mine eyes,
> But thou art ready there to catch
> My morning-soul and sacrifice:
> Then we must needs for that day make a match.

Herbert is fully prepared lovingly to yield to the partnership of that day, but he is deeply puzzled how God, himself, can demand his heart. Is it really so precious? What can it mean to God, that God, himself, can actively seek it, and want it?

> My God, what is a heart?
> That thou shouldst it so eye, and wooe,
> Powring upon it all thy art,
> As if that thou hadst nothing els to do?

All that Man is and has is meant to serve God. It was not Man who created the world, yet Man dares to study the world, rather than the Creator of the world. Then Herbert turns to God, begging fervently, his one desire to love, that the scales may fall from his eyes, and he may see the true light, by way of the Light:

> Teach me thy love to know;
> That this new light, which now I see,
> May both the work and workman show:
> Then by a sunne-beam I will climbe to thee.

Faced by the love of God, Herbert feels that there can remain only one wish, and that wish is to experience gratitude unceasingly. In *Gratefulnesse,* he writes:

> Thou that hast giv'n so much to me,
> Give one thing more, a gratefull heart.
> See how thy beggar works on thee
>   By art.

The beggar's cunning lies in his ability to make the gifts, already given, be the occasion for one more. He argues, if this one gift of gratefulness is withheld, then the others will be meaningless. God knew the consequences of Man's longing for his word. He anticipated the constant demands, the *perpetuall knockings* at his door. Had Christ not told his people to knock and knock again? The demands, the sighs, the tears, the laments, all these did not annoy, but caused God joy. In his love, God tenderly accepts every discordant murmur from below, surrounded as he is by the harmony above of heaven. And, so, Herbert has no compunction to persist in his disturbing demand:

> Wherefore I crie, and crie again;
> And in no quiet canst thou be,
> Till I a thankfull heart obtain
>   Of thee . . .

No normal thankful heart will, however, suffice. It is not a question of being thankful for some particular occasion. Whatever it may seem to us, the love of God is never absent, and it is not for us to choose our moments of gratitude. Such gratitude is no gratitude. The real gratitude, the gratitude which Herbert begs for, depends on nothing but his own continued life, for the gratitude must be the very breath and beat of his existence. Love for love:

> Not thankfull, when it pleaseth me;
> As if thy blessings had spare dayes:
> But such a heart, whose pulse may be
>   Thy praise.

In *Even-song,* again Herbert feels overwhelmed by the measureless love which God showers upon Man, and which he knows he can not, and does not, sufficiently answer. It is the end of the day, and he sings to the God of love who has given him all the faculties for enjoying the day, now passed, and, in particular, his sight, which he suggests God has denied for himself. If God would see, then there would be no hope for us. But, immediately, Herbert recognises God's greatest manifestation of love. There is hope, for he has given us his own Son, making us richer than himself. And the Son is the light of the day, and the light for us to see:

> But much more blest be God above,
>   Who gave me sight alone,
> Which to himself he did denie:
> For when he sees my waies, I dy:
> But I have got his sonne, and he hath none.

He has returned nothing but empty air to God for his precious gifts of the day, and his brain is on fire with his thoughts of contrition. But, with the day, the love is not exhausted. It is now the time to give Man the possibility of rest. The night takes on the image of the *ebony box*, the enclosure of darkness, and, because box so often refers to the heart, or soul, it would seem that night here is the container of God's Grace of rest. It must be a Grace for it gives the time for recovery:

> Put our amendment in our way,
> And give new wheels to our disorder'd clocks.

Herbert wonders whether day or night demonstrates more than the other the love of God. Day is the time of storms, of activity, night, of rest and shelter: but, whichever it is, he is convinced of the total love of God, of his omniscience and omnipresence; and, because God is Love, he is equally convinced that Grace is sent down unceasingly upon Man. The constant fear of arbitrary and erratic Grace is therefore alleviated only when Herbert concentrates on the love of God, and closes his mind to all other implications:

> Not one poore minute scapes thy breast,
> But brings a favour from above;
> And in this love, more then in bed, I rest.

The Call is the cry of love on Herbert's part to Christ, that he may take Christ into himself, and, thereby, reciprocate his love. Herbert invites Christ to himself, Christ is his all, Christ is his way, his truth, his life, his light:

> Come, my Joy, my Love, my Heart:
> Such a Joy, as none can move:
> Such a Love, as none can part:
> Such a Heart, as joyes in love.

The last line is the triumph of the ecstasy. Christ rejoices in our love. He not only pours his own love upon us, but he does not despise the little which we can offer.

In *The Pearl*, Herbert accounts for every aspect of his life, every possible achievement, every worldly success, every merit, and, measures each by only one measure: his love for Christ.

First of all, Herbert claims that he knows *the wayes of Learning*: the world of scholarship is open to him, the world of the intellect, of astronomy, of Discovery:

> All these stand open, or I have the keyes:
> Yet I love thee.

Herbert is thus undeterred by Science in his love of Christ. And, equally, he is undeterred by Society, the claims of gallantry, of sword-like repartee, of politics, of competition, of every form of worldly loyalty and disloyalty:

> Yet I love thee.

And, furthermore, he knows sensuous delights, soothing and pleasing, the demands of youth, gaiety and music. A sudden cry of natural desire so stringently straitened in his normal austerity:

> My stuffe is flesh, not brasse; my senses live,
> And grumble oft . . .

But, even so:

> . . . that they have more in me
> Then he that curbs them, being but one to five:
> Yet I love thee.

Fully aware of his potential scope in learning and at court, far from blind to the demand of his senses for some alleviation, Herbert insists that, whatever the cost, and he is far from underestimating the price, yet he knows that in all he has been guided by God alone, and he will be guided by God to God:

> Yet through these labyrinths, not my groveling wit,
> But thy silk twist let down from heav'n to me,
> Did both conduct and teach me, how by it
> To climbe to thee.

These are the poems, as it were, on the up-surge of love. But, equally, faced by the love of God, Herbert experiences the depression of his conviction that he can not in any measure return God's love, and, even worse, that the reason is his own lack of gratitude. Shame fills him.

In *Ungratefulnesse*, Herbert sees, as if in a new vision, the goodness of God, who, in the first place, re-directed Man from his pagan ways. God has dispensed the richness of his love to us from two containers of Grace: the *two rare cabinets full of treasure.* One cabinet contains the gift of the Trinity, the other, of the Incarnation. And, with these two gifts, God binds Man, whom he has created, to himself. Of the two cabinets, the Trinity is the more majestic one, aloof from our eyes as long as we are alive: only the dust of death can clear our eyes so that we may look upon its incomprehensible light. But, and here Herbert makes the greatest use of his beloved word *sweet* in reference to Christ, all delight, all joy, all peace and rest:

> . . . all thy sweets are packt up in the other;
> Thy mercies thither flock and flow . . .

Where the Trinity fills us with dread, Christ Incarnate draws us to him, for he had deigned to accept the same cabinet of flesh in which we too are encased:

> That as the first affrights,
> This may allure us with delights;
> Because this box we know;
> For we have all of us just such another.

And this is the mean ungratefulness in Man. For all the good which he bestows on us, Christ only asks our love in return; and immediately we quibble and draw back. We keep our sins carefully locked up in a separate box, within the cabinet of our body, and then we guard them jealously, refusing the key, and cheating God who gave us the two cabinets, the Trinity and the Incarnation, and, in return, only asks the one, our heart:

> But man is close, reserv'd, and dark to thee:
> When thou demandest but a heart,
> He cavils instantly.
> In his poore cabinet of bone
> Sinnes have their box apart,
> Defrauding thee, who gavest two for one.

Herbert takes up the same theme in *Unkindnesse*. If he had any consideration for an ordinary friend, he would never use the friend as he behaves to God. He would defend his friend's good name, it would be his personal responsibility to see that no slander touched his friend: and, even if his friend behaved outrageously, spitting on his expensively patterned floor, yet he would still lend him any money he needed: not so with God:

> But let the poore,
> And thou within them, starve at doore.
> I cannot use a friend, as I use Thee.

So, to the crux: if his friend would aspire to a particular position, he would vacate it for him, but, when God, himself, pleads for his heart that Grace may enter, far from leaving his heart free, he repels God's entrance. It is the same box, the cabinet, the heart, the seat of Grace, and the seat of sin:

> But when thy grace
> Sues for my heart, I thee displace,
> Nor would I use a friend, as I use Thee.

How can we be so un-natural? What friend has been crucified for us to ransom us? to draw our love to him? to free us from sin? Better than to own a heart of brass, to write in letters of brass, which may never be erased, the truth of our debt and of our ingratitude:

> O write in brasse, *My God upon a tree*
> *His bloud did spill*
> *Onely to purchase my good-will.*
> Yet use I not my foes, as I use Thee.

The consciousness of Christ's love leads into another aspect in *Sighs and Grones*. This is the self-identification with the love of Christ to avoid destruction for sin:

> O do not use me
> After my sinnes! look not on my desert,
> But on thy glorie! then thou wilt reform
> And not refuse me: for thou onely art
> The mightie God, but I a sillie worm;
> O do not bruise me!

Worm of the Psalms, and serpent under the heel of God, Herbert is also the wicked steward, he has mis-used and embezzled and stolen:

> O do not scourge me!

He deserves all punishment, the darkness which fell on the land of Egypt, for his sensuality has of itself excluded the light of God: he is as Adam, himself sewing on the fig-leaves of his fall. Ground to the dust already, he pleads:

> O do not grinde me!

The love of Christ is his shield. How can God turn the vials of his wrath against him, when the vials are already filled with blood?

> A part whereof my Saviour empti'd hath,
> Ev'n unto death: since he di'd for my good,
>   O do not kill me!

God Judge, God Saviour, the scales are weighted with love, the love of God; in one box is that which heals, in the other, that which burns:

>   . . . put not thy hand
> Into the bitter box; but O my God,
>   My God, relieve me!

The self-identification with the love of Christ may obtain forgiveness for us as in *Sighs and Grones*, but, it can also go further, it can obtain for us the power to love him in return, as in *The Reprisall*.

It would seem at first glance that there is actually no possibility of even beginning to return Christ's love for us. How can we compete with the agony of his Crucifixion?

> I have consider'd it, and finde
> There is no dealing with thy mighty passion:
> For though I die for thee, I am behinde;
>   My sinnes deserve the condemnation.

Whatever efforts he may make, yet he can not rival Christ:

> And yet thy wounds still my attempts defie,
>   For by thy death I die for thee.

Obviously, it is impossible to think of attaining to Christ in the glory of his resurrection, yet, it would have seemed possible to triumph in the greater suffering on earth: but, still, this also was not permitted:

> Couldst thou not griefs sad conquests me allow,
>   But in all vict'ries overthrow me?

What then remains? Only one solution: no more attempt to compete on the one hand, and the overcoming of sin on the other, in the total yielding, through love, into the love of Christ:

> Yet by confession will I come
> Into thy conquest: though I can do nought
> Against thee, in thee I will overcome
>   The man, who once against thee fought.

It is the same energy of the yielding of love into love which allows for the self-identification into the suffering of Christ. Personal suffering is raised up into the divine suffering, within the Grace of the love of God, and not outside it. It is not even only imputed suffering but redemptive suffering, in as far as the human cross is taken within the Divine Cross. The justification of Man's apparently meaningless pain, through finding it this place within the scheme of salvation, finds explicit and emphatic expression in *Affliction* (III).

Personal suffering is given a meaning, in human terms, by allowing it the Grace of the Cross in a direct aspect of redemption. The limited personal suffering is allowed, it seems, to join, according to its measure, the Divine Suffering in the work of salvation. Payment to God for Man's sin would seem here to be taken to its extreme, Christ and Man uniting in the work of ransom in mortal love:

> My heart did heave, and there came forth, *O God!*
> By that I knew that thou wast in the grief,
> To guide and govern it to my relief,
>   Making a scepter of the rod . . .

The suffering was a real suffering, a real pain, a torment, but, in the knowledge of its common redemptive quality, the suffering becomes sovereign. He, who suffers, is not the chastised servant, but the benevolent Monarch. Of this, Herbert is convinced, otherwise the suffering would be unbearable:

> Hadst thou not had thy part,
> Sure the unruly sigh had broke my heart.

God, who gives life, alone knows the span of each man's life. If the suffering prove too great, it is no cause for lamentation, for such a storm only thereby brings the peace of the haven nearer and sooner. The life of God Incarnate, of Christ, was a life of unending suffering, of this we are certain, and, in his love for us, Christ persists in this suffering, identifying himself with the suffering of each one of us. We are the body of Christ, and in each member he continues to his death:

> Thy life on earth was grief, and thou art still
> Constant unto it, making it to be
> A point of honour, now to grieve in me,
>   And in thy members suffer ill.

It is indeed no fit homage to Christ to think of his having died once upon the Cross. Christ, for Herbert, repeats his death day by day, in his love for us, and, hence, in his identification with our pain. So, we on our part, are drawn, each by our own little cross, into his One Cross, and our suffering ceases to be pointless:

> They who lament one crosse,
> Thou dying dayly, praise thee to thy losse.

Imputed Righteousness and imputed suffering are raised up into the sphere of love, and, thereby, are freed partially from the shame of passivity. It is indeed a matter of the deepest shame (*Dialogue*) to know one's own total inadequacy, and, yet, be forced to acknowledge a salvation outside one's own volition:

> Sweetest Saviour, if my soul
>   Were but worth the having,
> Quickly should I then controll
>   Any thought of waving.
> But when all my care and pains
> Cannot give the name of gains
> To thy wretch so full of stains,
> What delight or hope remains?

Back comes the Divine answer, putting the questioner austerely in his place as the child of the Father. It is not for Man to dispute his salvation, it is not for Man to evaluate himself, and put himself in the scales of Judgment. If God claims Man, then Man may not meddle with the expenditure of God's riches on him; it is not for Man to count the cost:

> *What, Child, is the ballance thine,*
>   *Thine the poise and measure?*
> *If I say, Thou shalt be mine;*
>   *Finger not my treasure.*

Christ, alone, paid for Man. The profit of buying Man out of the grasp of sin and death Christ alone knows; he bought Man, and he transferred to God the statement of purchase, cost and conditions. The supreme act of love may not be questioned:

> *What the gains in having thee*
> *Do amount to, onely he,*
> *Who for man was sold, can see;*
> *That transferr'd th' accounts to me.*

Herbert still persists in his argument; the full force of unanswerable love has not finally struck him. He pleads that not only is he incapable of seeing his merit for such salvation, but equally he can not see his way to making himself fit for receiving such a Grace. Faced by the arbitrary salvation of imputed Righteousness, he denies all responsibility. He can only see, in the face of his obstructive sin, a course of uncreative passivity open before him. There is nothing he can do within the plan of his own salvation:

> But as I can see no merit,
>   Leading to this favour:
> So the way to fit me for it
>   Is beyond my savour.
> As the reason then is thine;
> So the way is none of mine:
> I disclaim the whole designe:
> Sinne disclaims and I resigne.

But, the passive dead-end of imputed Righteousness suddenly bursts into active life in the loving reproach. What he says would indeed be rational and sufficient, had Christ obtained what he obtained without effort, if there were nothing in his Incarnation and Crucifixion for Christ to remember without pain; if Christ had been as passive as Herbert now intends, then Man would indeed be free to be as passive as he liked. But, there was nothing of passivity in Christ's redemption of Man. What he gave, he gave actively, generously, and he had all to lose and nothing to gain. The Righteousness imputed to Man was won in active agony, which could only spring from self-identifying love:

> *That as I did freely part*
> *With my glorie and desert,*
> *Left all joyes to feel all smart* . . .

Christ is not left to finish his reproach of comparison. Surely the least that Man can do is to follow in his own slight measure? Herbert interrupts. The hardness dissolves. Only love remains:

> Ah! no more: thou break'st my heart.

The most forceful expression of the Person of Christ as Love overcoming the whole passive aspect of redemption comes in the image of *Love* (III). But, in the context of *Love* (III), it would seem relevant here to mention first the translation of *The 23rd Psalme*.

Above all, the 23rd Psalm is the tender pre-view of the Eucharistic Feast. The God of Love leads the beloved to safe pastures. He gives his beloved both food and drink for his nourishment. He keeps him carefully from erring. And, he shelters him from the fear of death. The love is *sweet:* the love that is and was and will be of Christ, our Saviour. *Love* (III) would seem the direct sequence of the New Covenant:

> Love bade me welcome: yet my soul drew back,
> Guiltie of dust and sinne.

Thus, immediately, once again, the proud assumption of self-judgment in the false self-appraisal. To avoid passive redemption in imputed Righteousness, it would seem necessary to have some assurance of merit in oneself, some yard-stick of progress. Or, some guarantee. Herbert had no such guarantee and so his soul, in the knowledge of impurity, tried to withdraw from Love:

> But quick-ey'd Love, observing me grow slack
> From my first entrance in,
> Drew nearer to me, sweetly questioning,
> If I lack'd any thing.

His passivity is answered by the activity of Love. Sweet Love. Why was he retreating? Did he need something? Was something missing? His answer comes bitterly. Something is indeed missing: his own worthiness:

> A guest, I answer'd, worthy to be here . . .

The reply is instantaneous:
> Love said, You shall be he.

All the terror of inadequacy overcomes him. He has no right to be here. He has no guarantee whatsoever of his claim to be present. He can only feel his own unnatural guilt, his sins, his ingratitude. He can not bear to be in the presence of the most precious:

> I the unkinde, ungratefull? Ah my deare,
> I cannot look on thee.

But Love, in His self-limitation, only takes his hand and gently reminds him that without Him, he would be blind. It is not really for him to choose whether or not to look on his Creator:

> Love took my hand, and smiling did reply,
> Who made the eyes but I?

Herbert persists. God indeed made Man, but Man, of his own accord, blurred and blemished the image. His place, according to what he deserves, is not in the sight of God:

> Truth Lord, But I have marr'd them: let my shame
> Go where it doth deserve.

And, back comes the answer, the ransom of love. Salvation loses all its potential impersonality, as some kind of scheme divorced from the Person of God and the person of Man. Salvation turns to a personal sacrifice of Personal love and the passive sting of imputed Righteousness is drawn:

> And know you not, sayes Love, who bore the blame?

Love now answers Love. There is only one answer, to stay, and to adore, as a servant:

> My deare, then I will serve.

But, how can Man's love vie with the love of God? It is not for Man to serve at the table of God, but it is for him to eat, to eat the body of his God and, in Him, find salvation. The body and the blood of Christ is the body and the blood of Love: not merely of the act of loving, but of actual Love. Love answers love, and there can be no effort of self-judgment, no self-evaluation, and, above all, no passivity. The work of love begins in the answer to Love:

> You must sit down, sayes Love, and taste my meat:
> So I did sit and eat.

Herbert has again, as in his relationship to God, overcome the possibility of restrictive theological margins by means of leaving the widest space for the person: the Person of God and the person of Man. And, he faces the Person of God again with the one factor of love, seeing God as Love, Love as a Person, and thus he is released into free and creative activity, from out of dull and passive relativity. He will not merely suffer the love of God, nor does he even feel himself permitted to do so. Love is a work.

CHAPTER II

PARTICIPATION IN CHRIST

The positive recognition of the love of God, of Christ's redeeming action as that of Incarnate Love, inevitably leads out of any dark apprehension of passive redemption into the light of released and free reciprocal activity. Incomprehensible passivity to an arbitrary dispensation of Grace can now be interpreted as participation in Love. The two worlds of Grace and Nature remain, and the confession of Imputed Righteousness outside our merit or volition; and, again, there can be no assurance of salvation, no guarantee by the Authority of the Church; faith can not be proved as faith. All this remains. But, the possibility of atrophy, of despair, of passive numbness, is overcome by the accompanying acknowledgment of the Mystery of Love.

This Mystery of Love is inalienable and inexorable in its powerful demand of our activity. The Mystery of Love claims our practical life of spirituality not on a foundation of fear, nor of mute hope, nor of dependence on the Church, but on the explicit promise of the Mystery of human love going forward, in total trust, into the Mystery of the Divine Love. Disciplinary fear is replaced by the far more potent, and inescapable, experience of facing Love. Sin becomes, already in this world, the agony of hell, for it can not bear the confrontation with Love. Repentance takes on another meaning, and, so too, daily morality is drawn into its transcendent rather than social dimension. Death too is seen with different eyes. And, as long as we live, life is re-orientated. In fact, theology, faced with the Love of the Person of Christ, becomes a practical spirituality.

But, the theology and the spirituality may only remain one as long as the Mystery of the Love, the Mystery of the Person of Christ, and the Mystery of the person of each human being, is acknowledged and accepted as the foundation of life.

i. *Sin*

When sin, sin as an objective fact, and the sin of each one of us, is seen in this light, that is, not merely as a culpable act but as an affront against the Mystery of Love, its terror and meanness becomes far more potent. Sin is no longer in any sense an idea, but it is a manifest denial of the Person of Love. Sin becomes an actual enemy, and a despicable one to be feared and scorned at the same time.

In *Sinne* (II), Herbert can not even imagine how Sin can be described or drawn. He sees God, in his care for us, shielding us from the terror of the sight which would make us mad. Herbert only knows that Sin must be *flat opposite* to God, in as much as it can not be said to have either power or actual existence:

> It wants the good of *vertue,* and of *being.*

Sin, as Evil, in effect is a parasite on Good, on which it preys. Any other concept would of course lead to the heretical notion of Manichaeism, the two equal powers of Good and Evil. This is why Herbert is careful to see the Devil himself only as a fallen angel:

> We paint the devil foul, yet he
> Hath some good in him, all agree.

God, indeed, spares us from the full onslaught of the sight of Sin, but, one glimpse, in one dimension, we can catch, when we look upon devils. They can not show the whole of Sin, but they can suggest a partial view:

> Yet as in sleep we see foul death, and live:
> So devils are our sinnes in perspective.

Such, then, is the nature of Sin, the enemy of Love. Sin is a powerful enemy, lying in ambush, never fully to be recognised. But Sin is the enemy of God, and only God, in his love, shields us. It would seem that in the encounter of love between God and Man, Sin also takes on something of a personal quality, sufficiently at any rate to be feared for the terror of its aspect, and despised for its inability to survive on its own. Wherever love is, there Sin lurks, ready to feed and distort. In the Mystery of Love, Sin has its inalienable place.

This intimate connection of Sin, with the person of Man, is brought out clearly in *Decay.*

There was a time when Man was a friend of God, and the poem opens with the nostalgic:

> Sweet were the dayes . . .

As always, *sweet* holds the whole connotation of the bliss and delight of the presence of God. Then God was present in person, lodging with Lot, and wrestling with Jacob, sitting with Gideon, consulting with Abraham. Those were the sweet days, when the Person of Love could not withstand the pleading of love for his people:

>   . . . when thy power could not
> Encounter Moses strong complaints and mone:
>   Thy words were then, *Let me alone.*

The Person of God could actually be seen, immediately, without effort, at the oak, or in a bush, or cave, or by a well. One could ask where God was, and be told precisely where he had gone, and one could follow. Person to person:

> Is my God this way? No, they would reply:
> He is to Sinai gone, as we heard tell:
>   List, ye may heare great Aarons bell.

All this has changed. Sin and Satan have found a sure home for themselves—in our hearts. And, there, God too seeks to enclose himself. Once again, the image of the heart is that of a container—a box—a cabinet, now one which holds two enemies and the Person of Love: and, the two enemies fight with every stratagem to oust Love. The days of outer Presence have gone. The Person of God finds his place in the heart. The World of Nature and the World of Grace are no longer one. But, inner Grace is not a theological term, it is the Mystery of the actual presence of the Person of Love, inside our hearts, where Sin has its strong-hold:

> But now thou dost thy self immure and close
> In some one corner of a feeble heart:
> Where yet both Sinne and Satan, thy old foes,
> Do pinch and straiten thee, and use much art
>   To gain thy thirds and little part.

The last lines are the vision of the final meeting and triumph of God over Sin. Love is warm and Sin is cold. Sin forces and constrains Love to retreat further and further and into more and more narrow confines. Or, so it would seem to Man. But, the radiant heat of Love can not be quenched by Sin, and it will break out, on the Day of Judgment, to burst into the flames of the last conflagration, when all that is sinful will be destroyed by the fire of Love. Sin, again, is seen as an illusion of power, only to delude us into giving it reality by our harbouring and nourishing it:

> I see the world grows old, when as the heat
> Of thy great love, once spread, as in an urn
> Doth closet up it self, and still retreat,
> Cold Sinne still forcing it, till it return,
>   And calling *Justice,* all things burn.

The connected pattern of sin, Herbert sees to his shame in *Sinnes round*. He sees himself as contemptible before God because he can not put a stop to this evil sequence:

> Sorrie I am, my God, sorrie I am,
> That my offences course it in a ring.

It is indeed a vicious circle. First the thoughts, for Sin is always hatched in the heart, and his evil thoughts *are working like a busie flame*. The thought, inevitably, gives rise to the flavour of his words, what he says is now also as infected as what he thinks:

> My words take fire from my inflamed thoughts.

And, as if the words are not sufficient as the vehicles of sin, breathing out and scattering the evil around, the course must be fully run, and the words finally turn to action:

> My hands do joyn to finish the inventions.

Having built his three-tiered house, he must needs begin again, for the sinful deeds beget more sinful thoughts. He faces God, not a God of Wrath, not a fearsome Judge, but his own dear God, and he prays to Him:

> . . . wherefore, to my shame,
> Sorrie I am, my God, sorrie I am.

And, finally, in *Sinne* (I), Herbert faces the incontrovertible truth, that, as long as we live, we sin. We sin in the face of love and protection of God. The sin is in us and nothing can be stronger than the sin of the heart. We are first prepared by our parents, then taught by our school-masters what is right and what is not; we learn to think reasonably and we have sermons to help us, and every week Sunday; we have Sorrow to chase away sin, all kinds of distress and grief; God has countless measures of snares and art whereby he may in his love catch us and keep us safe. There is the Bible, waiting, open, for us but to look upon it. There are sudden assaults of God from all quarters. He pours his favours on us, and we hear the distant sound of the Glory to come. God gives us minds to be vigilant and aware of his presence. Everywhere we look is calculated to make us feel ashamed. He surrounds us with his guardians, he gives us the hopes and fears of eternity. What else can he do? In his love, he gives all, freely, every defence, and the whole host of heaven. And, all he gives is for nothing, for the sin is not from outside but from within. We sin in our hearts, against him alone, the person of Man sinning against the Person of Love. And, Love does not fight. Love must be sought by love:

> Yet all these fences and their whole aray
> One cunning bosome-sinne blows quite away.

ii. *Repentance*

Repentance for sin therefore again comes in the same light of confrontation with the Person of Love. It is a direct encounter and a direct reaction. Sin is a matter of shame when faced by Love, and repentance is an act of personal contrition.

> *Lesse then the least*
> *Of all thy mercies*, is my posie still. (*The Posie*)

And, then, in *The Method* comes the turn to the question of inexplicable with-holding of Grace, the question which so often would seem to torment Herbert.

This arbitrary coming and going, Herbert can see as capable of explanation inside the Mystery of Love. The explanation can be entirely simple. God could never not hear our prayer, or be either incapable or unwilling to hear it. How could he, who is Love, not listen?

> Thy Father could
> Quickly effect, what thou dost move;
> For he is *Power:* and sure he would;
> For he is *Love*.

The answer evidently lies in our own hearts, the known container of sin. Should we not, before despairing at God's defection, first seek diligently in ourselves?

> Go search this thing,
> Tumble thy breast, and turn thy book.
> If thou hadst lost a glove or ring,
> Wouldst thou not look?

The Love of God meets the love of Man: the Mystery of Person to person. And, where the love in Man is lacking, then he loses the sound of God's voice. The fault of communication lies solely in us. How can God hear our careless or indifferent prayers? How can God hear us when our actions deliberately follow where He does not lead? God is Love. What seems His inattention is our own distraction, not His. This is the step further on from

A Parodie, with the hope that Grace has only apparently gone. It is a re-direction upon our own lack of love as the root of the estrangement:

> Then once more pray:
> Down with thy knees, up with thy voice.
> Seek pardon first, and God will say,
> *Glad heart rejoyce.*

Inner Grace again takes upon itself the Mystery of the Person of God in *The Sinner*.

The possible container of God in the human body is the heart. This should be His dwelling-place. But, once more, comes all the shame of having no place suitable for giving God his due lodging. Shaking, as in a fever, Herbert reviews what he has accounted as precious, all the accumulated rubbish which fills up his heart and leaves no room for God. The Treasure of the Person of God is ousted by vain treasure. Heap upon heap of useless vanities rear up inside him, and only the slenderest traces of holiness, which hardly dare acknowledge themselves as holy, knowing how God's laws have been transgressed. Herbert's body is as the world, and the heart should be as heaven, the seat of Love. But, what room is there left for the innermost essence?

> There the circumference earth is, heav'n the centre.
> In so much dregs the quintessence is small:
> The spirit and good extract of my heart
> Comes to about the many hundred part.

Only repentance is left. Only the pleading of love to Love. Nothing is beyond God, no miracle is impossible. Was not the first Covenant written on tablets of stone? Can God not then still use Man's heart, hard and obdurate as it may seem to be, if there is but one true sigh of repentance?

> Yet Lord restore thine image, heare my call:
> And though my hard heart scarce to thee can grone,
> Remember that thou once didst write in stone.

The Storm again gives full value to the personal assault of repentance. The winds and waves of a tempest are likened to the sighs and tears which assail God; the one amazes Man by its intensity, the other may well surprise God. Nothing can be more potent than the pulse of conscience brought to life:

> It quits the earth, and mounting more and more
> Dares to assault thee, and besiege thy doore.

There is nothing of theory here, it is an actual daring effort at meeting God on the part of Man. And, such is Man's temerity, in the knowledge of the Love that awaits him, that he even ventures to make sufficient noise to spoil the sound of heavenly music, and drown the worship of angels and of saints. Did not Christ himself tell us to knock, and knock again? Have we not the importunate widow for our example?

>There it stands knocking, to thy musicks wrong,
>   And drowns the song.
>Glorie and honour are set by, till it
>   An answer get.

Herbert's confidence in the loving hearing of God is unsurpassed. So wild a storm of repentance will not go unanswered and the peace will follow, the fresh tranquillity of the air when the storm is over. Only a total trust in the God of Love could have evoked such an image of repentance:

>Poets have wrong'd poore storms: such dayes are best;
>They purge the aire without, within the breast.

All troubles can be turned into the creative work of repentance. In *The Water-course*, Herbert accepts the tribulations of this life as inevitable. Life and strife are indeed alternative synonyms. But, they can be turned to fruitful tears. The tears can become *sov'raigne tears*, holding mastery over God's compassion precisely as in *The Storm*. God equally dispenses salvation and damnation, but where there is true remorse, the issue is in no doubt. Thus, again, any problem of the Elect is denied totally. The person of Man, loving and repentant, confronts the Person of God, of Love, and there can be no doubt, nor fear. The tears are sovereign.

It is only through repentance that it is possible to bring back unity into the multiplicity of sin. Repentance is the vehicle of healing, repentance must begin with an open awareness of sin.

Thus *Repentance* begins unequivocally:

>Lord, I confesse my sinne is great;
>Great is my sinne.

There is no question of mitigation, no excuse. The approach can only be made to the love of God. God is implored to deal carefully and tenderly with Man, a living flower at the moment, but one whose life is short, whose fading follows instantly on his blossoming. The image of the flower, with its association of sweet scent surely suggests how dear Man is to God, and how connected in the sweetness of Christ. The plea can not be in vain:

> Oh! gently treat
> With thy quick flow'r, thy momentarie bloom;
> Whose life still pressing
> Is one undressing.
> A steadie aiming at a tombe.

The span of Man's life is short, and his conscious experience of joy is certainly short; his conscious experience of sorrow, however, is longer, if it is reckoned from Adam, for Man inherits the sensations of the common grief of the Fall. Every man feels that he carries within him the sadness of the experience of Adam, of the exclusion of the Fall and the subsequent spiritual and physical disintegration:

> . . . but we are all
> To sorrows old,
> If life be told
> From what life feeleth, Adams fall.

So, Herbert pleads for God's compassion on his short span of life that God does not bring death upon him before he has fully repented:

> Cut me not off for my most foul transgression:
> I do confesse
> My foolishnesse;
> My God, accept of my confession.

The bitterness of grief permeates his soul. Only God can turn the wormwood sweet, can change sorrow to dancing. And, if he delays, there is no possibility but death. This grief, which has fallen upon him, Herbert can not help but see as God's chastisement; and, he argues, such chastisement is beyond endurance; the pain flooding the spirit, overflows in to the body, sickness of heart turns to sickness of body:

> When thou for sinne rebukest man,
> Forthwith he waxeth wo and wan:
> Bitternesse fills our bowels; all our hearts
> Pine, and decay,
> And drop away,
> And carrie with them th' other parts.

Then, again, comes the clear conviction of God's love. God will himself destroy sin and grief. He will take the insoluble situation into his own hands and give it a solution. Then the dead bones will live, and will joyfully unite. Out of disharmony, will come harmony, the harmony of worship. Dead passivity of sin will rise into live activity of adoration, and only through the merciful love of God, for no other reason. And, Herbert sees, as in a vision, the truth of the experience of love. The dead bones will live, unity will come out of multiplicity, grown stronger in its trial of love, tested as by fire. There is no room for doubt in these lines, only the serene confidence in the Mystery of salvation:

> But thou wilt sinne and grief destroy;
> That so the broken bones may joy,
> And tune together in a well-set song,
>   Full of his praises,
>   Who dead men raises.
> Fractures well cur'd make us more strong.

Gods afflictions: these are the feared intruders in *Confession*. What are these afflictions? It would seem that they are the sorrows and griefs which God sends to us when we have yielded our life to sin: perhaps the pangs of thwarted ambition, or the pains of denied sensuality, in one form or another. But, whatever their precise nature, the afflictions are heavy to bear and not to be divorced from a worldly life. There is no possibility of defence against them, probably because, as a cancer, they emerge from the very tissue of the life which breeds them. There is no point whatsoever in making secret hiding-places in the heart for one's self-indulgence, for the indulgence, in itself, opens the doors to pain:

>   O what a cunning guest
> Is this same grief! within my heart I made
>   Closets; and in them many a chest;
>   And, like a master in my trade,
> In those chests, boxes; in each box, a till:
> Yet grief knows all, and enters when he will.

The affliction follows the condition of sin precisely, at the exactly vulnerable spot, for the very reason that it is the vulnerable spot. And, the affliction will not desist for an instant from probing into every nook and cranny of our hidden soul. As long as our soul is closed, there is work for the grief: to dig, and to probe, and to open the sores. We are our own helpless victims:

> We are the earth; and they,
> Like moles within us, heave, and cast about:
> And till they foot and clutch their prey,
> They never cool, much lesse give out.
> No smith can make such locks but they have keyes:
> Closets are halls to them; and hearts, high-wayes.

Man's heart is the thoroughfare of grief as long as he denies the love of God, and, in sin, shuts himself away as from an alien presence. But, if, in contrition, he opens his heart to the love of God, if he returns love by love, then the widened thoroughfare of his light heart has no room for the griefs which want dark corners and narrow lanes. There is no place for them, and they go on seeking new victims. Lies and falseness alone give affliction something to which to cling, and where to settle:

> Onely an open breast
> Doth shut them out, so that they cannot enter;
> Or, if they enter, cannot rest,
> But quickly seek some new adventure.

The grief, in effect, is the direct outcome of the closed heart. And, so, again the triumph of the victory of love: let all affliction go, for, his love has won, he opens himself fully to God in trust and in love, and the brightest day is gloomy compared with the clarity of his heart. Herbert knows, of a surety, that he is forgiven even as he asks forgiveness, and his evidence is nothing but this one conviction of the Mystery of the love of God for his creature. It only needs the effort of love on our part to draw upon us all the joy:

> Wherefore my faults and sinnes,
> Lord, I acknowledge; take thy plagues away:
> For since confession pardon winnes,
> I challenge here the brightest day,
> The clearest diamond: let them do their best,
> They shall be thick and cloudie to my breast.

Trinitie Sunday can be seen as a dedication of personal repentance. Each step of human life has been taken by God, in the three Persons of the Trinity, in direct relationship to the one person of each single man. In the creative act of Love, there can be no generalisation. And, on the part of Man, there too can be no generalised reaction. It must be a personal reaction of the personal load of guilt and debt, but so also the personal confidence of the ultimate peace, through Christ, in Christ:

> Enrich my heart, mouth, hands in me,
> With faith, with hope, with charitie;
> That I may runne, rise, rest with thee.

This is the confession of the wealth of the Beatitudes, the poverty of the world, which alone allows for the full putting on of Christ.

Defeat turns to the greatest triumph in *Sion*. Once again, as in *Decay*, it would seem superficially that God has been ousted by sin and corruption of Man. Previously God was not only immediately present, but he was worshipped with the utmost of Man's wealth:

> Lord, with what glorie wast thou serv'd of old,
> When Solomons temple stood and flourished!
> Where most things were of purest gold;
> The wood was all embellished
> With flowers and carvings, mysticall and rare:
> All show'd the builders, crav'd the seeers care.

But, this was not to the pleasure of God. Was not God Love? And, as Love, his aim was only the salvation of Man. God must meet the enemy, Sin, in its own stronghold. And, so, God moved his temple into the temple of the heart of Man, where he would share his home with the destroyer:

> Wherefore thou quitt'st thy ancient claim:
> And now thy Architecture meets with sinne;
> For all thy frame and fabrick is within.

God has left his isolated throne in the Holy of Holies, where Man did not dare to enter, and he has limited himself to one *peevish heart*, in order to save one soul from its own sin. God has condescended to enter into battle, and in his love, one sigh of repentance means more to him than the whole fabulous erection of worship constructed by Solomon. Such outward adoration means nothing, but, the submission of penitence of one soul means everything:

> The fight is hard on either part.
> Great God doth fight, he doth submit.
> All Solomons sea of brasse and world of stone
> Is not so deare to thee as one good grone.

Brass and stone of the Temple, and the hardness of the unloving heart, become one, both inimical to God. What can Love do with the riches of the world? Temple of stone, or heart of brass are both unworthy of God, for in them the Spirit of life is missing and they are indeed:

> Tombes for the dead, not temples fit for thee . . .

God can not dwell either in a glorious Temple built for his isolation, nor yet in a heart of adamant. But, repentance is not dead. The penitent heart is alive, and greatly equipped for the flight to heaven. The penitent heart is inspired with the living breath of the Spirit which must return to heaven, his home:

> But grones are quick, and full of wings,
> And all their motions upward be . . .

The groans of a penitent heart rise to heaven. They may sound to our ears as agonised, discordant in grief, thick with sobs; but, for God, they are the most beautiful notes of harmonious music, rising and singing, singing and rising, as a lark in all its disembodied joy. Tears: the laughter. Weeping: the gladness. Defeat: victory. God: the King of Glory:

> And ever as they mount, like larks they sing;
> The note is sad, yet musick for a King.

iii. *Morality*

The next step can not be avoided. Once the Person of Christ is the centre, and all is directed in love to him, then sin takes on forthwith a more real substance of an actual denial of the Person of Christ; then, comes the living desire for repentance. And, so, a day-to-day way of life must follow. Such a system of morality, however, is not a representation of an ethical principle, but is derived solely from the intention of living in accordance with what would seem the precepts of the loved Person of God. Thus, Herbert's poetry, when it is directly connected with morality, need not be seen as something alien to his other poetry, or indeed to poetry in general, because its source and purpose, far from being alien, are identical with the whole source and purpose of his spirituality: the Mystery of the Love of God.

The Church-porch presents a series of instructions on the godly life. But, Herbert makes precisely this point of unity between morality and Love in the opening lines. It is Herbert's evident intention to catch souls to God and he may be better able to do so in verse, than by a sermon.

A young man still has *sweet youth* to make him receptive: and *sweet* suggests the kinship somewhere in his innocence to Christ.

So, Herbert instructs him on the basis of the sacrificial love of Christ:

> Beware of lust: it doth pollute and foul
> Whom God in Baptisme washt with his own blood.

Then, he must keep sober:

> Drink not the third glasse, which thou canst not tame,
> When once it is within thee . . .

If he does not abstain, let him at least not boast of his mis-doings and let him not swear:

> Take not his name, who made thy mouth in vain . . .

He must tell the truth:

> Lie not; but let thy heart be true to God,
> Thy mouth to it, thy actions to them both . . .

He must avoid sloth of any kind:

> Flie idlenesse, which yet thou canst not flie
> By dressing, mistressing, and complement.

It is a sad mis-use of the Grace of the Spirit within us, if we let our wings lie idle:

> God gave thy soul brave wings; put not those feathers
> Into a bed, to sleep out all ill weathers.

Herbert instructs fathers to teach their sons real values:

> The way to make thy sonne rich is to fill
> His minde with rest, before his trunk with riches:
> For wealth without contentment climbes a hill
> To feel those tempests, which fly over ditches.

Constancy of purpose is to be prized, and open, honest work, as in the presence of the King of Kings. Gluttony must be avoided:

> Look on meat, think it dirt, then eat a bit;
> And say withall, Earth to earth I commit.

Self-discipline is essential, and so is solitude for self-examination:

> Who cannot rest till hee good-fellows finde,
> He breaks up house, turns out of doores his minde.

Thriftiness is of value. Wealth is suspect. Debts are dangerous. Modest dress is advisable. Gambling should be moderate. Conversation should be discreet. And in behaviour, again the memory of our Saviour: *Be sweet to all.* Quarrels should be avoided. Overmuch mirth is not profitable:

> Laugh not too much: the wittie man laughs least:
> For wit is newes onely to ignorance.
> Lesse at thine own things laugh . . .

Subservience to the great is not necessary, nor is envy. The position may still be respected, if not the person occupying it. And, because all derives from the Person, friendship has a place of eminence in this moral code. The Friend, the Holy Spirit, in our hearts, can turn into the love of a friend, to be retained constantly:

> Thy friend put in thy bosome: wear his eies
> Still in thy heart, that he may see what's there.
> If cause require, thou art his sacrifice;
> Thy drops of bloud must pay down all his fear:
>   But love is lost, the way of friendship's gone,
>   Though *David* had his *Jonathan, Christ* his *John.*

The family, however, should not be sacrificed for the friend. Speaking should be adapted to the audience; and, the best points kept back as extra ammunition. Whatever else, losing one's temper in discussion does not help. It is far more rewarding to keep calm and let the other rave. Wild vapouring gets us nowhere:

> Truth dwels not in the clouds: the bow that's there
> Doth often aim at, never hit the sphere.

It is important to listen to other people, and pick up particles of truth wherever they are to be found. Then, it is only right to care for others living in the same district, to seek out those in need, and give help where possible. Humility of behaviour should go together with spiritual enterprise. And, the spiritual effort should be unceasing. It is of supreme importance to be open to all; we can never tell where our advantage lies. It is easy enough to discard the ill from the good. But, at the same time, it is equally important to keep one's own way, and not follow after every newcomer's will. Cleanliness is essential, and so is the giving of charity. It should never be forgotten that the poor man is stamped with the image of Christ:

> Let thy almes go before, and keep heav'ns gate
> Open for thee; or both may come too late.

Tithes should be paid accurately, and Services attended regularly. Decent behaviour is essential in Church, and careful attention to what is happening. Fugitive thoughts should be restrained and the priest not criticised, for he is the emissary of God. Above all, in Church, none should partake of Communion without the deepest reverence. Holy Communion is the one healing medicine, and if the medicine turns to destruction, through our own fault, what help can there be for us?

> None shall in hell such bitter pangs endure,
> As those, who mock at Gods way of salvation.
> Whom oil and balsames kill, what salve can cure?
> They drink with greediness a full damnation.

And, Herbert's final injunction is for a nightly act of self-examination and repentance:

> Summe up at night, what thou hast done by day;
> And in the morning, what thou hast to do.
> Dresse and undresse thy soul: mark the decay
> And growth of it: if with thy watch, that too
>   Be down, then winde up both; since we shall be
>   Most surely judg'd, make thy accounts agree.

The series of exhortations ends with the reminder of the shortness of life, and our inadequate values. Joy and pain both have their incomprehensible place in eternity:

> If thou do ill; the joy fades, not the pains:
> If well; the pain doth fade, the joy remains.

So, *The Church-porch* has set out a programme of morality fully centred on the Person of Christ, for fundamentally it denies the world, the gains of the world, and demands of Society. The only demand it acknowledges is that of those loved or in our care: friends, family and the poor. The only overall command is to worship God in the Church which he has given us. This code of behaviour, Herbert sees as indivisible from the theology of his Church, for it is the Church-porch to the Church.

Various other poems, which would appear primarily moral in tone, pick up and elaborate on these themes set in *The Church-porch*. And, perhaps, it is worth noting how reminiscent both the virtues and the vices, and their consequences, are of the axioms found in the Old Testament, particularly in *Proverbs*. The teaching would seem to follow directly the teaching which found its earliest sources in the days when God and men were friends. Thus, even more, the moral themes are orientated upon the Person of God, and neither on social nor on ethical principles.

Church-monuments takes up the theme of Man's mortality, the short duration of life on earth. The tombs are the reminder that the body is only the container, the measuring glass of dust, holding death within itself. Sensuous pleasure is fleeting:

> Deare flesh, while I do pray, learn here thy stemme
> And true descent; that when thou shalt grow fat,
>
> And wanton in thy cravings, thou mayst know,
> The flesh is but the glasse, which holds the dust
> That measures all our time; which also shall
> Be crumbled into dust.

No lust remains in these last ashes. And, during life, it were well to prepare for this last flesh-less eventuality:

> Mark here below
> How tame these ashes are, how free from lust,
> That thou mayst fit thy self against thy fall.

Charms and Knots, in brief epigrammatic form, recapitulates several of the aspects, namely, of reading the Bible, of a simple array, of generosity, of prayer, of calumny, of humility, of vanity, of the efficacy of preaching, and, lastly, of the dangerous vice of drinking: the climax:

> In shallow waters heav'n doth show;
> But who drinks on, to hell may go.

The Foil epigrammatically contrasts heaven and earth; if only we could see the virtue of heaven as clearly on earth, then earth would be *the better skie, the brighter place*. God has placed the stars in the sky, that, in their reflection, we might see virtue reflected, bright and clear. And, God has given us *griefs* that we might see sin equally clearly. Again, we have here the allusion to affliction and grief as the companions of sin, either in the pain of the train of desires to which sin gives inception, or to the consequences in a variety of ill. But, we are blind. We labour on, equally heedless of the signs of virtue, and the signs of sin; of the repulsion of sin-induced grief, and the attraction of virtue:

> Yet in this wretched world we toil,
> As if grief were not foul, nor vertue winning.

The Church-floore sets out the pattern of virtues, which can be seen as the basis of Christian behaviour, not of the belief, but of the consequent way of life: *the go and do likewise* of Christ's teaching. The paving stones are patience, humility, confidence:

> But the sweet cement, which in one sure band
> Ties the whole frame, is *Love*
> And *Charitie*.

It is the *sweet* cement: the binding together by Christ and, in Christ, of morality into love. Morality is not a dissociated code of behaviour, but the daily, practical expression of Love. Otherwise, it would be nothing but an empty Law. And, the floor of the Church is the floor of each single heart. Again, the heart is the seat not only of God, but of Sin, and of Death. Repentance is the answer to Sin. Death, too, is only a cleansing. God has chosen to leave the great Temple, he has his home in a corner of a frail heart, and he has it there because he is Love, and loves and redeems each person singly (cf. *Sion*):

> Blest be the *Architect*, whose art
> Could build so strong in a weak heart.

Humilitie emphasises the pre-eminence of self-criticism and the danger of seeing one's virtues, in effect, as absolute and unassailable. *Humilitie* shows the necessity for constant vigilance against the pride lurking within virtue. There sat the Virtues, expecting and receiving homage. And, the sensual passions, in the form of beasts and birds, appeared to be totally subjected, each presenting its particular strength to the victorious Virtue. Humility handed round the gifts of homage: the lion's paw of strength to Meekness, the hare's hearing to Endurance, the turkey's licentiousness to Sobriety, the cunning of the fox to the Law. All went well, until the crow brought the peacock's plume. This, the Virtues could not withstand. Each vied for the pride of place, and, immediately the beasts of passion were let loose. Only Humility, weeping in repentance, held up the spoiled plume, and the beasts were routed. Penance must follow. But, without humility, what hope could there be of no further outbreak?

> They drive them soon away;
> And then amerc'd them, double gifts to bring
> At the next Session-day.

The temptation of the riches of the world, ambition, success, splendour, is stressed in *Frailtie*. The world can not just be swept away as of no significance. It is a daily death to die to the world. The attraction persists and can not be overcome once and for all. As long as we live a fully retired life, it is possible, without difficulty, to scorn the world. But, when the world is actually met in its reality, its glamour pitted against the simplicity of the religious life, then:

> That which was dust before, doth quickly rise,
> And prick mine eyes.

The dust, which will decay and return to dust, nevertheless temporarily takes on the semblance of vital life, and blinds our eyes, with its own particles, to the eternal Truth. This worldly attraction is *quick,* with all the suggestion of the appearance of true life, hiding the inherent death, and so too of a swiftness of movement, slipping in slily like a thief, to cheat and deceive, and then vanish into nothing. The prayer is for God's intervention that this seduction may not be permitted. Orientation on the joys of God must somehow remain steadfast. The soul is wedded to God, but the world can still interrupt with its manifold confusion of attraction and its multiplicity of aims, if once the single self-direction on God swerves from its purpose:

> It may a Babel prove
> Commodious to conquer heav'n and thee
> Planted in me.

Thus, once more, morality is no ideal but the actual experience, and continued and re-lived experience, of God's love to us and our love to God. And, again, God and heaven are within the heart of Man, in the infinite condescension of God, Love and Sin skirmishing for position.

The picture of the steadfast man in *Constancie* summarises the possible virtues of life, as suggested in *The Church-porch*, where a man's primary interest is in neither himself nor his own advancement in the world. It is not the picture of the successful, in any sense, righteous man, but the picture of a man living his religion in the moral sphere. The premise is of truth in intention:

> Who is the honest man?
> He that doth still and strongly good pursue,
> To God, his neighbour, and himself most true:
> Whom neither force nor fawning can
> Unpinne, or wrench from giving all their due.

The prevailing characteristic of honesty is this indifference to any form of popularity. An honest man goes on, regardless of what surrounds him, and he keeps his own pace. Accidents, demands, crises, all are faced by him with the same careful indifference. Each is given its due attention, but he remains unaffected and unshaken. Nothing will move him from the vision and aim of Truth. Day or night, encouragement or temptation, have no effect on him. He is not touched by outward circumstances which would either strengthen or weaken. The help of the light of day, or the hindrance of the dark of night, mean nothing to him. He knows where he is going:

> The sunne to others writeth laws,
> And is their vertue; Vertue is his Sunne.

He is equally unaffected by the frailty of others, not yielding to easy deflecting pity. His will is within the Will of God, so:

> Whom nothing can procure,
> When the wide world runnes bias from his will,
> To writhe his limbes, and share, not mend the ill.

The honest man must and does keep his integrity by this total non-involvement. He knows that if he plunges, out of false sentimentality, into the evil, he will be caught in the whirlpool himself. He will be inside the trap, unable to help. But, his work is the work which might seem aloof, might seem cold and unloving, and, yet, retains the power, thereby, to *mend the ill*. Or, if not mend it, yet keep the way open to the greater aim. The honest man has only the one mark, and the mark is God. Morality again is not a separate or social condition, but the direct outcome of this inflexible movement towards the Truth. And, the movement is only possible on the impulse of love:

> This is the Mark-man, safe and sure,
> Who still is right, and prayes to be so still.

Avarice succinctly expresses the paradox of money, for this drudge of ours, money, which we dig out of the earth, we then elevate into sovereignty, stamp with our image, and, then, worship it. The result is inevitable:

> Man calleth thee his wealth, who made thee rich;
> And while he digs out thee, falls in the ditch.

But, this falling in the ditch is again the folly of the blind man who will not look upon the real world of God, but follows his own corruptible aim.

All things, in the daily routine of life, may indeed turn to gold, as they do in *The Elixir*, if the aim once ceases to be immanent. All things not only turn to gold, but change their meaning entirely if they are directed to God in willed intention. The whole of life can, thus, be lifted out of the psychological into the spiritual sphere. *The Elixir* is the explicit plea for retaining unswervingly this self-orientation:

>Teach me, my God and King,
>In all things thee to see,
>And what I do in any thing,
>To do it as for thee . . .

The soul can only thrive in this austere and strict attention on God; for, then, the world falls away as meaningless; poverty or prosperity are one and the same:

>A servant with this clause
>Makes drudgerie divine:
>Who sweeps a room, as for thy laws,
>Makes that and th'action fine.

But, there is nothing *moral* in this, in the sense of a respectable social code. However it may sound, in isolation from the other poems, *The Elixir* remains a simple statement of love to the Person of God, and the consequence of the love. There is no reward for conscientious piousness divorced from love. It is the love which is the active agent in the elixir:

>This is the famous stone
>That turneth all to gold:
>For that which God doth touch and own
>Cannot for lesse be told.

iv. *Death*

There now remains one aspect of this series of consequences to Herbert's theological emphasis on the Person of God, the Person of Christ, and, hence, the work of love. He has directed the consciousness of sin to Love, and, hence, came repentance. The whole moral sphere has lost its autonomous achievement, and becomes important predominantly in relation to living within and towards the loved presence of God. But, now, death must be faced on the same premise of Love. How can transitory life be approached? And, then, death? And, then, eternity? And, always, with the one immutable criterion of the near presence of the loved Person of God.

There is a delicate serenity in the face of death in the expression of *Life*. The sweet-scented flowers, so swiftly withering, are an unavoidable reminder of the swiftness of the passage of time. Time inexorably destroys within the finite life:

> But Time did beckon to the flowers, and they
> By noon most cunningly did steal away,
> And wither'd in my hand.

This was the warning and Herbert sees it as a kind warning, it was *Times gentle admonition*. There is nothing hard, nor ugly, in this presentiment of death, because of the connection with the fragrance of the flowers. And, where there is sweetness, there is Christ:

> Who did so sweetly deaths sad taste convey,
> Making my minde to smell my fatall day;
> Yet sugring the suspicion.

The flowers are dead, but even in death they can still be used medicinally. Now, it is his turn, and, gently assured of the natural sequence of death, he feels no fear:

> I follow straight without complaints or grief,
> Since if my sent be good, I care not if
> It be as short as yours.

If my sent be good: but why should it not be good in the knowledge of Christ's ransom paid that Man might once more be pure?

Mortification follows the same way of awareness of the brevity of life. But, this life, brief as it is, yet need not be wasted. It can be seen positively, as a time of preparation. The infant's swaddling clothes may already be tiny winding sheets; and the sleep of boys is as in a grave, only their breathing differentiating sleep from death; and the gaiety of young music is but the reflection of the death knell. But, here, is the first clear hint that this is no conventional exposition of the temporary nature of mortality, for Herbert sees the harmony in this music of death:

> That musick summons to the knell,
> Which shall befriend him at the houre of death.

The two significant words would appear to be *befriend* and *houre:* both have for Herbert a special connotation. The *Friend* is ever the Spirit, and *the houre* connected directly with the Passion of Christ. So, each one of our deaths is already seen in the context of the Love of God. It is not a lonely death, nor a sterile one. In the next stage of life, a man has his home, and his home pre-figures the enclosure of the coffin. And, finally, in old age:

> A chair or litter shows the biere,
> Which shall convey him to the house of death.

The road is straight from birth to death, with unmistakable sign-posts on the way. But, this is no passive road. It is an active road within the personal direction of God, and it is a road which leads into the eternal life of death, if only we practise daily, already in life, that final death of the body, the inception of the emancipated life of the soul:

> Yet Lord, instruct us so to die,
> That all these dyings may be life in death.

There is no fear in this poem, only a trust, a loving submission into the willingness to be unmoved by temporal motives, but ever to be aware of the guiding presence of God.

The brief *A Dialogue-Antheme* between Christian and Death reiterates the final defeat of death, through the love of Christ. Death can boast that he has killed the Christian's King, but Christian retaliates by commiserating with this fruitless attempt which has turned back on Death. Has not Christ destroyed death by death? Death can threaten Christian how one day he will crush him, but Christian retaliates in the full certainty of his salvation, through the Sacrifice of Christ:

>   Spare not, do thy worst.
> I shall be one day better then before:
> Thou so much worse, that thou shalt be no more.

Death comes out even more explicitly in this movement of denial of any terror in death because of Christ's act of redemption. In fact, here the negative becomes actively positive: Death is not only not feared, but it is welcomed.

There was a time when death was strange, grotesque and horrifying in its flesh-less finality. Where there were only bones, what life could there be? Only the skull, with its travesty of a fallen under-jaw:

> Death, thou wast once an uncouth hideous thing,
> Nothing but bones,
> The sad effect of sadder grones:
> Thy mouth was open, but thou couldst not sing.

Death was seen as a continuation of old life, but intensified: the extended condition of skeleton-like emaciation: the extended condition of mental decay:

> For we consider'd thee as at some six
> Or ten yeares hence,
> After the losse of life and sense,
> Flesh being turn'd to dust, and bones to sticks.

This was the mistake. And the mistake lay in apportioning to death what still lies on this side of death, the last remnants of this life; whereas, death is not the end of this life, but the opening into the new. We saw death in relationship to the old, dis-used life of the body, instead of the hardly hatched new life of the soul:

> We lookt on this side of thee, shooting short;
> Where we did finde
> The shells of fledge souls left behinde,
> Dry dust, which sheds no tears, but may extort.

If the souls are seen in the image of birds, then the Holy Spirit is present. And, the Spirit is indeed present, for the death of Christ has revolutionised the truth of death. Death is no dusty end. Death is beautiful. Death is not feared, but courted and awaited eagerly, for the colour in the face of Death is the redeeming blood of Christ, and the beauty is the Grace of the Spirit:

> But since our Saviours death did put some bloud
> Into thy face;
> Thou art grown fair and full of grace,
> Much in request, much sought for as a good.

The old picture in our minds of Death has been discarded for the new one. We see Death as at the Day of Judgment. And, the Day of Judgment must be a Day of Joy, not of terror, because we rest secure in the redeeming love of Christ. The Day of Judgment will see Death finally destroyed, as the bodies will be dressed again in all the physical beauty of flesh. There is nothing to fear. Love and trust are the pass-words to serenity. Sleep or death—there is little difference. We need not fear to lend our bodies, the half of us, temporarily to the grave, any more than to our beds. Therefore, we can die, as sleep, and trust:

> Half that we have
> Unto an honest faithfull grave;
> Making our pillows either down, or dust.

Dooms-day goes further than *Death*. Here comes the actual incisive invitation for the Day of Judgment to come, on a lyrical note which would normally be associated with a conventional love-lyric:

> Come away,
> Make no delay.
> Summon all the dust to rise,
> Till it stirre, and rubbe the eyes;
> While this member jogs the other,
> Each one whispring, *Live you brother?*

Human bodily remains are dispersed throughout the world, waiting for the healing sound of the one music which they can recognise: the Trumpet of the Last Judgment. The blowing of the trumpet will be the signal for the dispersed to assemble, for unity and harmony to replace all the disintegration of death; the graves must not be allowed, by the Day's delay, to imagine that they have a permanent claim on the dead. Corruption must be purified. But, the trumpet is not merely a signal of the Last Day, it is the call of Christ himself, raising up his Bride, the Church, that she too might join in the eternal worship. No wonder that the song of death is a lyric of joy, the final loving re-union of life in the presence of God:

> Come away,
> Help our decay.
> Man is out of order hurl'd,
> Parcel'd out to all the world.
> Lord, thy broken consort raise,
> And the musick shall be praise.

The ironic conversation with *Time*, once more, reverses the normal attitude to life. How often Time is reproached for the swiftness of its cutting short the days of life! But, how often is Time reproached for the reverse? In daring anticipation of the joy of eternal bliss, Herbert rebukes Time for its tardiness. He suggests that Time could sharpen his scythe and, thereby, gain a little more efficiency in dealing with its own slow passage. Time remonstrates that this is not the usual rebuke, indeed:

> But where one man would have me grinde it,
> Twentie for one too sharp do finde it.

But, Herbert speaks enthusiastically of the vast difference which has come to Man in the Sacrifice of Christ. There was, of course, the time when the scythe of Time would have seemed the executioner's axe, final and inexorable death, but, now, this same scythe is the one means of giving renewed life. Cutting off the old life, as unfruitful branches, with a pruning knife, Time gives the means for the continuation of the real and healthy life:

> Christs coming hath made man thy debter,
> Since by thy cutting he grows better.

It is Time's envied and respected prerogative to conduct Man from this life to eternity:

> An usher to convey our souls
> Beyond the utmost starres and poles,

The thought of the eternal life is so joyous, that this life becomes more and more burdensome and irksome. It is like a fore-taste of hell in its forced separation from God. It is a punishment to continue living, on this side of life. So-called pleasures become penance:

> And this is that makes life so long,
> While it detains us from our God.
> Ev'n pleasures here increase the wrong,
> And length of dayes lengthen the rod.
>   Who wants the place, where God doth dwell,
>   Partakes already half of hell.

For a moment, Herbert pauses on the thought of hell. He sees hell as the lack of the presence of God and he can not imagine the duration, in terms of time, of hell, if it is ever excluded from Eternity. But, his cogitations on hell are rudely interrupted by Time, who in the meanwhile has thought over what Herbert has been saying and who has suddenly understood the paradox. Herbert's longing to die is in order to live! Time has been wasting his time, believing that he had come across a man who really wanted him to hurry. And, what he has met, is a man waiting for

Eternity in glad confidence. Time is affronted before this vision of timelessness which, being finite, he can only comprehend as an extension of himself:

> Then chafing said, This man deludes:
> What do I here before his doore?
> He doth not crave lesse time, but more.

One image remains of Herbert's attitude to death in the diagram of *Heaven*. How can Man write but in hints on Heaven which he has not seen? And, so, Herbert writes, as it were, artificially. But, the artificiality of the conversation with Echo seems the very means of emphasising the impossibility of a natural comprehension of Heaven. We can only guess, and so the less rationally that we express ourselves, the more true we are to our human limitation. But, what emerges? One thing is certain, and that is Herbert's conviction of the bliss of heaven which awaits us. It is a real joy, of which we only have a reflection, an Echo, in the Holy Scriptures. And, from the Holy Scriptures, we know that Heaven is preeminently light. Where we now comprehend darkly, there all will be revealed. And we also know that the joy of heaven is a joy which we can not now comprehend. There will be peace. The anxious questioning is drawing to its end. The answers have been given: Light: Joy: Leisure. There is only one more word of consolation to be added. There will be no more time, and, hence, no more end:

> Light, joy, and leasure; but shall they persever?
>   *Echo.*   Ever.

Heaven is open to us. Yet, we live. And, we continue to live. Face to face with the love of God, Herbert has considered the moral sphere. He has presented sin and repentance in direct confrontation with the loved Person of God. He has suggested the life of virtue, again, turned to God as the centre. He has faced death in the same context. But, it is not possible to live, in the world, always at this point of death. There must be some return to life. And, in the return, Herbert turns fully to the one active spiritual work which he can find satisfying for himself as long as he lives: the *creative* work of the worship of God, who first loved us.

CHAPTER III

THE OFFERING OF PRAISE

Face to face with the Person of God, Herbert sees his work in the world as the unceasing labour of praise. And, because he is a poet, his way of expression will inevitably lie in his verse. But, this weapon of prayer proves a double-edged weapon, for poetry brings with it the echoes of the world which he rejects. As a poet, he must find a way for dissociating his medium of worship from all sensuous connotations. He claims, unequivocally, that poetry may be used for the praise of God, and denounces any counter-claims that poetry is only of this world, and concerned primarily with the events and emotions of this world. Praise of God, in the form of poetry, becomes, for Herbert, a challenge to society, and a reiteration for himself, that the life, not turned to God, is no life, and that the words, not addressed to God, are vain.

i. *The duty of praise*

The work of praise is not the work of fear, nor, as it were, of empty duty. It is a duty, but a duty of love, which is not only unavoidable, but which there can be no wish of avoiding. God is a loved Person, not an idea, and to praise his goodness is a work of gladness.

Prayer (I) sees this duty of worship as the greatest fulfilment and wealth of Man:

> Prayer the Churches banquet, Angels age,
> Gods breath in man returning to his birth,
> The soul in paraphrase, heart in pilgrimage,
> The Christian plummet sounding heav'n and earth . . .

These opening lines are a clarion-call of challenge. Prayer becomes not the *expression* of the Church on earth, but the *nourishment*. Without Prayer, the Church would become thin and emaciated. Yet, it is no mere meal, it is a banquet, a feast. And where there is a feast, there is the Bride-groom present. With the Eucharistic feast, time verges on no-time. In the worship of Prayer, we come nearest to the timelessness of the angels, whose worship is unceasing. But, even more, Prayer is the Grace of God, returning as a loved gift to God. The Holy Spirit breathes into us, and, when we pray, that breath returns to God, a breath which in ourselves we could not contain. In prayer we are already therefore linked with Christ, with the Angels, with the Holy Spirit. No wonder that our soul expands to its potential fullness and begins its journey to heaven, seeking its first home. Prayer unites heaven and earth, sounding one and the other; heaven sounds earth; and earth seeks to sound heaven.

But, Prayer is even more potent. For in Prayer, again, we turn God's own machines of war against him, in our assault of love upon him, as upon a besieged city:

> Engine against th' Almightie, sinners towre,
> Reversed thunder . . .

And, the most powerful weapon in our grasp in Prayer is as the sword which pierced the side of Christ: in the hour, his hour, the whole face of creation was altered. The earth shook, in that hour, and there was a mighty storm. The thunder of that storm reverberates in our single prayers:

> A kinde of tune, which all things heare and fear . . .

The power of our prayer is not dependent upon itself. It is a power of Christ himself. The power of Christ is the power of Love:

> Softnesse, and peace, and joy, and love, and blisse . . .

The manna, which fell from heaven, is now the bread exalted into heaven in his glorious Resurrection. Christ has brought heaven to us, as something natural, accessible to all. Now Man raises himself from the dust. Man, in Christ, sees the sky, the stars, the bird of Paradise. Man's prayer on earth is answered by the ringing of the bells of the Church in heaven. The blood of Christ is the very blood of our souls, and the promised land is sweet and near. At the instant of prayer, the glad solution is ours, for the dreaded division, in vision, seems no more:

> Church-bels beyond the starres heard, the souls bloud,
> The land of spices; something understood.

The souls bloud: the land of spices: the Presence of Christ is the clue to the vision: the ransom of love: the blood of Passion and Crucifixion, the spices of the entombment which overcame death.

Providence explains precisely why it is Man's debt, beyond all other creatures, to praise God. How can Herbert even write, if it were not for Providence?

> . . . through whom my fingers bend
> To hold my quill? shall they not do thee right?

Man, alone, has the capability of extolling God in words, and this capability was given by God. How can Man then even consider using his power of words for any other end?

> Of all the creatures both in sea and land
> Onely to Man thou hast made known thy wayes,
> And put the penne alone into his hand,
> And made him Secretarie of thy praise.

Other creatures, even if they wish to, are incapable of giving coherent utterance to this praise. It is Man's duty to offer the sacrifice of praise on behalf of all the incoherent world. If Man withdraws from his duty of praise, he betrays all the other creatures dependent upon him for their expression. The Holy Spirit moves throughout all the created world, *strongly* and *sweetly*, with inestimable power, and with inestimable gifts of delight and joy. Nothing is outside the Providence of the Spirit. And the music of the Spirit is the sweetest harmony. Sin is the discordant note. The Spirit infuses harmonious balance. We mar it:

> . . . all must appeare,
> And be dispos'd, and dress'd, and tun'd by thee,
> Who sweetly temper'st all. If we could heare
> Thy skill and art, what musick would it be!

The power of the Spirit is ever great, nothing is too mean for his careful Providence. It is the Spirit who stills the storm and feeds the beasts. The whole of nature is ordered and disposed for survival. Every creature knows only as much as it need know to live and rear its young. Nothing is wasted:

> Sheep eat the grasse, and dung the ground for more:
> Trees after bearing drop their leaves for soil:
> Springs vent their streams, and by expense get store:
> Clouds cool by heat, and baths by cooling boil.

Herbs and flowers are both beautiful and medicinal. Metals are hidden in the earth for the use of Man, and where poison grows, the antidote is near at hand. Seas and winds are at the service of the sailor. The whole world is again carefully divided, allowing for its own special offerings in vegetation and animals. Light, warmth, mobility, all is provided for Man. And, if one country lacks anything, this is all to its benefit, for the need leads to trade with other countries. Man reigns supreme in the world. He alone needs clothes, he alone uses fire showing his kinship to heaven. God created a world where Man could live, with dry land and water, and mountains. Winds bring the rain and the rain gives life to the flowers. Each thing has its use. Perhaps thorns seem sharp, but they make a hedge; stones and sticks may not seem as soft to the touch as silk, but they construct the foundation without which silk would be useless. Some things have one purpose, others many. The creatures themselves are separate in identity, but some combine more than one quality, for Providence is not tied by any rules, and this He shows by sudden deviations from normal behaviour in His creatures:

> Most things move th' under-jaw; the Crocodile not.
> Most things sleep lying; th' Elephant leans or stands.

So, Herbert, in this poem of gratitude and praise, takes upon himself, as Man, the double duty of thanking God, not only for himself but for the creatures of the world which can not speak for themselves:

> All things that are, though they have sev'rall wayes,
> Yet in their being joyn with one advise
> To honour thee: and so I give praise
> In all my other hymnes, but in this twice.

All creatures have some means of honouring the Creator, but not the means of speech; the poem ends in this sense of double duty of explicit devotion:

> Each thing that is, although in use and name
> It go for one, hath many wayes in store
> To honour thee; and so each hymne thy fame
> Extolleth many wayes, yet this one more.

Creation rejoices in the Creator. *Antiphon* (I) is not concerned with the variety of creatures. It sees the whole creation as one, and it sees the work as one:

> *Cho.* Let all the world in ev'ry corner sing,
>   *My God and King.*

It is the praise for God, God the Creator, and my *King*, my Sovereign, him to whom I owe my duty and my worship. Heaven

and earth are united by the chorus of praise, for the praise rises
from the earth and reaches to Heaven. It is the link. But, even in
such an explicit and objective poem of praise, where the Church
breaks through every barrier of sound with its psalms of worship,
Herbert retains the final and deepest importance for the heart. We
must not be lost in generalisations. God, the Person, is Love. And,
each one of us, the person, returns the love of God with his own,
particular love. The love in the heart, the seat of God in each
person, even as it may be the seat of sin:

>But above all, the heart
>Must bear the longest part.

>*Cho.* Let all the world in ev'ry corner sing,
>   *My God and King.*

Employment (II) persists with the awareness of the work, the
duty, of worship, but with the hint of uncertainty in the achieving
of the work. Herbert has no desire for idleness; let the weary rest,
and those who are cold by constitution wrap themselves in their
furs, he wants to be active, alive, not keep his thoughts to himself,
but spread them abroad:
>My soul would stirre
>And trade in courtesies and wit . . .

Man is made of fire. Is not the Holy Spirit within him? If he
does not breathe upon the charcoal to keep the flame glowing, it
will turn to ashes. Man is equally made of earth. Without the
creative Spirit, he can soon revert to ashes. To live is to work, not
to exist at ease. The sun shines constantly, it is the stars which
come and go opportunely. The Spirit in us must live, returning light
to Light, breath to Breath. Herbert's dread is to be barren in
worship. The fig-tree withered. But, an Orange-tree bears much
fruit. God has planted, and pruned, and cultivated him. He longs
to give back the fruits:

>Oh that I were an Orenge-tree,
>   That busie plant!
>Then should I ever laden be,
>   And never want
>Some fruit for him that dressed me.

Herbert deplores the cold sterility within the heart which prevents
the warmth of creative worship. There is always some excuse for
failing God; we are first too young, and then too old. And, then,

it is too late. We keep back our goods, all that we could offer in worship and praise, coldly avaricious:

> The Man is gone,
> Before we do our wares unfold:
> So we freeze on,
> Untill the grave increase our cold.

But, sometimes, the employment of praise does become possible, and then comes the joyful grasping of the opportunity while it lasts, in all its urgent insistence, as in *Praise* (II). Herbert has prayed for the mercy of God that the love, that is, the expression of the love, may not cease, and:

> Thou hast granted my request,
> Thou hast heard me:
> Thou didst note my working breast,
> Thou hast spar'd me.

Set free into creativity, by the permission of God, and the permission signifies the inspiration of the Spirit which brings with it the full spurt of creative activity, Herbert seizes on the rare moment. Not only has dry numbness left him, but he is positively alive:

> Wherefore with my utmost art
> I will sing thee,
> And the cream of all my heart
> I will bring thee.

It is the cream, the best of his *heart*. This once again emphasises the seat of the Spirit. The gift, the Grace, is of God, but the work can be ours. But, without the Grace, nothing is possible. Sin always battles with God for pride of place in the human heart. This time it has been ousted:

> Though my sinnes against me cried,
> Thou didst cleare me;
> And alone, when they replied,
> Thou didst heare me.

So, Herbert has been, at least temporarily, released from the paralysis of sin, and in loving reply, his one desire is to worship. There can be no doubt here how Herbert associates lack of creativity with sin, that is, there is no place for the Spirit when sin has priority in his heart. Now, however, in the joy of release:

> Sev'n whole dayes, not one in seven,
>   I will praise thee.
> In my heart, though not in heaven,
>   I can raise thee.

God has compassion on him. Where so often Herbert feels his own heart hard, God is *soft and moist with tears* towards him. Love replaces Justice. Time and Eternity, both are not long enough for the praise of God:

> Small it is, in this poore sort
>   To enroll thee:
> Ev'n eternitie is too short
>   To extoll thee.

Praise (III) opens with the determined intention:

> Lord, I will mean and speak thy praise,
>   Thy praise alone.

Herbert's heart, again the heart, not the mind, for the praise is the work of the Grace within him, will not cease to be industrious. And, if by chance, it would seem to become dry, he will extract what already may seem not to be there by means of his grief, his sighs and his groans, which are the mark of repentance. If the heart is dry, then only repentance can bring it to activity again, ousting the sin:

> My busie heart shall spin it all my dayes:
>   And when it stops for want of store,
> Then will I wring it with a sigh or grone,
>   That thou mayst yet have more.

With the breath of the Spirit, with the Grace of God, impossible things become possible. All takes on a divine and miraculous impetus of movement. But, if the Spirit would wish to quench the flames of activity with his breath, then it is indeed an apathy. Nothing moves, and nothing can make anything move:

> Legs are but stumps, and Pharaohs wheels but logs,
>   And struggling hinders more.

It is the dreadful picture of the proud Egyptian charioteers in the waters of the Red Sea. How could they struggle against the will of God? God's care and attention are demanded from all sides. It can not be otherwise:

> Thousands of things do thee employ
> In ruling all
> This spacious globe . . .

Angels, Devils, the sea, the winds, all equally can do nothing without God. But, and this is the miracle, God is yet attentive to his single cry:

> . . . and yet when I did call,
> Thou heardst my call, and more.

God not only hears the actual cry, but he hears what we ourselves do not even know that we need. Not a cry is lost, and not a moment of sorrow. The compensation for all our suffering awaits us. The bottle of the Psalm, which contains our tears, for Herbert has grown to a size far in excess of his needs. How can his tears either fill that bottle or be worthy to fill it? In ourselves, there can never be sufficient merit, not even of sorrow or suffering. But, through the love of Christ, the deficiency is more than adequately compensated. One drop of the tears of Christ's Passion, and: *The glasse was full and more*. What love and praise can repay such love? Christ, for Man, wept blood, not tears. His Crucifixion was his Victory, and the flag on a Church waves bravely, blood-red, proclaiming the victory. Christ's victory of blood makes good our lack. We can only answer by worship:

> Wherefore I sing.

But, what is one man's praise? Herbert yearns for others to join, that his meagre effort might swell, that his one talent could at least be put out to usury and gain more. When his Lord returns, will he not offer him some profit?

> Yet since my heart,
> Though press'd, runnes thin;
> O that I might some other hearts convert,
> And so take up at use good store:
> That to thy chest there might be coming in
> Both all my praise, and more!

ii. Language of sacred verse

Praise is the work, and the vehicle of Herbert's praise is his poetry. Thus the value of the poetry, in critical terms, no longer affects nor even concerns him. He denies that he is in the least perturbed by an adverse judgment of his apparent loss of poetic expression or singularity. It is as if he denies for his poetry, precisely what he denies for himself, that is, any kind of worldly vanity, worldly achievement, worldly attraction. His life is turned inwards to God, and his poetry will follow suit. This turning inwards, the stillness of contemplation directed to God, away from all possibility of achievement, Herbert describes in *Content*.

Wandering and discursive thinking must be gathered into a unity. Things outside must cease to seem inviting and exciting. The heart should not follow every spurt of ambition, chasing frivolous and unreasonable desires and hopes which can not be fulfilled. Every casual eventuality, which happens fortuitously, should not be an immediate object of sensuous distraction:

> To court each place or fortune that doth fall,
>   Is wantonnesse in contemplation.

The greatest strength would always appear restrained and hidden. The highest mind is flexible, equally ready to respond to every kind and manner of life, be it royal court or monastic enclosure. A receptive soul is at home throughout every corner of the world. No part of the world is uncomfortable for him. Wherever he finds himself:

> He lies warm, and without adventure.

Above all, worldly achievements are the most transient of all things. A few days of wild excitement, and all is over:

> And after death the fumes that spring
> From private bodies make as big a thunder,
>   As those which rise from a huge King.

The only loss is worldly reputation. But, the eternal Book of Life is more important, and more dangerous. And, worldly reputation does not depend on us, but on those who chew us over when we are dead. It is what they say about us that remains, not we ourselves. If fools write about us, then whatever we have done, and suffered the consequences, will indeed in their mouths seem equally foolish. After we are dead, our reputation depends on the intelligence of our biographers!

> When all thy deeds, whose brunt thou feel'st alone,
> 	Are chaw'd by others pens and tongue;
> And as their wit is, their digestion,
> 	Thy nourisht fame is weak or strong.

So, the soul must surely cease from all out-going dispersing efforts. The soul must carefully and serenely farm its own land, facing inwards, living within its own boundaries, disturbing neither himself nor his friends. This is a state of true wealth and contentment, the life recollected upon itself, away from the world, and therefore free and ready to please God alone. It is a life of *the soul:*

> Then cease discoursing soul, till thine own ground,
> 	Do not thy self or friends importune.
> He that by seeking hath himself once found,
> 	Hath ever found a happie fortune.

The Forerunners is a poem not of passive acceptance but of strong, active taking up and turning into life what may seem decline and death:

> The harbingers are come.

The forerunners, the messengers are not to be mistaken. Herbert prevents the inevitable coming on of age, and with age, the apparent decline in his poetic power. The brilliance of his mind would seem to be losing its sparkling wit, and a gray uniformity dispels the bright light. But, is this prophecy of imminent loss of splendour, equally a condemnation to non-productivity, to the death of the creative genius within him? Or is it merely the change from the service towards Man, to the service towards God, in his poetry? It can not be an easy decision for a poet to choose between writing for Man and writing for God. Writing for God will certainly not give pleasure to Man, nor success for himself. But, the problem is unavoidable:

> But must they have my brain? must they dispark
> Those sparkling notions, which therein were bred?
> 	Must dulnesse turn me to a clod?
> Yet have they left me, *Thou art still my God.*

The harbingers have come but, thinking that they have requisitioned the best rooms for the worldly king, they have left by far the best room for the heavenly King. They have left not the rooms of wit and cleverness and scintillating verse, but they have left the heart, the seat of the Spirit, and that is why, whatever happens, the one simple verse can be repeated, again and again:

> *Thou art still my God.*

And, for God, this suffices and, if it suffices for God, then it must be the greatest poetry:

> He will be pleased with that dittie;
> And if I please him, I write fine and wittie.

So:

> Farewell sweet phrases, lovely metaphors.

His wide vocabulary, attractive images, turns of phrase, all must be sacrificed. He had begun by trying to use the common poetic language for his divine poetry. He had thought that if he used the whole battery of secular love imagery for sacred verse he would be able to rid the language of its sensual associations, and yet retain its virility and strength for God:

> Then did I wash you with my tears, and more,
> Brought you to Church well drest and clad:
> My God must have my best, ev'n all I had.

But, it had not proved possible. The attractiveness of the secular language was not to be dissociated from its context, and it remained only sensually appealing, unrelated to the ultimate Beauty. Herbert could not find the means of raising the language of the senses into the sphere of the Spirit. The syrup charm must be abandoned, for this charm finds no home for itself in the Church. It can only tarnish what it touches with the stains of the senses. Wit and brilliance must be left to the world, where they belong:

> Let follie speak in her own native tongue.

True beauty is in heaven. There burns the real fire of the Spirit, and the real poet catches the sparks from this fire only in order that his poetry may return there, whence it drew its inspiration. Wit and brilliance for the world, but, for God, the beauty of words which are fitting and seemly to the beauty of God. His heart is free:

> Beautie and beauteous words should go together.

And, even, if the beautiful words, as Herbert sees them as beautiful, should desert him, it still means nothing at all. He can still repeat again and again the simple:

> *Thou art still my God . . .*

What can words say more however adorned? There is no fear. Far from it. There is an eager acceptance of what may seem to the world as old age, a loss of intellect, a decay of genius. This is how the world may see his work of praise from the outside. But, the world can not see inside the heart. And, inside the heart, the work of praise continues, ever more intensely, ever more alive, and serene, even as the outside grows less and less attractive, and more and more unproductive in worldly terms:

> Go birds of spring: let winter have his fee;
>   Let a bleak paleness chalk the doore,
> So all within be livelier then before.

The door is marked, not for the king of this world, but for the King of Kings. And the King of Kings is not concerned with outward appearance.

The dedication of praise is repeated in *A Wreath*. The wreath of praise is given to God, who knows every twist and turn of the human soul. Here is the Evangelical contradiction. The seeming life in these adventures of worldly life are, ultimately, death. Life only lives in the death to the world, in the straight, undeviating orientation to God. With God, there can be no equivocation of any kind. There can be no multiplicity of aim. He, who turns to God, above all must pray for this inflexible unity of purpose beyond the attraction of the world. He must pray for simplicity:

> Give me simplicitie, that I may live,
> So live and like, that I may know, thy wayes,
> Know them and practise them . . .

Praise of God can not come from an effort of wit, nor of intelligence. Praise of God can only come from having lived the experience of the praise in single orientation towards God. This Herbert knows, and so he prays for the Grace that he may offer his praise to God:

>   . . . then shall I give
> For this poore wreath, give thee a crown of praise.

His poetry is Herbert's direct means of communication with God. To write his poetry, he must be inspired by the Spirit, in a condition of the presence of Grace, and his poetry returns to God in the form of praise. This he claims in *The Quidditie* for his verse. It would be an astounding claim in itself if not for the general context, and, particularly, the constant acknowledgment that he can only write when the Spirit of God is free to work in his heart. Thus, the claim for himself is in effect the claim, not for his, but for God's sovereignty. Where God is, there is the essence of Majesty surpassing all possible human claim of achievement. The world is again discounted and, with the world, so too secular verse. It is only prayer and praise, for Herbert in his poetry, which essentially goes beyond all other wealth, property, or nobility in the world. A verse would not seem capable of competing with kingship, honour, foppery, hunting, feasting, heroism, love-poetry; moreover:

> It cannot vault, or dance, or play;
> It never was in *France* or *Spain;*
> Nor can it entertain the day
> With my great stable or demain . . .

A verse is indeed a poor thing, quite beneath the notice of gallantry. Nor can it even rival more mundane money deals and merchandise. What is this simple verse then? What can it bring in its defence? It can bring its prime universality, its final victory over all in its communion with God, not with Man. It can claim to be foremost, outpacing all else:

> But it is that which while I use
> I am with thee, and *most take all.*

Jordan (i) most clearly brings out this possible divine work and purpose of verse, but of verse strictly and soberly cleansed from the gaudy attraction of secular imagery.

There is a fine scorn in the opening lines, denying that poetry must be relegated to the world of fantasy, and claiming that the expression of truth has its own and greater beauty. Ingenious verse-making is not the only possible kind of verse. And verse, dedicated to the true King, is surely as valid as that written for the world of invention. The throne of Truth is no less an object of poetry, than the throne of art, some simpering, painted harlot elevated to sovereignty in a love-lyric:

> Who sayes that fictions onely and false hair
> Become a verse? Is there in truth no beautie?
> Is all good structure in a winding stair?
> May no lines passe, except they do their dutie
>   Not to a true, but painted chair?

And the following lines persist in this near-despair that all poetry must apparently be some form of love-poetry, impregnated with sly hints and innuendoes, all the romantic intricacies, to make the alluring wrapping for the unadorned sensual content. The suggestiveness of verse gives the extra spice of interest in the interpreting:

> Is it no verse, except enchanted groves
> And sudden arbours shadow course-spunne lines?
> Must purling streams refresh a lovers loves?
> Must all be vail'd, while he that reades, divines,
>   Catching the sense at two removes?

Herbert refuses to be involved in any poetic competition. As far as he is concerned, shepherds can pipe away their love songs, others can try to out-do each other in witty and epigrammatic rhymes. He is not interested in the charm of other men's poetic ability, nor youth. But, on the other hand, he claims for himself the prerogative to write as he wishes without reproach. His writing will remain steadfast, simple, and to one aim alone, whatever else may befall:

> Shepherds are honest people; let them sing:
> Riddle who list, for me, and pull for Prime:
> I envie no mans nightingale or spring;
> Nor let them punish me with losse of rime,
>   Who plainly say, *My God, My King.*

iii. *Verse as the medium of devotion*

The contention that it is not reasonable to retain poetry solely for secular purposes, but, that poetry, in fact, can be the highest medium of praise of God, persists emphatically in *Love* I and in *Love* II.

What can be more unfair? God is Love, God gave Man the capacity not only of loving but of giving expression to the love through the working of his imagination. And, Man, in return, has used both the love and the tools of expression to please his own sensual satisfaction. God is Love. And Man has taken hold of Divine Love and portioned out Love, which is One, into a multitude of little pieces, giving mortal love the same name and the same veneration as Divine Love. Even worse, this partial love, having imagination as its ally, has in effect ousted Love from His rightful place in the heart and mind of Man:

> Which siding with invention, they together
> Bear all the sway, possessing heart and brain,
> (Thy workmanship) and give thee share in neither.

It seems a complete victory on the part of sensuality. The intellect looks upon what is beautiful and is attracted by it, whilst beauty stimulates the inventive mind. They play into each other's hands. While the Author of all has no place. Was it not God who saved us from hell? But, this is quite forgotten. No poems of praise are raised to God, only some woman's frivolous possession can set alight our inventive genius, and, then, we write of love, what we call love:

> Who sings thy praise? onely a skarf or glove
> Doth warm our hands, and make them write of love.

In *Love* II, Herbert sees God as the Undying Fire, the Fire of Inspiration, the Fire of Creation, but equally the future Fire of Judgment and hell. Herbert prays that this fire can yet somehow control the wild passions of Man, and harness Man towards spiritual longing. If only this could come to pass, then sensual craving would change to spiritual seeking. Our hearts, free from lust, would turn all the energy of desire, breathless with sustained effort, thirsty with striving, to God. As the hart pants for cool streams, Man's heart will pant after the clarity of Love, instead of the muddiness of sensuality:

> Then shall our hearts pant thee; then shall our brain
> All her invention on thine Altar lay,
> And there in hymnes send back thy fire again:
> Our eies shall see thee, which before saw dust;
> Dust blown by wit, till that they both were blinde . . .

Then God will be re-instated in his rightful place, and what is his, will once again return to him. Then the scales will fall from our eyes and we shall see the Truth, and our minds will proclaim the Truth, and our faculties of mind and senses will be directed on God alone:

> All knees shall bow to thee; all wits shall rise,
> And praise him who did make and mend our eies.

There is nothing equivocal in either of these two poems. They both openly and fully and without reserve renounce any kind of creative art if it is not directed to God alone. All genius is for God alone, all powers of the intellect. It is hardly possible in the face of such assertion even to consider Herbert's poetry in any other light than as the conscious effort of using his verse, in some way, only for explicit worship or spiritual teaching. His problem could only have been whether or not it were possible to decontaminate language to the extent of making it the suitable vehicle of devotion.

iv. *Verse as the work of devotion*

Poetry is not only the vehicle for discussion of the praise of God, or for teaching about God. Because the poetry is for God, it, thereby, becomes in itself an act of devotion, an expression of love. Poetry is not merely the means of insisting that poetry should be the praise, but it becomes the praise.

So, *A true Hymne* breaks into the gladness of direct devotion. It is a *true* hymn, truth returning to Truth. It is a *true* hymn, not a licentious distortion. And, because it is a *true* hymn, the words derive from God, to return to him, and thus they possess and direct Herbert: it is not for him to manipulate for fine phrases:

> My joy, my life, my crown!

My crown: again the emphasis on the sovereignty, the true Kingship of God. The proof of the divine possession, and hence the freedom to write, comes in the next line:

> My heart was meaning all the day . . .

My heart: the seat of God, and hence the released potency of creativity:

> Somewhat it fain would say:
> And still it runneth mutt'ring up and down
> With onely this, *My joy, my life, my crown.*

Only three ejaculations, but fully sufficient in themselves. If then these sentiments are true, then they are entirely adequate. Their greatness even as poetry lies in their true expression of the soul's experience:

> The finenesse which a hymne or psalme affords,
> Is, when the soul unto the lines accords.

No effort of mind, nor of soul is sufficient to produce anything approaching satisfactory devotional poetry. Whatever the effort, there will remain the knowledge of something lacking. It must be so. No human effort can reach to God. But, if the poetry does not aim at its own perfection, if the poetry is content with the simple truth which comes from the heart, out of the Grace inspired into the heart open to Grace, then God himself will amply supply the deficiencies. *A true Hymne* is a confession of inadequacy, and a resting in the generous love of God:

> Whereas if th' heart be moved,
> Although the verse be somewhat scant,
> God doth supplie the want.
> As when th' heart sayes (sighing to be approved)
> *O, could I love!* and stops: God writeth, *Loved.*

How fitly express his love? *The Thanksgiving* must remain far away from the truth of the Love of God. God is the *King of grief*. He is the *King of wounds*. No song of tears can measure with the truth of the Sacrifice. What human words can re-capture the infinite grief:

> *My God, my God, why dost thou part from me?*

Should the thanksgiving not take the form of the grief then, but concentrate on the Resurrection, the *triumphant glorie?* Is it possible to deny the suffering to such an extent?

> Shall I then sing, skipping thy dolefull storie,
> And side with thy triumphant glorie?
> Shall thy strokes be my stroking? thorns, my flower?
> Thy rod, my posie? crosse, my bower?

But how then should Herbert imitate Christ, and:

> Copie thy fair, though bloudie hand?

So, this poem of thanksgiving turns to practical possibilities of praise, of giving to the poor, of denying reputation for himself, of dedicating his family to Christ, of discarding his best friend if he dare blaspheme the Name of Christ, of giving what remains of his wealth to the foundation of a Chapel. For the future, build a hospital, repair the roads, but first amend his own ways. Above all, use worldly things as but passing toys, and focus his whole creative energy on God alone. Not one part of him but will praise God. This is his promise of thanksgiving:

> My musick shall finde thee, and ev'ry string
>   Shall have his attribute to sing;
> That all together may accord in thee,
>   And prove one God, one harmonie.

The thanksgiving will be a constant return of God's gifts. All the fine craftsmanship of versifying will be turned back on Christ, after careful and diligent study of the Bible. Where else but in the Bible is it possible as deeply to study the art of love? Armed with the weapons of God himself, Herbert's thanksgiving takes on a note of ecstatic triumph. With God's power, not his own, he can give thanks:

> Thy art of love, which I'le turn back on thee:
>   O my deare Saviour, Victorie!

But, the suffering still remains. And, for this, there is no answer to be given openly in verse. Herbert draws back. It is not fit to be part of the challenge of thanksgiving:

> Then for thy passion—I will do for that—
>   Alas, my God, I know not what.

Christmas is the thanksgiving for the patience and self-limitation of God. Weary of worldly pleasure, Herbert at last finds rest in the inn where Christ is born, and where Christ awaits him, knowing that he will come when he is too exhausted to pursue his own ways any more:

> There when I came, whom found I but my deare,
>   My dearest Lord, expecting till the grief
>   Of pleasures brought me to him, readie there
> To be all passengers most sweet relief?

The thanksgiving for Christmas is also the prayer once again that God should so purify his soul that there may be space there for Christ to take up his dwelling, a better dwelling than the manger of his birth as man, and the grave in the death as man. It is Christmas, and as the shepherds sing, Herbert gathers his thoughts up as a flock of worship to Christ. But, the pastures, on which his thoughts feed, are not his own. The pastures are the Word of God, and the Grace of God alone can bring the water of life to make the pastures fresh and green. If God gives the Grace, then day will not be long enough to allow for his songs of praise:

> I will go searching, till I finde a sunne
>   Shall stay, till we have done;
> A willing shiner, that shall shine as gladly,
>   As frost-nipt sunnes look sadly.

The sun and he will conspire together, and inter-mingle to the praise of God:

> His beams shall cheer my breast, and both so twine,
> Till ev'n his beams sing, and my musick shine.

My musick shine: the prayer for illumination, that his verses may indeed be from God to God.

> Rise heart; thy Lord is risen. Sing his praise
>   Without delayes,
> Who takes thee by the hand, that thou likewise
>   With him mayst rise:
> That, as his death calcined thee to dust,
> His life may make thee gold, and much more, just.

Rise heart: Easter, the poem of Resurrection. It is the heart to rise with the risen Lord, the heart, which by his rising, has at least the possibility of purity. With the risen Lord, the heart is given its due place as the possible home of the Lord. If the heart rises with the Lord, then, freed from sin, the creative energy again is released into praise:

> Awake, my lute, and struggle for thy part
>   With all thy art.

The crucified Christ transfers the power of his redemptive suffering wherever he is duly received. His Grace will tune the lute to sing in accordance with his worth, as far as lies within human potentiality. But, without his Grace, without the strength of his suffering, there can be no energy of creativity. Verse there can be, but not true verse of the Truth:

> The crosse taught all wood to resound his name,
>   Who bore the same.
> His stretched sinews taught all strings, what key
> Is best to celebrate this most high day.

Again, the Spirit, if he is allowed the freedom of space within the heart, will in the combination of the harmony compensate for any deficiency in the poetry. Is it not the poetry of the Spirit?

> O let thy blessed Spirit bear a part,
> And make up our defects with his sweet art.

The Palms of the Entry into Jerusalem, the Myrrh-bearers of Easter Sunday, become irrelevant. Christ has risen and with him all, and more delight and fragrance than we can ever provide for him, by any means:

> But thou wast up by break of day,
> And brought'st thy sweets along with thee.

Sweets: always, for Herbert, the dear word for Christ. Was not the ointment of Mary Magdalene's repentance sweet? And the flowers on the shroud of his death sweet? And the fragrance of his Resurrection? In Christ was all sweetness contained, and from him comes all sweetness. The Sun rose on Easter-day. But, the light of the Sun can not compete with the One and Single Light—with Christ, the risen Son and Lord:

> We count three hundred, but we misse:
> There is but one, and that one ever.

v. *Self-dedication to devotional verse*

Herbert's poetry is for God, and so he can but pray again and again that God gives him the capacity for that uniting within himself which allows creative work. If his spirit is distracted, if his heart is torn, he can not write. Only God, for whom the poetry alone is intended, can help him. And, if he can not write, then somewhere, somehow, he is failing badly, for it can but mean that something in him withstands the entry of the Spirit. The actual pain of not writing, which every poet feels, is intensified by the accompanying sensation of guilt.

Affliction (IV) shows the initial condition of scattered multiplicity in which any form of creative writing is impossible. The torn awareness of multiplicity re-emphasises the unceasing knowledge of the division between the two Worlds, of Grace and of Nature. Man, like some grotesque monster at a fair, is suspended between the two, and relies for every positive motion on the inspiration of Grace. And, if the heart is not free from sin, the Spirit will not take up his abode. But, only God can make that essential initial purification, and so the imploring:

> Broken in pieces all asunder,
> Lord, hunt me not,
> A thing forgot,
> Once a poore creature, now a wonder,
> A wonder tortur'd in the space
> Betwixt this world and that of grace.

Herbert's thoughts, which could unify into a one, single, creative, incisive thrust, now, because they are disunited, turn their sharpness upon himself, rending and piercing his heart and his soul, raining death, not life. His attendant faculties turn upon him as enemies instead of willing servants. He is in a condition of total civil war. Each part skirmishes for supremacy. Only God can help. If God does not help, his thoughts, emotions, feelings, hearing, sight, touch, all that contributes to him as one man, will destroy each other and him. This is a work of darkness. God, alone, can shed the light of renewed harmony. If God condescends to re-establish harmony, then the warring elements will turn from hostility to unanimous praise, and he will be delivered from the agony of self-destructive forces. His work will be inflexibly directed to God to the end of his days in the world. Without the Grace, he can not move, and the Grace is in the sole and unaccountable dispensation of God:

> Then shall those powers, which work for grief,
>   Enter thy pay,
>   And day by day
> Labour thy praise, and my relief;
>   With care and courage building me,
>   Till I reach heav'n, and much more, thee.

The prayer for spiritual life rises again imploringly in *Dulnesse:*

> Why do I languish thus, drooping and dull,
>   As if I were all earth?
> O give me quicknesse, that I may with mirth
>   Praise thee brim-full!

And, again, the disdainful comparison with sensuous love lyrics. How can he be silent in praise of God, when another versifier can produce every kind of neat turn of phrase to a lock of hair? And make the hair seem doubly attractive by his image? While Christ, the one real Beauty, the one true Loveliness, the Perfect, remains unsung:

> Where are my lines then? my approaches? views?
> Where are my window-songs?

Lovers never cease from their attempts, and they can extract material even out of scornful rejection, whereas he, living for the Spirit, has lost all spirit. He feels himself encased in the body, his words unfitting his theme. God gave him a mind. Where is it buried?

> But I am lost in flesh, whose sugred lyes
> Still mock me, and grow bold:
> Sure thou didst put a minde there, if I could
> Finde where it lies.

Herbert prays fervently for the purification which will lead to the clarity of mind. Then he can re-orientate himself steadily in the one direction. He can look, even if his love must remain insufficient. But, with his gaze fixed, the gift of God will not remain unused:

> Lord, cleare thy gift, that with a constant wit
> I may but look towards thee:
> *Look* onely; for to *love* thee, who can be,
> What angel fit?

Praise (I) reiterates his one gift of praise, his poetry, and with the claim of the gift immediately comes the denial of its independent validity. Herbert can do nothing without the Grace, to fill and inspire him:

> To write a verse or two is all the praise,
> That I can raise:
> Mend my estate in any wayes,
> Thou shalt have more.
> I go to Church; help me to wings, and I
> Will thither flie;
> Or, if I mount unto the skie,
> I will do more.

Man on his own is a feeble thing. On his own he can achieve nothing, with God's help he can kill a giant. The courage of strong drink is nothing when compared with the power God can give to the meanest. The world of nature is yet the happier and more content. A bee need never cease from work, and shows its disdain for Herbert's tardiness by its passing sting. But, a man can do nothing without the Grace which he may not summon at will. Without the leaven of the Kingdom of Heaven within him, Man remains sour bread:

> O raise me then! Poore bees, that work all day,
> Sting my delay,
> Who have a work as well as they,
> And much, much more.

Employment (1) pursues the same theme of enforced idleness. Before death, a flower blossoms and opens fully, widely. Will not God allow Herbert this same expansion, or must he die, still in the bud? If God would allow him this blossoming width, the *sweetness* of this flowering, the praise for the flowering would be re-directed to God. Yet, at the Day of Judgment, the work of the space given would be accredited to him. He will not come, having buried his talent. The fabric is God's, but the use and extent of the use, the cutting out and the sewing, is our work. Yet, the work can not be done, again, without the Grace. If God grants the Grace, then on the Day of Judgment we shall be rewarded, although the fabric remains his:

> For as thou dost impart thy grace,
> The greater shall our glorie be.
> The measure of our joyes is in this place,
>   The stuffe with thee.

It is the same strange situation once more, deriving ultimately from the theology of the imputation of Righteousness, from the concept of the arbitrary descent of Grace. We find reward or punishment for what would seem outside our volition to initiate. The work is within our disposal, but not the power of work:

> Let me not languish then, and spend
> A life as barren to thy praise,
> As is the dust, to which that life doth tend,
>   But with delaies.

Herbert mourns that he, alone, is out of harmony. As a man, he can not join the industry of nature. He can only pray to God to release him from the inertia and bring him, ineffective as he may be, into the great orchestra of the worship of God:

> I am no link of thy great chain,
> But all my companie is a weed.
> Lord place me in thy consort; give one strain
>   To my poore reed.

Deniall shows once again the condition of creative uselessness without the direct inspiration of Grace. Again, there comes the awareness of the multiplicity, when Grace would seem absent, the broken, scattered faculties, quite incapable of re-assembling themselves. And, the condition violently aggravated by the disturbance being in the heart, suggesting the contaminating and exclusive presence of sin which will not allow the free room for Grace:

> When my devotions could not pierce
> Thy silent eares;
> Then was my heart broken, as was my verse:
> My breast was full of fears
> And disorder . . .

Herbert's thoughts, in this condition, wander off into every path of fantasy; was not anything better than this paralysis induced by the absence of Grace which would allow, if only it were present, for the gathering up into one, and the creative work of praise? His verse disperses. Still, he cries and cries again:

> *Come, come, my God, O come,*
> But no hearing.

The poetry of truth eludes him. How could God create Man and then not hear him in his crying? His soul is limp, dejected, impotent. The strings of his lute can play no melody:

> Therefore my soul lay out of sight,
> Untun'd, unstrung:
> My feeble spirit, unable to look right,
> Like a nipt blossome, hung
> Discontented.

Could there be a more vivid picture of dejected restlessness? And, still there is nothing that can be done of our own will. Fantasy and love lyrics we can write entirely when and how we please, but the poetry to God remains in God's jurisdiction. The poetry to God is a Grace. Therefore, Herbert can only pray for this Grace, as men pray for other things. His gift is not at his disposal. It comes from God and returns to God and from this austerity Herbert will not move. He will die in torment, but he will not write a single line of praise out of his own contriving. It must be inspired. It would seem the same austerity of spirit which possessed the true prophets of Israel who would not utter without the direct Word of God. Herbert demands of himself that his heart must revive with the in-dwelling of the Spirit:

> O cheer and tune my heartlesse breast,
> Deferre not time;
> That so thy favours granting my request,
> They and my minde may chime,
> And mend my ryme.

In *Easter-wings,* Herbert takes perhaps to its highest point his austerity of expression. It has become more and more apparent, how his verse is consistently the objective presentation of a specific spiritual condition. In *Easter-wings,* Herbert's consciousness of his poetry, solely as the means of conveying a theological or spiritual concept, becomes most explicit in the linear structure. *Easter-wings* appear as wings on the printed page. And, such a presentation would seem the conscious, even challenging, antithesis to a metaphysical conceit. The structure is enrolled as an extra aid to drive in forcefully the theological point. The point is the confession of the Holy Spirit, and the structure of the wings of the poem demands the concentration on the Spirit. Nothing can be achieved without the Holy Spirit. If the Holy Spirit descends into his heart, then Herbert can rise, and fly with the Spirit, in praise of God. If the Holy Spirit does not descend upon him, he will be left, the poor thing which he is:

> With thee
> O let me rise
> As larks, harmoniously,
> And sing this day thy victories:
> Then shall the fall further the flight in me.

On one level, here, Herbert seems to have gone to the limit of denying validity to poetry, *as* poetry, by this super-imposing of the visual image. But, the poetry remains poetry, a longing for the essential unity and harmony which alone will produce his song of worship and triumph in the victory of Christ. Herbert sees all times of non-creativity, as the absence of the Holy Spirit, and, conversely, the presence of sin. So, he wastes away in the devouring consciousness of his guilt. And, now, he prays for the miracle of Grace, that he be allowed to share in the Resurrection, that his heart may rise, that the pain of sin and repentance may turn to the impetus of his song of praise. Grief will become joy at the first movement of the Spirit, which will bear him up with it: to Christ, the Saviour:

> With thee
> Let me combine
> And feel this day thy victorie:
> For, if I imp my wing on thine,
> Affliction shall advance the flight in me.

A small bird, with a broken wing, he will be borne on high on the mighty wings of the Comforter. *Easter-wings* may be seen as a trick, but, if it is a trick, then it is surely a double trick. Is it not that Herbert is sometimes fearful for his pearls, fooling the fools with foolery?

The effect of movement in *Easter-wings*, of flight, and of descent, of coming, and, again, of forsaking, together with an immutable sense of presence, comes even more forcefully in *The Temper* (I).

There is an indomitable resolution in *The Temper* (I) not to be swerved aside into dejection, whatever happens. It is as if Herbert refuses to accept any more the absence of Grace as a punishment. He insists that even in the absence, he knows the presence. There is an immense effort of release in the poem, as if, for once, the whole constricting rope of imputed Righteousness, of arbitrary descent of Grace, is thrown off with one gesture of sovereign plunging into the innermost Mystery of Love. God is Love. Herbert will therefore not accept defeat and desolation and dejection. If God is Love, then such conditions are not possible:

> How should I praise thee, Lord! how should my rymes
>   Gladly engrave thy love in steel,
> If what my soul doth feel sometimes,
>   My soul might ever feel!

It would seem the same repetitive opening, the condition of wretchedness that the Grace is not constantly there to allow for the unending flow of praise. The complaint continues of the inconstancy, of the being debarred from the control of his own sensations:

> Although there were some fourtie heav'ns, or more,
>   Sometimes I peere above them all;
>   Sometimes I hardly reach a score,
>   Sometimes to hell I fall.

The complaint turns to imploring: Why must God torment him by such extremes of experience? From heaven to hell is surely beyond the human span. The world may be small for God, but for a man it is a vast tomb. And from imploring, comes an effort of reasoning with God. How can God condescend to meet the speck of dirt, which is Man, in what seems like equal combat? How can He allow Man even to glimpse the magnitude of His size?

> Wilt thou meet arms with man, that thou dost stretch
>   A crumme of dust from heav'n to hell?
> Will great God measure with a wretch?
>   Shall he thy stature spell?

From longing, to complaint, to imploring, to reasoning. And now, to the crux: Can not God grant him the assurance of constant Grace? When once he flies up, can he not remain within the nest of the Holy Spirit? If only this were possible, if he could remain in Grace, if Grace possessed his heart entirely, then there would be no room for sin. And, once there were no room for sin, there would equally be no false expectation of success in this world, and no dread of the future:

> O let me, when thy roof my soul hath hid,
>   O let me roost and nestle there:
>   Then of a sinner thou art rid,
>   And I of hope and fear.

So far, the poem has gone step by step of self-will. Suddenly the position reverses:

> Yet take thy way . . .

How can there be any doubt? God is Truth. And Truth is a Mystery for finite man. There can be no denying the ultimate Truth, therefore the way must be equally true:

> . . . for sure thy way is best . . .

Suddenly, there comes the clear intuitive certainty that whatever the apparent method or effect, what God does is not to be judged. It must be a positive and not a negative act, for God is Love. It is an error to see God's actions as in any sense possibly detracting from the potentiality of creativity. God can not destroy. Is he not the Creator?

> Stretch or contract me, thy poore debter:
> This is but tuning of my breast,
>   To make the musick better.

The actual immanent condition within the Mystery of God's Love is of no importance. It is a mistake to judge the cause and purpose of any human experience in divine terms. We do not know into the Mind of God. But, we know that he is Almighty, and we know that he is Love. Thus, all is one. All lies within the Mystery of Divine Providence. We can not in the last count distinguish between apparent joy and apparent grief, we can only experience them as such, but not their essential meaning of divine significance. The burden of intolerable sin is thereby lifted, the horror of the incalculable. Inner Grace, imputed Righteousness, assurance of salvation, the guarantee of the Church, faith alone, are the words of Man. The Mystery of Love is untouched:

> Whether I flie with angels, fall with dust,
> Thy hands made both, and I am there:
> Thy power and love, my love and trust
> Make one place ev'ry where.

The complaint of doubt falls away. The scrupulous tenets of theology are openly taken into common ground, the Mystery of Love.

PART III

KEY-POEMS OF THE MYSTERY

PART III

Key-poems of the Mystery

There comes a moment of self-identification with the poems of *The Temple* when one can be struck with a feeling nearly of dread before a Herbert of impersonal dimensions. Everything may begin to point to an immense diagrammatical system of theological, spiritual and moral exposition. Can all our accustomed, even instinctive, reaction to Herbert's poetry really be so wrong? Was his poetry, in effect, nothing but a scientific medium of an avowed and convinced Anglican priest? It can not be doubted that, on one level, *The Temple* is an exposition of a system of theology, and the rational application to daily life of the system. But, this, surely, is not an adequate appraisal. The immediate apprehension of warmth is not fallacious. Underlying all else, however stylised the laments, or the love, or even the compassion for Christ, the experience of the suffering of Christ, there surely lies another level of truth. This is the level which Herbert would seem even to guard, yet, in a few of his poems, he explicitly gives the hint of his conviction of the Mystery, which, within him, transcends all systems of theology. Herbert is an Anglican priest, firmly rooted in the Church of England, and he is a poet dedicated to the exposition of the Anglican faith as he lived and preached it, but, this is not all. Throughout Herbert's poetry, there is the unfailing awareness of what we can not touch, a reality beyond us, a Truth, a Beauty: Love. And, his own deep conviction of the presence of Love. And, his own yearning love towards Love. In what I call the key-poems, all the possible flatness of theology falls away and there stands out strongly and simply the fabric of Herbert's spirit, a fabric woven with the single thread of his unceasing prayer, his life, within the Mystery. Herein lies his greatness.

i. *The Mystery of God*

The first of these key-poems, as I see them, to *The Temple* is *Divinitie*. Here, it seems, Herbert lays the foundation of the incomprehensible Mystery. And, in the same movement, explicit dogma can hardly retain the same emphatic, didactic authority. Teaching, of any kind, loses its absolute contours. There is space for what we do not know, and the space is spiritually fruitful.

Man has over-reached himself in rational arrogance. He has defined and annotated the stars of the sky, as if they might lose their identity without his help. The stars would hardly lose their way, even if they were not labelled and given separate identities and fixed locations by scientists. And, not content with this, the theologians approach heaven, the transcendent sky, with the same set purpose of analysis, distribution and annotation: all seems within the scientist's and the theologian's field of assimilation and exegesis, within his competence, and, so, his responsibility. With what fine irony Herbert comments on this *hubris!*

> As men, for fear the starres should sleep and nod,
>   And trip at night, have spheres suppli'd;
> As if a starre were duller then a clod,
>   Which knows his way without a guide:
>
> Just so the other heav'n they also serve,
>   Divinities transcendent skie:
> Which with the edge of wit they cut and carve.
>   Reason triumphs, and faith lies by.

Christ is Truth. Christ is Wisdom. And Herbert demands some awareness of our intrusive insolence, which can get us nowhere. If Christ had wished us to know more, He could hardly be considered incapable of giving us the knowledge. It was His side which was pierced, and from His side ran the blood, the wine of our Eucharistic feast. But, He allowed the flow of blood simply. He did not deem it necessary to give additional substance to the stream of life with explanations of its nature. His seamless garment remained simple, He did not think it expedient to decorate the fringes with an intricate lace pattern of theological precious quibbles and innumerable pedantic niceties of dispute:

> Could not that Wisdome, which first broacht the wine,
>   Have thicken'd it with definitions?
> And jagg'd his seamlesse coat, had that been fine,
>   With curious questions and divisions?

Christ retained the Mystery of the Eucharist and demanded love, not scientific reasoning. His truth is beyond science, for His truth is Truth beyond finite teaching or finite comprehension. His truth is the light, the glimpse of the Spirit of Light and of Truth, the burning fire of Purity:

> But all the doctrine, which he taught and gave,
>   Was cleare as heav'n, from whence it came.
> At least those beams of truth, which onely save,
>   Surpasse in brightnesse any flame.

Christ teaches:

> *Love God, and love your neighbour. Watch and pray.
> Do as ye would be done unto.*

These are indeed transparent words. A child can understand them. But, here lies the shock. All the complications of the theologians are nothing compared with the simplicity of Christ's needs. It is the simplicity of His commands which act on us as the darkest of problems. We do not know how to love. There seems no solution:

> O dark instructions; ev'n as dark as day!
>   Who can these Gordian knots undo?

The central puzzle remains: the Eucharist. Christ orders us to drink his blood for wine. And, Herbert yields to the Mystery of Love. He confesses the salvation in the obedience and refuses the temptation of obscuring the issue by discussion on the Eucharistic elements. Is it not sufficient and clear enough that Christ gives the order?

> But he doth bid us take his bloud for wine.
>   Bid what he please; yet I am sure,
> To take and taste what he doth there designe,
>   Is all that saves, and not obscure.

The poem ends with a near-note of scorn. Man is a fool. Does he really think that faith in God needs propping up with human materials? With the tools of Science? Faith is the means and not the end. Faith *is* the means of the dark, incomprehensible journey towards the One Light. There is, within the Mystery, no question of definition of faith, of fear whether we have the faith. The faith is the faith. Faith is love and of love there need be no theological justification, nor proof. In faith, we move towards the ultimate point of meeting Truth, which we can not comprehend by any finite means:

> Then burn thy Epicycles, foolish man;
>   Break all thy spheres, and save thy head.
> Faith needs no staffe of flesh, but stoutly can
>   To heav'n alone both go, and leade.

ii. *The Mystery of continuity*

The Flower would seem the key-poem to the Mystery underlying the persisting terror of the inconstant position of Man.

Once again, as so often, Herbert writes of the sudden changes to which Man is exposed. Grace, inexplicably, is absent. The heart is hard and cold and impervious to any outside influence. But, suddenly, Grace returns, fragrant, pure, the Presence of Christ. And, the heart is tender and malleable again as Spring after winter, with the hardships of winter not wasted:

> How fresh, O Lord, how sweet and clean
> Are thy returns! ev'n as the flowers in spring;
> To which, besides their own demean,
> The late-past frosts tributes of pleasure bring.
> Grief melts away
> Like snow in May,
> As if there were no such cold thing.

While Grace was not present, it would have seemed that any future period of creativity was unthinkable. Grace absent, seems, while it lasts, an absolute condition of withering:

> Who would have thought my shrivel'd heart
> Could have recover'd greennesse?

It seemed impossible that he could revive, even as in winter it seems impossible that the flowers will grow again. And, here, is the first hint of the positive acceptance of the Mystery of the absence of Grace. Whatever the reason and pain of its real absence, equally real is the continuity of its presence, yet hidden from our practical experience. Grace, within the Mystery, is as hidden as the winter-living roots:

> It was gone
> Quite under ground; as flowers depart
> To see their mother-root, when they have blown;
> Where they together
> All the hard weather,
> Dead to the world, keep house unknown.

The apparent absence of Grace may in fact be a period of recuperation, of healing, not of sickness. But, still the strangeness of the arbitrary Omnipotence is upon him. Within the shortest span of time, God kills and gives life to the Spirit. The funeral toll can become the glad ringing of the wedding-feast. All can be done in one hour, the hour, the Mystery of the Passion of Christ, of the Crucifixion, of the Resurrection; enacted over and over again in our frail human frames:

> These are thy wonders, Lord of power,
> Killing and quickning, bringing down to hell
>   And up to heaven in an houre;
> Making a chiming of a passing-bell.

We may try to discriminate, and judge, to evaluate, but it all means nothing. If only we had the clue, we would know the meaning, for the meaning is in the word of God. But, we do not know how to read and interpret the word. We still live in darkness:

> We say amisse,
> This or that is:
> Thy word is all, if we could spell.

The longing grows more and more fervent and intense, for this time of revolution to end, for the peace of heaven:

> O that I once past changing were,
> Fast in thy Paradise, where no flower can wither!

Again and again, Herbert would seem as if he might be on the way of salvation, he can imagine some growth, watering his repentance with tears, his sins temporarily subdued into unity with him:

> Many a spring I shoot up fair,
> Offring at heav'n, growing and groning thither:
>   Nor doth my flower
>   Want a spring-showre,
> My sinnes and I joining together.

But, equally again and again, even as Herbert would seem directed towards heaven, ever climbing upwards, as if Heaven were his own, personal and indisputable destination, the desolation and the darkness of the absence of Grace descends once more upon him, the coldness with which no coldness in the world can compare:

> But while I grow in a straight line,
> Still upwards bent, as if heav'n were mine own,
> Thy anger comes, and I decline:
> What frost to that? what pole is not the zone,
> Where all things burn,
> When thou dost turn,
> And the least frown of thine is shown?

Suddenly, strangely, when there seemed no further possibility, the creative genius once more is awake within him. Grace gives the warm life. The air is fresh, filled with the sweet reviving scent of dew and rain. Joy enters his heart. His apathy is stirred:

> I once more smell the dew and rain,
> And relish versing . . .

It hardly seems credible that such darkness could have preceded this radiance of Presence:

> . . . O my onely light,
> It cannot be
> That I am he
> On whom thy tempests fell all night.

And here comes the final turn into the Mystery, not of negative, nor even of positive acceptance, but the consciousness of a creative work of love within the Love. It is the awareness that darkness is dark, and light is light, we can not escape from the finite limits of experience. We must experience all the transitory ills:

> These are thy wonders, Lord of love,
> To make us see we are but flowers that glide . . .

But, even as we become aware of these limitations, another realism opens to us, a realism which can not be touched by passing mutations. Here we can rest, within the commotion, creatively active, provided we do not make the impossible attempt to dissect the Mystery into dogmatic, comprehensible terms. Within the changes, there can be a secret place of Spring, until the harvest of the End:

> . . . Which when we once can finde and prove,
> Thou hast a garden for us, where to bide.
> Who would be more,
> Swelling through store,
> Forfeit their Paradise by their pride.

iii. *The Mystery of success*

The Answer is the reply to the reproach of non-achievement. It is the single claim of the right to live already on earth as if dead, suggesting the sole possibility of survival within the Mystery:

> My comforts drop and melt away like snow:
> I shake my head, and all the thoughts and ends,
> Which my fierce youth did bandie, fall and flow
> Like leaves about me: or like summer friends,
> Flyes of estates and sunne-shine.

All the pleasant, witty, attractive inter-change of his young days has forsaken him. As some tired, old horse shaking his head to rid himself of pestering flies, so Herbert shakes the world off, and, because he shakes it off, the world deserts him. The friends of this world will not stay where they are not comfortably entertained. They want wealthy surroundings and the semblance of good cheer, not grief, nor memories of death. However, even as they desert him, they reproach him. How could he have shown such promise in youth and then come to nothing? He has risen as some impetuous vapour, which then slackens in its pace, growing dull and slow, sinking extinguished into darkness, and remaining obscure, gray and damp, until the end. He is severely reproached for such a brilliant deception, and for such a waste of talent. But, for all who represent him in this light, and put him in this category, he has but one reply:

> to all, that so
> Show me, and set me, I have one reply,
> Which they that know the rest, know more then I.

What does Herbert mean by this last conundrum? He may mean that the answer does not ultimately lie with him. There may be actual people who know the whole circumstances of his retreat, and therefore can account better for it, than he can himself. But, alternatively, or perhaps as well, is there not once again perhaps a delicate irony? Can he not be addressing the very people who reproach him? If they know so much already, then they must also know the answer better than he does. But, and this seems the essential point, whatever the explanation, he guards the answer to himself. It remains his secret, within the Mystery of his love which is not directed to the world. And, again, this Mystery he guards jealously, on the deeper level, for himself, fobbing off all questioners with the equivocal answer.

iv. The Mystery of freedom

It is interesting to take *The Collar* in immediate conjunction with *The Answer*. The decision of retreat into the full asceticism of non-achievement was not an easy one. Why was the decision made and so irrevocably kept? *The Collar:* the mark of servitude to a worldly master, but equally the servitude to sin, and not without the suggestion of the releasing yoke of Christ. Was Herbert not subject to all three? And was it that he could not always distinguish satisfactorily for himself in which of the three collars the true freedom lay?

Herbert feels the collar suffocating him. He does not know the source of the suffocation, but he struggles violently, supposing that somehow, somewhere, the servitude is his deliberate abnegation from worldly achievement. He feels not only intellectually and spiritually suffocating, but physically circumscribed:

> I struck the board, and cry'd, No more.
> I will abroad.

The board: a table, presumably. But, does not this suggest the Holy Table of the Eucharistic feast? Is Herbert not denying the spiritual food which he sees as robbing him of all other nourishment? He challenges what he experiences as servility. He claims his freedom from grief, from the affliction of the awareness of sin, and the subsequent repentance:

> What? shall I ever sigh and pine?

He is no mean servant, nor is he without his own resources of gifts and talents:

> My lines and life are free; free as the rode,
> Loose as the winde, as large as store.

Why must he, who could be sufficient in himself, draw out the days of his life in constant pleading and imploring for favour? Once again, it is the wretchedness of the absence of Grace, and the uncertainty of its duration even when he knows that Grace has visited him. His life would seem a torment of unceasing petition for the Gift of the Spirit, with no guarantee that the petition will be granted:

> Shall I be still in suit?

There is no fulfilment, no reward for him. The most which he can reap is a thorn, to prick him and shed his blood, a reminder indeed of the Crown of Thorns, of the blood shed for him, but, still, holding no guarantee of salvation, that this blood is the blood to redeem him, personally. And, for this unsure and unconfirmed salvation, he has forfeited all the delights and health-giving nourishment of the world. He has no assurance that the wine which he now drinks at the board is the blood of salvation, but he has forfeited the worldly wine which at least he could have enjoyed:

>Have I no harvest but a thorn
>To let me bloud, and not restore
>What I have lost with cordiall fruit?
>   Sure there was wine
>Before my sighs did drie it . . .

How can he be assured that the Bread, which he eats, is the Body of Eternal Life? Yet, he has voluntarily and rashly discarded the earthly food, which, at least, would have nourished him:

>   . . . there was corn
>Before my tears did drown it.

Is he alone in this quandary? Why must he be the only one to refute any recognised triumph of worldly success, and, to deny seeing the triumph even as triumph, but merely as the sign of withered and decayed mortality?

>Is the yeare onely lost to me?
>   Have I no bayes to crown it?
>No flowers, no garlands gay? all blasted?
>   All wasted?

The answer comes directly and only from his heart. Such an answer could only come from the heart, not from any process of ratiocination. His heart denies the contention of waste and sterility:

>Not so, my heart: but there is fruit,
>   And thou hast hands.

His heart claims that there is reward, there is the fruit, and he has the hands, the capacity of gathering the harvest, if he would desist from squandering his time on lamentation, seeking his aim in two directions simultaneously:

> Recover all thy sigh-blown age
> On double pleasures . . .

His heart, as ever the seat of the Spirit, begs him:

> . . . leave thy cold dispute
> Of what is fit, and not.

His heart sees his so-called freedom as the actual prison. He is being choked by his own scattered thoughts of immanent good, building his house on sand, with no foundation and with nothing strong to attach it securely. His own self-delusion and self-deception convince and entice him to submit to the lie that this flimsy anchor is really a strong and enduring one, and he remains wilfully inattentive and blind to the blatant falsehood:

> Forsake thy cage,
> Thy rope of sands,
> Which pettie thoughts have made, and made to thee
> Good cable, to enforce and draw,
> And be thy law,
> While thou didst wink and wouldst not see.

But, Herbert repeats, obstinately, ignoring the prompting of his heart, his wild claim to freedom. He demands that his heart should accept his decision:

> Away; take heed:
> I will abroad.

His heart, however, will not yield to this decision. The living Spirit within him knows the weak spot in this argument. Such freedom brings with it inevitably the terror of death, and the daily burden of fear, not only of death, but of anything and everything which can mar so easily the fragile immanent pleasure. If he would only once take the daring step, his heart tells him, he can for ever forget all this heavy oppression of fear of losing his so-called happiness. But, if he does not wish to petition for his necessity, and work for it, then he deserves the burden. It is entirely within his capacity to put an end to the burden of worldly success, ever at the mercy of failure and death:

> Call in thy deaths head there: tie up thy fears.
> He that forbears
> To suit and serve his need,
> Deserves his load.

Fury overcomes Herbert at the prompting of his heart. He will not listen. He will make such a fiendish noise that he will even be unable to hear:

> But as I rav'd and grew more fierce and wild
> At every word . . .

At the height of the storm, comes the voice, gentle and quiet, and unmistakable. A voice, which, if we hear, we can not ignore, because we could not hear it amidst the turmoil, if it were not in our hearts to hear it. The submission is not the submission to the collar. It is the joyful discarding of the collar. Love is answered by love. And, there can be no greater freedom. The voice calls, but it calls within his own consciousness and he can not even prove the presence of the voice. This is not a dominating assault from outside. Herbert turns to the direction to which the voice calls him. There is no need for assurance, for guarantee. The Love is the inner evidence, and that is the highest knowledge. But, it remains inner evidence. It is a Mystery. The voice might equally not be heard. Proof is denied. The answer is given to a voice which is not certain, but the answer is certain: the movement into freedom:

> Me thoughts I heard one calling, *Child!*
> And I reply'd, *My Lord.*

v. *The Mystery of presence*

In *Miserie*, Herbert follows this thread of Man's blindness and deafness to the presence of God.

Man is a fool. The Angels praise God, while Man, amidst a scene of destruction, continues to revel, singing the lewd songs induced by folly and sin, drinking and carousing in the face of death. Is Man not as the grass of the field, blossoming and withering?

> Lord, let the Angels praise thy name.
> Man is a foolish thing, a foolish thing,
> Folly and Sinne play all his game.
> His house still burns, and yet he still doth sing,
> *Man is but grasse,*
> *He knows it, fill the glasse.*

But, what is even more despicable is Man's meanness. He will not curb a single extravagance for God. How can God suffer such mad folly? Man dares to boast that he can find more profitable employment than in the worship of his Creator:

> How canst thou brook his foolishnesse?
> Why, he'l not lose a cup of drink for thee:
> Bid him but temper his excesse;
> Not he: he knows where he can better be,
> As he will swear,
> Then to serve thee in fear.

Man is corrupt, and thinks that he can hide his corruption from God. Nothing can penetrate his thick head that God can see through his efforts at secreting his sins. The curtain he draws over his corruption is made of cloth:

> Where never yet came moth.

Never yet: the promise of destruction is for the future, at present he feels safe, with his treasure precisely there where the moth will eat away to nothing.

Any reminder from God, some small sorrow or affliction, however inadequate in punishment for the actual sin, offends even the best of men. Such is their pride:

> They would not have their actions scann'd,
> Nor any sorrow tell them that they sinne,
> Though it be small,
> And measure not their fall.

But, it is not possible to fall out of the love of God, for He is Love. This is the strange revelation. Man, of his own bad will, can deny God, but God will not deny him. The Comforter holds all men within his sheltering wings, whatever the eventuality, whatever the appearance to the contrary. The theological question of assurance of the presence of Grace is irrelevant. Love can not cease to love:

> They quarrell thee, and would give over
> The bargain made to serve thee: but thy love
> Holds them unto it, and doth cover
> Their follies with the wing of thy milde Dove,
> Not suff'ring those
> Who would, to be thy foes.

It is possible, however, to look at it yet from another perspective. Man denies the praise which he owes to God, but could he give it? Corrupt and contaminated as he is, how dare Man approach the Perfect? The sun, itself, the radiance of the world:

> . . . holds down his head for shame,
> Dead with eclipses, when we speak of thee:
> How shall infection
> Presume on thy perfection?

How dare we come anywhere near with our dirty hands and untransparent and impermeable hearts? But, there is no alternative. God must bear with our mean praise, which we even dare to grudge, or He will have none, for we are capable of no better in ourselves. There we crouch, as some beast in his lair, offering to God what we audaciously presume to be praise worthy of Him:

> So our clay hearts, ev'n when we crouch
> To sing thy praises, make them lesse divine.
> Yet either this,
> Or none, thy portion is.

If, listening to the word of God annoys and bores Man, then why must God persist in loving the Prodigal? Can not God lose patience once and for all and expel Man, where he belongs, to feed the swine? If Man refuses virtue, why does not God deliver him up to wallow in the mud where he belongs? Man is a fool. Dazed with a tangled mob of immanent anxieties, he has lost sight of the Truth. He will not stir out of bed for a glimpse of heaven. There is always some excuse for not going to Church, such as sleeping or eating. And the greatest sin of Man is that he is not unaware of what he does. A bird praises its Creator in song, but unknowingly:

> But Man doth know
> The spring, whence all things flow:

> And yet, as though he knew it not,
> His knowledge winks, and lets his humours reigne . .

His whims and fancies, his impulses of sense, govern Man's life and make it a foul thing. While Christ died. How can Man refuse that memory? What verse can adequately describe such perfidy?

There was a time when Man was God's most precious possession, his heart enclosed the rarest riches for God; God wore Man on his finger as a ring and the motto inscribed was: *My pleasure*. Man was the garden of Paradise, in him grew all beautiful things for God, and no rank weeds choked the fresh purity:

> Glorie and grace
> Did crown his heart and face.

Man, before his fall, was wise. In seeking knowledge, he became a fool, fooled by sin. And now his spirit has left him, he is but:

> A lump of flesh, without a foot or wing
>   To raise him to a glimpse of blisse:
> A sick toss'd vessel, dashing on each thing;
>   Nay, his own shelf . . .

It is not God who denies the Grace, but it is Man who in his body, without the leaven of spirit, can not rise to God; he is tossed on the storm of his sensual passions, flung about, wrecked on the reef of his own making. And, then, the invective stops. From loud condemnation, Herbert turns to calm of confession. Has he not harangued sufficiently against others? Thus *Miserie* is not the wretched plight of any other man. He alone is he who has sinned. In full communion with God, Herbert turns to God:

> My God, I mean my self.

My God. *My* self. The Mystery of the union between God and Man, God who condescends to allow Man to claim Him as his. God who gives the freedom to Man to make the willed choice of self-dedication. There is no servitude in love, and there is no judgment of others. One God and one man.

vi. *The Mystery of praise*

Man is mean. He will not sacrifice anything of his pleasure to God. And God demands little from him. God only wants love in return for his love. In *Jordan* (II), Herbert argues how little necessity there is, in praising God, to write exquisite verse, with all the possible precious tricks and devices. The love is enough. And, what is more, there is even here no question of God, supplying the deficiency in skill or content. In the Mystery of love, there is no measure.

When Herbert first began to write poetry to God, he thought that he must produce the very best which he could, the most intricate, subtle, unusual, full of strange imagery; he thought that the sentiments must be ornamented to the full, everything made to appear splendid, as if the poetry were destined for a competitive market! He was extremely particular in the choice of words, picking and choosing the thoughts and then fitting the words, discarding some images as too alive, others as not sufficiently evocative:

> Thousands of notions in my brain did runne,
> Off'ring their service, if I were not sped:
> I often blotted what I had begunne;
> This was not quick enough, and that was dead.

Thinking in worldly terms, Herbert could not believe that anything he produced could be adequate for approaching the glory of heaven. If we can hardly find the right words for the radiance of the sun, how can we for Him who transcends the sun, far above, using the sun, as it were, as a floor to walk upon?

> Nothing could seem too rich to clothe the sunne,
> Much lesse those joyes which trample on his head.

Looking back with some dry humour, Herbert re-lives the commotion which he made to praise God as he felt that He should be praised. Herbert twisted and turned and contorted his verse to the exact meaning with a great deal of unnecessary agitation!

> As flames do work and winde, when they ascend,
> So did I weave my self into the sense.
> But while I bustled . . .

In the midst of the noise, again there came the still, small voice. Was not Christ baptised in the waters of the Jordan? And did not the Spirit of Truth descend upon Him in the shape of a Dove? The Spirit of Truth witnessed to Christ, and now the Spirit of Truth, the Comforter, the friend, whispers the warning and advice of Truth:

> . . . *How wide is all this long pretence!*
> *There is in love a sweetnesse readie penn'd:*
> *Copie out onely that, and save expense.*

All his efforts were wide of the mark. Herbert realised that he had missed the Mystery of praise. Praise is no praise without love. And love bears within itself, without more effort, the presence of Christ. There is nothing left to write. It is only a question of repeating, in oneself, the love of Christ. The yoke is light, the cost is little. Vociferous praise is merely ridiculous in the stillness of His presence, in the fragrance of His sacrifice. Christ was baptised in the Jordan, and with the baptism, he began the human road which would lead to sweet spices of his burial. High-sounding words ring false in the face of love:

> *There is in love a sweetnesse readie penn'd.*

But, if he must write, then let him write only of that love, without pretence or vanity, let him write again and again of that love which died for us. It is sufficient:

> *Copie out onely that, and save expense.*

vii. *The Mystery of affliction*

Josephs Coat is one of the most apparent poems of reversal, that is, reversal on the explicit level. Repeatedly, Herbert's recurring fear and sorrow have been the creative paralysis induced by the absence of Grace, as he saw it, and, thence, the consequent agony of mind. He persisted in seeing affliction and grief as the outcome of the withdrawal of the Spirit, and, from this, the double anguish, not only for the benumbing condition of withdrawal, but for the cause of such withdrawal, the excessive sin which would leave no space for the presence of Grace, the creative Spirit. But, now:

> Wounded I sing, tormented I indite,
> Thrown down I fall into a bed, and rest . . .

In the actual condition of affliction, which he knows so well, the paralysis has turned to creativity, the distraction, to peace:

> Sorrow hath chang'd its note . . .

What has happened? Herbert sees it as the mercy of God to prevent his utter destruction. But how has he come to experience the mercy? Once again it would seem the breaking through the dogmatic theology by the inner conviction of the unassailable sovereignty of Love. If God is Love, then He can not be the God of Anger. Then He can not chastise, however much we may try to justify the chastisement as for our good. How can Love destroy or disunite? Love is ever the healing force. This affliction, the torment, the grief, whatever the cause, is not the punishment from God. It can well be the reflection of the presence of sin in the heart; it can also be the despair and repentance for the presence of sin. But, it is not sent by God. This, Herbert finally denies. The estrangement can only come from us, our own constriction:

> . . . such is his will,
> Who changeth all things, as him pleaseth best.

It is not God's will that Man should perish, but it is his will that Man should be saved:

> For well he knows, if but one grief and smart
> Among my many had his full career,
> Sure it would carrie with it ev'n my heart,
> And both would runne untill they found a biere
> To fetch the bodie; both being due to grief.

The sorrow and the pain would kill him, competing as to who would get him first to his funeral, and it is God who has intervened to save him, not God who has brought the grief, and sorrow, upon him:

> But he hath spoil'd the race . . .

God prevented the death-race. And, instead, he has given a coat of many colours to the anguish besetting him. Herbert does not see God as interfering by miracles and removing pain from us. Evil persists in the world, and we are free to sin. But, God is merciful. He, in love, bestows a sheltering garment to Man. It is a coat of Joy: Joseph's coat: the Coat of the Beloved Son. Shielded by Christ, the anguish persists, but it can not kill, relieved by the presence of Joy, of Love. Herbert feels reprieved from death. And, in his reprieve, he knows that he lives only to confess the power of God: there was a time when what he thought was joy turned to grief: but that was not the real joy, now within him. The real joy, unlike hope, turns the grief to joy without removing the grief. Herbert feels himself held within the Mystery of the unspeakable Love, which has taken all grief, all sin upon himself:

> I live to shew his power, who once did bring
> My *joyes* to *weep* and now my *griefs* to *sing*.

viii. *The Mystery of renewal*

The hint of the Mystery of suffering, the suggestion that God is indeed present, not absent, in affliction and pain, that there is no question of punishment, nor of anger, emerges more forcefully and unmistakably in *Love unknown* and *The Pulley*.

Love unknown

The identity of the *Deare Friend* of the opening of *Love unknown* is uncertain. It might even be a friend to whom Herbert wrote of his vision, but this seems unlikely in view of the interpretation which the Friend gives at the end of the poem. It is also doubtful if the Friend is simply a fiction to give a shape to the poem. Such a contrivance would seem a little clumsy. Perhaps, the suggestion could be of a split within himself. The Friend could then be the antithesis of deluding Hope. The Friend might be the truest spiritual part of himself, because both *dear* and *friend* consistently hold for Herbert the connotation of Christ, and of the Holy Spirit. In this dialogue, he, the doubting finite creature may be confiding in the part of himself which is centred on God. But, this is of course problematic. At any rate, at the outset of the poem, Herbert does not anticipate any practical help from the Friend in his problem. He only wants the comfort of the affection.

Herbert presents the image of himself as the tenant of a Lord, as in the parable. He has been given the estate and he is meant to do something profitable with it. He is entrusted with the estate on behalf of two lives, and both lives are his. In other words, what he does with the land, or the talents, given to him, will not only affect him now, but in eternity. He, as sole tenant, is free to prepare the present and the future harvest of his labour. But, he has not bought the land. However rich he may be, however much he overcomes the world, Man can not discard his Creator:

> A Lord I had,
> And have, of whom some grounds, which may improve,
> I hold for two lives, and both lives in me.

Some payment clearly must be rendered to the Lord from the tenant. So, one day, Herbert decorated a most attractive gift for his Master. It was a dish of fruit. He presented a token, the best sample, of what he had produced. He had not wasted his time. His days had not been barren. There lay his offering, the mark of his devoted creativity, on a dish, the working of his mind, displayed, as the head of St. John the Baptist, for the pleasure of his Lord. But, he knew that this was not enough. The fruit was of the mind. But, what of the spirit? So, he carefully placed his heart inside the circle of fruit. Could it not slip past as the real offering in its splendid setting?

> To him I brought a dish of fruit one day,
> And in the middle plac'd my heart.

How is it possible to deceive God? However brilliant and rich the service, does not God see into the innermost recesses? The Lord did not even answer the presentation. He merely looked at a servant. Perhaps an Angel of the Lord, who waits upon him. But, certainly one who instantly knew his Lord's mute command, better than his Friend, or Herbert knew himself. The parenthesis (*which is one*) seems to tend towards the interpretation that his Friend is the spiritual part of Herbert himself:

> But he
> (I sigh to say)
> Lookt on a servant, who did know his eye
> Better then you know me, or (which is one)
> Then I my self.

The servant knew precisely and immediately what to do. The fruit was ignored, it was the deception of the heart which mattered, and, because the Lord is Love, the heart must forthwith be purified:

> The servant instantly
> Quitting the fruit, seiz'd on my heart alone . . .

The servant seized the heart, extracted it from the exhibition of achievement, which was worth nothing, and subjected it to an agonising purification. Once, he had been baptised in water. Now, his heart was subjected to a new baptism, not invalidating but re-newing the first. The first baptism made it possible. His heart was plunged into the agony of the Crucifixion. Only the blood of Christ, streaming from His pierced side, could save him now. And the blood was the wine of the Eucharist and, at Christ's command, the blood was dispensed by the servant, from out of the great rock: the Church and the celebrating Priest. The Blood of the Saviour drew the tears of repentance, the repeated baptism of penitence:

> And threw it in a font, wherein did fall
> A stream of bloud, which issu'd from the side
> Of a great rock: I well remember all,
> And have good cause: there it was dipt and dy'd,
> And washt, and wrung: the very wringing yet
> Enforceth tears.

The Friend interjects:

> *Your heart was foul, I fear.*

And he replies:

> Indeed 'tis true.

His sins are heavy, he has transgressed repeatedly against the Law and more than deserves to lose his tenancy, his life now and his life to come, but, washed in the blood of Christ, he dare ask forgiveness, and the forgiveness is not denied:

> I did and do commit
> Many a fault more then my lease will bear;
> Yet still askt pardon, and was not deni'd.

The story, however, is not ended. This was the first trial: his gifts refused in the revelation of their worthlessness. Only the purity of his heart was deemed of any significance. And, this first trial was experienced and understood. Now for the second.

The second trial, as all trials, came unexpectedly, and at the very instant of a consciousness of well-being and spiritual relaxation. The soul was clean, and therefore particularly ready for the new invasion of seven more devils:

> After my heart was well,
> And clean and fair, as I one even-tide
>   (I sigh to tell)
> Walkt by myself abroad, I saw a large
> And spacious fornace flaming, and thereon
> A boyling caldron, round about whose verge
> Was in great letters set *AFFLICTION*.
> The greatnesse shew'd the owner.

Herbert saw what seemed hell on earth. He saw suffering as the antithesis of Love. He saw suffering as the work of cruelty, of hatred, of punishment. And, he believed that God in his anger could somehow be appeased. At the moment of cleansing, when he knew God to be Love, for God had forgiven him and purified him, he was faced by the worst temptation of all: the confrontation with suffering. Was the Love a lie? Could God waver in his love for Man? He dared to judge God by his own human measures and fell headlong into the trap of denying the Mystery in the Love of God. The answer to the joy of purification, and the answer to the terror of the affliction, are equally not within his comprehension. But, his immediate reaction was that he could circumvent the suffering, revive, by bribes, God's lack of love, as if an offering could re-focus God's wandering attention. He went to fetch a sacrificial lamb from his flock. Was this not also a reminder to the Father, of the ransom paid by his Son?

> So I went
> To fetch a sacrifice out of my fold,
> Thinking with that, which I did thus present,
> To warm his love, which I did fear grew cold.

And, he offered the lamb as the gift of his heart, not as he had the fruits together with his heart, but as the offering of his spirit, purified only recently by the blood of Christ. This was a spiritual sacrifice, far removed from the worldliness of the first offering. But, it could not be as easy as that. The heart might be purified, but it must also be tried and refined in the furnace. It must learn the Mystery of suffering and take it up joyfully, creatively, not mutely acquiescing:

> But as my heart did tender it, the man,
> Who was to take if from me, slipt his hand,
> And threw my heart into the scalding pan;
> My heart, that brought it (do you understand?)
> The offerer's heart.

This was the crucial question. Why? It was not just any person who was subjected to the pain of suffering. That would have been bad enough. But, it was the heart of the very person who was, as he thought, giving himself, his gifts, to God. *The man* (again, perhaps, the Angel of the Lord, the Lord himself who condescended to wrestle with Jacob) knew better what should be the gift. He knew why the lamb was proffered. And, he refused passive imputed Righteousness. The Friend also understands, and intervenes again, with his precise and unsentimental comment:

> *Your heart was hard, I fear.*

And, Herbert acknowledges the truth of this explanation:

> Indeed it's true.

Herbert had not realised himself how his heart, the box, the cabinet, the sole container of the Spirit, had lost the living pliability for housing the Spirit, for listening to the whisper of the Spirit. The heart was hard: unreceptive, impermeable, and unknowing of its own condition. It was a discovery for Herbert to see and recognise the condition of his heart, he watched his heart as a thing detached from himself, and he joined in the objective work of repairing and healing. He found that he himself knew the exact materials to use for the treatment:

> I found a callous matter
> Began to spread and to expatiate there:
> But with a richer drug then scalding water
> I bath'd it often, ev'n with holy bloud,
> Which at a board, while many drunk bare wine,
> A friend did steal into my cup for good,
> Ev'n taken inwardly, and most divine
> To supple hardnesses.

The salves, which he applied for the hardness of his heart, were not only outward, not only the positive acceptance of suffering as a Mystery somehow connected with Love, but, he applied the greater medicine of reviving the inward life. There, at the Holy Table, he drank the wine of Communion. And, because he drank it in the fullness of faith that it was indeed divine, the Holy Spirit made it so. The Mystery of the Eucharist remains for Herbert a Mystery, not only sacramentally a Mystery, but also in the reception. Some drink wine, but, others, through the working of the Spirit, in a way totally inexplicable, do indeed drink of the blood of Christ, and with the blood they drink eternal life. At this single moment, Herbert knows beyond all doubt that for him it has been made possible to taste of the blood, but how or why he will not, nor can, hazard the explanation. And, it even remains doubtful if he is sure that the experience is inevitably repeated. Exhaustion overcomes him. He has recognised and somehow worked through the revelation of the foulness of his heart, masquerading under a pleasant appearance of generous worship, and the hardness of the heart, equally dissembling with spurious sacrifice whilst denying any real experience of suffering. Both conditions were only remedied by open acknowledgment of repentance and the receiving of the life-giving blood of Christ. Was the ordeal still not finished in all its intensity? He longs for rest:

>   But at the length
> Out of the cauldron getting, soon I fled
> Unto my house, where to repair the strength
> Which I had lost, I hasted to my bed.

But, instead of the anticipated softness of a bed in which he could at last lie down, sleep, and forget, he found not ease and comfort, but, *thorns:* thorns, which pricked, and tore, and irritated: thorns, which prevented one moment of relaxation. He had foregone everything in the first two movements of repentance, the world and all the delights of the world, he had accepted suffering and pain as within the Love of God, was he not even allowed to rest in peace?

> But when I thought to sleep out all these faults
>   (I sigh to speak)
> I found that some had stuff'd the bed with thoughts,
> I would say *thorns*. Deare, could my heart not break,
> When with my pleasures ev'n my rest was gone?

No-one but One, could have intruded into the privacy of his

peace. Only One had the keys, and that was the Master, his Lord. It could only be God himself who tormented him thus. The thorns of his crown must pierce his heart. And, the Friend, again, knows the reason:

> Full well I understood, who had been there:
> For I had giv'n the key to none, but one:
> It must be he. *Your heart was dull, I fear.*

This was the reason and the third effort of heart must be made. Confession, repentance, awareness, all this, and one thing more, constant and unceasing living vigilance. He must day and night bring his wandering and scattered multiplicity of thoughts into unity, and, once gathered, orientate them as one upon the Saviour:

> Indeed a slack and sleepie state of minde
> Did oft possesse me, so that when I pray'd,
> Though my lips went, my heart did stay behinde.

He had dared to rely upon the redeeming Sacrifice as sufficient with no effort of his own. He had accepted the dogma of imputed Righteousness and refused participation, denying the Mystery of the person, permitting himself to lapse into an attitude of passive redemption. There could be no assurance of salvation, not even through the releasing Cross. He must work. He is finally and triumphantly free from any theology which would deny the responsibility of the person. No-one is righteous on his own, no works can suffice, there is no guarantee, but equally, Man is not a passive creature, unable to control his own destiny of faith and work. There is faith, and there is the active freedom of the work of love. It has not been sufficient to hide behind the excuse:

> But all my scores were by another paid,
> Who took the debt upon him.

And, the last words are from the Friend, now addressing Herbert as Friend. The Friend has listened carefully, it is his turn now to comment on all that he has heard:

> *Truly, Friend,*
> *For ought I heare, your Master shows to you*
> *More favour then you wot of. Mark the end.*

And, he repeats what has taken place, through the love of God:

> *The Font did onely, what was old, renew:*
> *The Caldron suppled, what was grown too hard:*
> *The Thorns did quicken, what was grown too dull . . .*

Every one of the events was calculated to put right what Herbert had himself spoiled:

> *All did but strive to mend, what you had marr'd.*

And, what remains, in the face of such love, is not difficult. It is the returning of love to Love: to worship God, instant to instant, day to day. For God is not the God of Anger, God does not punish, God only wills our instant to instant spiritual renewal, our openness to him, the life and vigilance of the spirit:

> *Wherefore be cheer'd, and praise him to the full*
> *Each day, each houre, each moment of the week,*
> *Who fain would have you be new, tender, quick.*

The Pulley

The Pulley again strongly integrates suffering into the Love of God. Here, the Mystery is even partially explained, in as much as the suffering is seen as the means of release from absorption in the world. The suffering, as it were, helps towards the sense of disgust, and, thence, to the renewal of re-orientation.

The opening lines are fresh with the joy of God in his new creation. It is as if God did not know how to show his infinite love for the creature whom he had made. The creature had not yet turned on his Lord with treachery and hatred. It is the time of intimate relationship. God wanted to give Man everything possible for his pleasure, the world and all it contained, to be concentrated into Man's grasp, and at his disposal. Nothing was too much:

> *When God at first made man,*
> *Having a glasse of blessings standing by;*
> *Let us (said he) poure on him all we can:*
> *Let the worlds riches, which dispersed lie,*
>   *Contract into a span.*

It seemed that of the world God wished to do for Man, what Man, in his turn, should wish to do for God, that is, draw all into one, orientated upon him. All the multitude of the resources of the World of Nature should be directed, as one, upon Man. It is creation as described in *Genesis:* all given to Man for his use. But, the resources were not only material, they were also the faculties for ruling and enjoying the material world:

> So strength first made a way;
> Then beautie flow'd, then wisdome, honour, pleasure . . .

Yet, in his wisdom, God suddenly stopped. He had poured the best that he could upon his creature. One gift remained, and one gift he withheld:

> When almost all was out, God made a stay,
> Perceiving that alone of all his treasure
> Rest in the bottome lay.

Rest was at the bottom. *Rest,* therefore, was the foundation for the fulfilment of any other one of the gifts. God gave the gifts but he withheld the one gift which would make them so satisfying that there would be no more need for effort. It was not only the sense of rest, of peace, in itself, which God would not give to Man, but the sense of rest, of achievement, in all the other gifts. If God withheld rest, then it would for ever be missing from everything. Strength would never be experienced as fully strong, beauty would always be just out of reach, wisdom unattainable, honour passing, pleasure unsatisfying. In fact, in the giving of the blessings, God not only denied the autonomous value of any one of the blessings, but, far more, he removed for ever absolute validity from any finite condition.

Within the finite realm, all must remain relative, and, in the last count, unfulfilled. Herbert recognises that if God had given Man *rest*, that is an absolute knowledge of any kind, in any sphere, then Man would for ever be circumscribed by the finite, he would find his God *within* creation. The absolute must remain a Mystery, outside Man's grasp and only thus Man is free to work and live and grow inside the finite world. Had God given the absolute possibility *within* the world, Man would have been a paralysed slave to himself, and to the men and things surrounding him.

Rest is the most precious of all the gifts, for it remains the transcendent goal in every sphere of life:

> For if I should (said he)
> Bestow this jewell also on my creature,
> He would adore my gifts in stead of me,
> And rest in Nature, not the God of Nature:
> So both should losers be.

All the other gifts, God freely leaves to Man, but always in the knowledge of final non-achievement. Absolute perfection within the world remains impossible. And this realisation, either through reason, or through experience, may, if nothing else, force Man to face the inevitability of his source and his destination. Man, created of God, longs for the Perfect, and he will struggle on and on, within the enforced torment of ever-seeking the unattainable Perfect, in the agony of creative work, when the created object consistently falls short of the creative intention, in the bitterness of love, which is never pure, in the attaining of knowledge, which ever remains inadequate. All this, God intends. In his love, the Mystery of the incomprehensible transcendent is present so that Man may not perish:

> Yet let him keep the rest,
> But keep them with repining restlesnesse:
> Let him be rich and wearie, that at least,
> If goodnesse leade him not, yet wearinesse
> May tosse him to my breast.

ix. *The Mystery of Eternity*

Mans medley

The Pulley has suggested how nothing in this world can be absolute. *Mans medley* suggests that Man belongs neither to this world nor yet to the World of Grace. This consciousness has frequently throughout the poems proved a source of uneasiness and even terror, particularly in the realisation that the World of Nature, separated as it is from the World of Grace, yet is assured of constancy. Man, alone, fluctuates between the happiness of the presence of Grace, and the grief of the withdrawal. Now, this isolation from the constant World of Nature, an isolation which has caused the misery of fluctuation and has presented Man frequently as the victim of arbitrary Providence, becomes the source of the deepest joy. If Man belongs, even partially, to this world now, yet, he is not tied to it. The future is his.

Nature is happy. But, the happiness of Nature, consistent as it may seem, ends here, in this world. If we evaluate correctly, and not in temporary and fleeting measurement, then we find that Man's happiness lies in the future. In effect, the comparison between the happiness of Nature and the happiness of Man is invalid, one ceases and the other continues and temporary satisfaction can not reasonably be put on the same level as eternal joy:

> Heark, how the birds do sing,
> And woods do ring.
> All creatures have their joy: and man hath his.
> Yet if we rightly measure,
> Mans joy and pleasure
> Rather hereafter, then in present, is.

The sensible world lays claims to this world:

> To this life things of sense
> Make their pretence . . .

The Angels inherit the right to the World of Grace:

> In th' other Angels have a right by birth . . .

But, what about Man? Man made of flesh, Man with the bodiless life within the encasing senses? Is Man not suspended between the two, the uniting link, sharing the constitutions of both?

> Man ties them both alone,
> And makes them one,
> With th' one hand touching heav'n, with th' other earth.

The soul, the spirit in man, yearns to be in the other world, its home. The body has no such longing, for this other world is not its home. It is not only that the spirit inherits eternal life, while the body, as we know it, perishes, but it is also the two-fold contradictory attitude in Man's nature; as far as he is body, he has no desire to live on as spirit, and as far as he is spirit, he can not tolerate the earth-bound body. Spirit and body, in this context, are mutually exclusive and highly antagonistic:

> In soul he mounts and flies,
> In flesh he dies.

This duality may be seen in the image of a garment. At first appearance, the garment is coarse and thick, a material insufficient in itself for it would normally be used as canvas on which to embroider. But, incongruously, this poor, uncouth and ungainly material is decorated with exquisite and unusual, delicate lace, seemingly quite inappropriate to the stuff to which it is attached. And, even more strange, Man is destined by nature to take his stand not in accordance with the preponderate, coarse material, but with the far less discernible, delicate lace. By nature, he is meant to be fine, not brutish:

> He wears a stuffe whose thread is coarse and round,
> But trimm'd with curious lace,
> And should take place
> After the trimming, not the stuffe and ground.

It is not that Man may not temporarily enjoy what the world offers; but, he must not linger. He can taste of the good things of the world, but ever be alert to the world to come, as some migrant bird of passage. This sense of transitory life is his prerogative and his strength:

> Not that he may not here
> Taste of the cheer,
> But as birds drink, and straight lift up their head,
> So he must sip and think
> Of better drink
> He may attain to, after he is dead.

It is Man's joy that this world is not the end. But, is it not also his terror and grief? The creatures of the world, all nature, which has no soul, blossoms, withers, and dies once. But Man, in his double nature, is faced by the possibility of a double death. When he dies, will he then live? Or, when he dies, will his life on earth have been such, that he will die again? Now, into eternity. Will he rise to a second life, or to a second death? And, so too, there is the dreaded preliminary to the first death: the double winter. Other things grow old, but without the consciousness of the significance. Man grows old, in the consciousness of the death which follows. He dies twice already in this life, in the anticipation and in the death. And, always, he lives without the assurance of what will be. He is a man, not an Angel. Suspended between Heaven and Earth, how can Man know for certain that Heaven will be his?

> But as his joyes are double;
> So is his trouble.
> He hath two winters, other things but one:
> Both frosts and thoughts do nip,
> And bite his lip;
> And he of all things fears two deaths alone.

Suddenly, the entire position is reversed, and, as it were, taken into another dimension. Life, death, happiness, misery, what does it all mean? In this new dimension, all falls away into the joy of love: into the Mystery of love. This is the real, the lasting happiness, the happiness which stretches from earth to heaven without question. Within this new dimension of freedom, evil crumbles to nothing. Speculation ceases. Life or death, the nature of Man, is it not insignificant? The new dimension is the release of the spirit, where nothing can affect it any more; but every single thing, good or bad, finds its rightful place to contribute to the willed and conscious growing out of the world, into the love of God. This is the beginning of the impatience with this life as we know it, and even more, our constant and distracting reaction to this life:

> Yet ev'n the greatest griefs
> May be reliefs,
> Could he but take them right, and in their wayes.
> Happie is he, whose heart
> Hath found the art
> To turn his double pains to double praise.

Home

The overt impatience with the reactions and demands of this life is becoming more explicit. And, in *Home,* this impatience becomes even more marked, the longing for emancipation from the world, whose whole achievement remains a delusion, becomes more intensified.

This life is the daily work, but there comes a time when we are weary, we yearn to be finally relieved from this task of living. The lingering in this world produces a sensation of physical sickness. It is a fever of the heart. Can not God either give some direct explanation for the delay, disclose something of his secret plans, or, if not, give speedy release? It hardly seems possible any longer to drag one day into another:

> Come Lord, my head doth burn, my heart is sick,
> While thou dost ever, ever stay:
> Thy long deferrings wound me to the quick,
> My spirit gaspeth night and day.
> O show thy self to me,
> Or take me up to thee!

It hardly seems possible that God can delay now, leaving Man to his torments, when He once bore such agony for the same man whom He now seems to abandon. The blood was not slow which poured out of Him. There was no stint in the pain which He endured for Man:

> How canst thou stay, considering the pace
> The bloud did make, which thou didst waste?
> When I behold it trickling down thy face,
> I never saw thing make such haste.
> O show thy, &c.

And God was not slow to save Man, when Man fell away in sin. There was only one remedy, the uncreated Son, in the bosom of the Father, and the Son was sent to redeem Man, who, with all the wealth of the world, could not refrain from the one mean apple forbidden to him. The Son left the nest, the home of the Spirit. He exchanged the sweetness of Heaven for His death, that Man might be saved from the slavery of sin. He came to save us, for Heaven He substituted the world: for sweetness, gall: for Man He exchanged the feast of the fruits of Paradise for the bread of His own body:

> There lay thy sonne: and must he leave that nest,
>   That hive of sweetnesse, to remove
> Thraldome from those, who would not at a feast
>   Leave one poore apple for thy love?
>   O show thy, &c.

The Redeemer, his Redeemer, the personal Redeemer of each person of Man, came. How can He now keep aloof? Baptised into Christ, Herbert can not accept the estrangement. Of the love of Christ, he is sure:

> He did, he came: O my Redeemer deare,
>   After all this canst thou be strange?
> So many years baptiz'd, and not appeare?
>   As if thy love could fail or change.
>   O show thy self to me,
>   Or take me up to thee!

Now, the impatience becomes more vehement. If Christ delays, then he will not. Herbert is sick of the world, of the enshrouding sorrow, of the clouds which obscure heaven. He will no longer be content to see darkly. He will see clearly, face to face:

> Yet if thou stayest still, why must I stay?
>   My God, what is this world to me,
> This world of wo? hence all ye clouds, away,
>   Away; I must get up and see.
>   O show thy, &c.

The world is tired, worn out; what right has it to keep us chained to it when we long to be free? It is merely a feeding-place for our stomachs:

> What is this weary world; this meat and drink,
>   That chains us by the teeth so fast?

The world has no interest for him; but, then, what does Herbert mean by the next lines?

> What is this woman-kinde, which I can wink
>   Into a blacknesse and distaste?
>   O show thy, &c.

It is hardly likely that at this point of ecstatic denial of life, Herbert is referring to his indifference to the possible worldly attraction of women. It would be more interesting to see a hint of a denial of the Bride of Christ, that he even has no more time for the *deare Mother,* his Church on earth. But, probably, whatever may be implicit, this statement is more directly concerned with his active indifference to all life, to man born of woman, *woman-kinde:* humanity, made all the more despicable in his estimation by the emphasis that man is naturally the offspring of woman, she, who first betrayed her God, by stupidity.

Herbert's scorn for the so-called joys surrounding him becomes more and more apparent. He sees these joys as insolent temptations. He withers them with a look, and then challenges them to dare to re-appear. The breath of his disdain is engendered by the faintest whisper of the Spirit, by one slight consciousness of presence:

> With one small sigh thou gav'st me th' other day
>   I blasted all the joyes about me:
> And scouling on them as they pin'd away,
>   Now come again, said I, and flout me.
>   O show thy, &c.

Herbert can see no glimpse of relief wherever he looks around him: all is dry, arid, stunted. Perhaps, in sleep, some pretence is still possible; but, waking means the immediate rising up into re-orientation to God alone:

> Nothing but drought and dearth, but bush and brake,
>   Which way so-e're I look, I see.
> Some may dream merrily, but when they wake,
>   They dresse themselves and come to thee.
>   O show thy, &c.

And, now, comes the full confession and active acceptance of non-achievement. No achievement in this life can be final. Any achievement is merely a step, and in its achievement is already the substance for the non-achievement, the beginning of the next effort. The only achievement lies in the illumination of the non-achievement and, hence, the ceasing from the discussing of its possibility:

> We talk of harvests; there are no such things,
> But when we leave our corn and hay . . .

When we once do forget what seems success to us, and the materials of the success, then we have begun our pilgrimage. We must know that there is no reward, nothing which we have created or made or attained, except one: the one year of harvest is that which contains the Day of Judgment: the last day: the day to be dreaded because we can not know our own value, however productive we may seem to have been: the day to be loved because it marks the end of the temporal daily works and opens time into eternity, death into life:

> There is no fruitfull yeare, but that which brings
> The last and lov'd, though dreadfull day.
> O show thy, &c.

Impatience turns to prayer: will not God hear him and hurry on the dragging days? Herbert feels himself as a bird, tied by the leg to its perch. If this knot of life were only loosened, then his soul would fly in the spirit, away from mortality, clogging, dragging down, into the freedom of death, the emancipation of the body, into life eternal:

> Oh loose this frame, this knot of man untie!
> That my free soul may use her wing,
> Which now is pinion'd with mortalitie,
> As an intangled, hamper'd thing.
> O show thy, &c.

Man is suspended between the two worlds. But, Herbert's contention is far more important and personal than the theological appraisal. His whole spirit yearns for death, he feels as if he is already a stranger in this world, a tenant who, with his baggage sent on, outstays his welcome. Some minor accident defers his going. And, his lodging has been rented already to the next comer. He waits impatiently for the carriage to fetch him. His mind, all his happiness, have preceded him, and they miss his presence, demanding the re-union. What is this inexplicable and annoying delay?

> What have I left, that I should stay and grone?
> The most of me to heav'n is fled:
> My thoughts and joyes are all packt up and gone,
> And for their old acquaintance plead.
> O show thy, &c.

So, the last plea to God: his whole body joins in this prayer that he may, even now, immediately be summoned to heaven. And, his gift, with a sudden turn of irony, his poetry, joins in the pleading by refusing to rhyme! Rhyme will keep him in the world, no-rhyme is the invitation to death:

> Come dearest Lord, passe not this holy season,
> My flesh and bones and joynts do pray:
> And ev'n my verse, when by the ryme and reason
> The word is, *Stay,* sayes ever, *Come.*
> O show thy, &c.

The Pilgrimage

The long journey of life must end in death. It is possible, as in *Home,* to anticipate death. But, in fact, it is not possible, in any sense, to comprehend it. Strive as we will, we can not go beyond the point of death. We can not in our finite minds take the step from this side of the finite, into the non-finite. The goal is beyond what we can imagine as the goal. So, *The Pilgrimage* makes this further movement out of emotion and speculation into true reason, which knows its limitation. *The Pilgrimage,* above all else, is a sober poem of delicate balance as far as the mind can reach. And, it is a fine expression of humility, in the joyous awareness of what the mind can not comprehend.

Hope and expectation are words of delusion. Both boost up a confidence in reaching an aim which might seem the real aim, but is, in fact, a mere temptation of apparent achievement. Hope would put the end within the finite, comprehensible realm. Herbert thought that he knew his destination. It was not easy to reach, but his determination was unshaken. His journey led upwards, out of the vale of the world, of daily experience, through ambushes and assaults:

> I travell'd on, seeing the hill, where lay
> My expectation.

Thus, already, in these opening lines, the flaw of the pilgrimage may be discernible, the seductive delusion of the expectation. How could he, as a finite creature, *see* his destination? But, so it seemed possible to him:

> A long it was and weary way.
> The gloomy cave of Desperation
> I left on th' one, and on the other side
> The rock of Pride.

He steered successfully through this Scylla and Charybdis of spiritual ascent: seduction of despair in non-sense, and seduction of pride in seeming-sense. Doggedly he continued, now to enter the most attractive stopping-place: the region of poetry. Here Imagination had her dwelling-place, with all the charm of her fantasy growing in pleasing abundance of variety. He wanted to linger, to stay and entertain himself with his own gifts:

> And so I came to Fancies medow strow'd
>   With many a flower:
> Fain would I here have made abode . . .

But, he rejected the delights of his poetry. He must go on. His hour had come and his passion was at hand. He, too, must go up to his Jerusalem and he could not linger; he was spurred into activity by this conviction:

> But I was quicken'd by my houre.

Then, Herbert found himself beset with a variety of concerns and anxieties, as some over-grown spinney, tangled with briar and nettle, catching at his legs, impeding his movement in the one, set direction. Yet, still, he managed to continue his journey, although with difficulty:

> So to Cares cops I came, and there got through
>   With much ado.

Out of the tract of tangled undergrowth, he came to a more open plain, a desert stretch, the home of tearing sensual desires, howling winds with nothing to bar their warring onslaught on this wide expanse of level ground:

> That led me to the wilde of Passion, which
>   Some call the wold;
> A wasted place, but sometimes rich.

It was a desert of spirit, but with all the temptations of worldly success, of rewards and of praise. Herbert stayed there long enough to lose all that he possessed. His riches dropped away as worthless, except for one piece of gold. One reserve was left to him so that he had the physical possibility of continuing, and that reserve was not, however, entirely of his own earning: it was carefully hidden on him, on his side. He was, thus, not left comfortless. One gold coin was still his. But it was the gift of the Holy Spirit, secretly bestowed on him. Somehow it was, as gold, a sovereign remedy, but, at the same time, he was still in this world, and it still savoured of worldly values. He was now rid of all incumbrances: despair, pride, imagination, anxieties, desires and wealth. All that remained of worldly possessions was this one Angell:

>> Here I was robb'd of all my gold,
> Save one good Angell, which a friend had ti'd
>> Close to my side.

Perhaps this *good Angell* could yet prove, being yet of this world, the well-used talent, which he could offer to account for his life on earth. So, free and unencumbered, he thought his journey over, the promised end reached:

>> At length I got unto the gladsome hill,
>>> Where lay my hope,
>> Where lay my heart . . .

This was the highest moment of expectation. Hope had led him to this high spot, the point of death. Already his heart, his very life, his very soul, were there. Another moment, and he would face his God, as he believed he knew Him. He would stand before his Judge, and his Saviour, and offer himself as he was. He had climbed and climbed on the ascent of sanctification. In the ascent he had lost all, even what he had thought that he could offer. Nothing remained beyond his naked self, and perhaps his few deeds of merit, in the one gold coin. He had reached the longed-for end. Now he would see the ineffable light: his Love, his Lord:

>>> . . . and climbing still,
>> When I had gain'd the brow and top,
> A lake of brackish waters on the ground
>>> Was all I found.

Stagnant, foul water: the last desolation. Had the whole journey been in vain? Was it all a sham? a lie? Was there no joy of everlasting promise?

>> With that abash'd and struck with many a sting
>>> Of swarming fears,
>> I fell, and cry'd, Alas my King!
>> Can both the way and end be tears?

And, then, praying in despair, Herbert understood how he had deceived himself. Hope had led him on and brought him to a finite end within his attainment. But, there can be no ascent such as this for the non-finite end. He must make another ascent, this time beyond the way which he could comprehend. And, he still thought that this at least he could do. He still believed that the further way of sanctification was possible. So, he started off again, courageously:

> Yet taking heart I rose, and then perceiv'd
> I was deceiv'd:
>
> My hill was further: so I flung away...

It was then that the mercy of God showed itself to him. Then he heard the voice of God, and he was faced with the truth. No assurance of salvation could be given to him. There was no sure ascent of sanctification. Not even the *good Angell* tied to his side could lead him. He could not go any further, alive: he could not reach the peak, the last point, face to face with his Lord, as long as he believed that he could reach it. He must die to this last satisfaction of knowledge:

> Yet heard a crie
> Just as I went, *None goes that way*
> *And lives:*

Herbert's answer is immediate, for he has indeed reached the last point before the end. And, so, he is prepared to die to his own knowledge of his destination, to his own estimation of the destination which he seeks. He accepts to the full his human limitation and sees in radiant joy the life inherent in what seems death to us: to die to one's autonomy, to one's own evaluation of sanctity, to any pre-conceived notion of the process of sanctification, or assurance of such sanctification, is not death, is not servitude, but it is true wisdom, a mighty sovereignty, a spiritual transcending of our human limitation, the dying into life. Herbert turns his back, even contemptuously, upon all worldly success, however spiritual it might seem, he can only now see the beauty of the Kingdom of Heaven before him: the throne of his King:

> If that be all, said I,
> After so foul a journey death is fair,
> And but a chair.

Hope

One poem remains, which I have left to the last, because I know that I can never fully understand it. Yet, I shall make this last attempt to suggest how I have come, at least partially, to follow the theme.

I see *Hope* as pre-eminently a joyous poem of death, of the anticipated meeting with God. It seems to go further than *The Pilgrimage* in the precision of its movement, with no extraneous matter whatsoever. And, in this last poem of Hope, it would seem to be finally conclusive that, for Herbert, Hope is ever the source of delusion, the inviting seduction to think that we know what we do not know, and that we can achieve what we can not achieve, with the subsequent torment of despair at failure. In this connection, it may be of interest to refer to the ascetic writings of the Eastern spiritual Fathers, particularly in *The Philokalia*. Here, we frequently find the Fathers warning the young monks against a particular threat, in Greek, πλάνη, and in Russian *prelest*. Translators have always had difficulty in finding a single word in English to suggest the condition, the seductive charm, the drawing on into the final disillusionment. Herbert's use of *Hope* would seem to me very close indeed in significance.

It was to Hope that Herbert gives his watch:

> I gave to Hope a watch of mine . . .

In the giving of the watch to Hope, it is possible that Herbert may not mean that Hope was the actual recipient of the watch, Hope, in effect being a personification capable of receiving his gift, but that in the giving of his watch to Hope, he is suggesting the potentiality of hope in relation to his watch. The watch, on which Herbert would then be directing his hope, could be an actual watch, which tells the time, but it might also be the watch on board ship: the sailor who keeps watch. This would perhaps be more relevant to the anchor which follows. Herbert is putting his hope, he is nourishing his hope, with the watch: the passing of time, either in hours, or in the long waiting of the sailor on lookout duty. Is not this long interval of time something to offer the hope within himself for the longed-for end? Can not the enduring of this passage of time be the grounds for release? But, on this occasion, the voice of *The Pilgrimage* is silent. Without speaking, the voice only answers image with image. He presents Herbert with an anchor. Did Herbert think it time to leave off work? But, the ship had not even set sail, it was still at anchor. The journey had not begun. The hope of completion was a delusion, the passing of time gained him no release.

Yet, Hope persisted within him, enticing him into another effort to give himself the courage of success and achievement, that his work was done. Optimistically, Herbert fed the flame of hope within him, flickering as it might be, by presenting as proof to himself an old prayer-book. Had he not prayed for years and years? Was this time of service in the world still not completed? Again, there was silence. But, the prayer-book was exchanged for a telescope. It was nearly a scornful action. His years of worship receded further and further into the distance as time completed. The perspective before him stretched immeasurably further than the past.

Then Herbert made his third attempt to claim that this irksome servitude in the world was successfully accomplished. He proffered the hope of conclusion, *a viall full of tears*. Had he not endured enough sorrow and grief? And had not God, himself, promised to Man that the bottle would be filled to the brim, where we ourselves lacked? But, again, the silent answer: *a few green eares*. The Spirit reminds him, inwardly, that no harvest is possible, nor assured in this world. Far from the harvest of Autumn beginning, the season of Spring had hardly begun. We can not know the values of God.

What can Herbert do? He can not pretend, even to himself, that there is any validity in the Hope which he has tried to foster in himself by proof of his efforts. He had waited long, he had prayed, he had wept:

Ah Loyterer! I'le no more, no more I'le bring . . .

If God will not accept his gifts, if God will not agree that his work is finished, he can do no more. And, then, at last, the voice, the Spirit, speaks within him. What Herbert has offered is of no value, for Herbert valued it himself. It is not for us to evaluate. We may only love, and give ourselves to God, not on the way of progression, but in the circle of eternity. God is Perfect Love. There is nothing to offer him, but ourselves. There is no beginning and no end to the Mystery of holiness. We must die to our gifts, to our knowledge of knowledge, to every virtue as to every evil. We are free, no more servants but sons. And, we are God's most precious jewel. And, because we are free, we, alone, can give ourselves in all the joy of love:

I did expect a ring.

The vanity of travelling has found its destination in the Mystery of the circle of love, of death into life, of the point beyond which we can not go. All is over in the perfect freedom of submission from out of slavery. The yoke is, indeed, light, in the radiance of the Son. The wedding feast at Cana is joyously alive, and the wine of the marriage is the Mystery of salvation to which we have no key:

I did expect a ring.

PART IV

SYNOPSIS OF THE IMAGERY

PART IV

Synopsis of the Imagery

i. *Introduction to Imagery*

I was in doubt for some time as to what might prove the most useful way of presenting, within the context of the book, certain aspects of Herbert's imagery. I decided finally, in view of the complexity of the inter-relationship of the imagery, that it might be more clear to use diagrams, and this I have tried to do. In the diagrams I have attempted to suggest the width together with the total lack of prolixity in Herbert's imagery.

Herbert has taken the whole world, created and uncreated, as his source for imagery and he, himself, has given the clue to the net-work of intricate connotation in his insistence on the importance of *harmony*. This would suggest that his poetry can be seen as some immense symphony, with every aspect of the World of Grace and the World of Nature contributing its particular variation and consistency of melody. Herbert was a great poet and a great craftsman. But, and this I see as the vital point which I would emphasise above all else, Herbert's *words,* images single and complex, may not be considered as in any sense autonomous or merely relevant to each other in the psychological (associative) field. On one level, they can not escape from such an impression because of their close-knit relationship to each other, but, in spirit and practice, there is no intellectual nor artistic positivism involved, no question of preciousness, nor of conceit.

Herbert's relationship of imagery is not primarily the inter-relationship of the sensible world seen through symbols (images), but it is the expression in words, his one medium as a poet, not of the relationship of the images to each other as words, but the relationship of the inherent ideas within the words, and, thence, the active inter-connection and derivation of idea from idea to idea. There is little doubt possible that Herbert fully accepted the inadequacy and limitation of words, and for this reason, if none other, he was careful and fastidious in his choice of images. Thus, his thoughts speak as clearly, as he can make them, by means of a meticulous labour of composition. Every word would seem to have a particular part, but the part is its single contribution to a complex idea.

What, then, in practice, would seem the purpose and effect

of this inter-relationship of image, constructed out of carefully selected words?

By means of a practical visual demonstration in the diagrams of a few of the complex relationships of words, I have tried to show how the complexity of a principle or concept may be reflected in the representative complexity of verbal expression. In such a connection from diagram to diagram, the co-relation of the complex of idea and image, the inner coherence of an idea's singular complexity within each simple component, should become both evident and evocative. It is my hope that the diagrams may help to suggest how critical analysis can avoid absolute terminal evaluation and, at the same time, stimulate an active pursuit of secondary connotations, each of which, in itself, is the primary centre and source of a further related system. This may help, as a suggestion, that, as illustrated in Herbert's poetry, critical analysis need not be severed from philosophical (theological) process of reason, and that literary criticism fully participates, with philosophy and theology, in the free acknowledgment of its own limitation. Literary criticism may yet be released from its age-long conflict, on the one hand of the idealism which would refute the relevance of the word, that is, matter and event, and, on the other, of the positivism which would allow autonomous, that is, immanent, significance to the word (matter or event). I would suggest that there is still much work to be done in the integration of literature into philosophy and theology, as an acknowledged medium of truth (reason), and, hence, the consequent re-valuation of the critical approach. It is a pity to deny the full significance of their thoughts to the most sensitive thinkers, because they express their thoughts in poetry.

I am giving here a few examples of how I approach the diagrams although, of course, both diagrams and interpretation are far from complete and remain merely a suggestion.

ii. *Index to diagrams*

Diagram 1: World of Grace

Diagram 2: Finite and Infinite

Diagram 3: World of Nature

       3(a) World of Nature: sky

       3(b) World of Nature: elements

       3(c) World of Nature: produce

       3(d) World of Nature: creatures

Diagram 4: Properties of Nature

Diagram 5: Constitution of Man
        5(a) Constitution of Man: soul
        5(b) Constitution of Man: body

Diagram 6: Nourishment of Man

Diagram 7: Man: Rank and Activity

iii. *Examples of use of diagrams*

1. *The Fall-Redemption*

Example: Easter-wings: Then shall the fall further the flight in me.

a. *Analysis*

  i. The Fall: 5(a), 5(b), 1, 3(a-d), 2, 4, 7.
  ii. Apple: 1, 3(c), 6.
     Fruit: 3(c).
 iii. Tree: 3(c).
     Wood: 3(c).
     Ashes: 3(c).
 iv. Death (decay): 2, 5(b).
  v. The Cross: 3(c), 1.
     The Crucifixion: 1, 5(b).
 vi. Flight: 1, 4, 3(d).
vii. Me (Man): 5(a), 5(b).

b. *Exposition*

Then shall the fall further the flight in me.

    The fall (expulsion of Man from the World of Grace—Paradise) into the mortality of the World of Nature retains the potentiality of life (Grace) since Man was created in Paradise and the apple derives from a tree from which the Cross of redemption also derives. Thus the potentiality of life, for fruit is also the means of nourishment, of redemption, becomes realised in the redeeming act of Christ. His resurrection from death on the tree, the image of finite life and nourishment and thence synonymous with death, opens the heart of Man to the reception of the Holy Spirit and the consequent possibility of flight, the upward movement of the reverse of the Fall, to heaven. By implication, the tree (i.e. the World of Nature) is also potentially redeemed.

It is interesting how this suggests that Herbert in no way subscribes to any notion of the Fall as Man's emancipation into the freedom of will and hence to a more conscious and potent religious capability. He sees the Fall as a Fall, and only redeemed through the redeeming act of Christ which allows for Man's return to Heaven, a freedom forfeited by Adam. Cf. *The H. Communion:* Adam moved freely from heaven to paradise as from one room to another.

The Fall, as *my* Fall, removes the barriers of past, present, and future. We do not suffer the consequences of a Fall which took place in the past, but we participate in the Fall now. This suggestion of the individual participation both in the Fall and in the Salvation is, on another occasion, very delicately expressed in Herbert's reference to the Sycamore tree.

The World: Then enter'd *Sinne,* and with that Sycamore . . .

Herbert is apparently using the Sycamore tree here as synonymous with the fig-tree, but the synonymous use would seem evocative. When Zacchæus (Luke 19, 1-10) wanted to see Jesus, he climbed into a Sycamore tree: already the suggestion that Man is not utterly depraved but retains some capacity for ascent (flight) by the inspiration of the Spirit. At Jesus's command, Zacchæus came down from the tree: the obedience of his descent thus becomes the ascent (flight) out of the disobedience of the Fall. And did not Jesus then himself explicitly tell him: *this day is salvation come to this house?* It is *this day,* the particular event in time, and *this house,* the particular person. Thus, Fall and Salvation, are real, yesterday, today, and tomorrow, and personal through the working of the Holy Spirit in each individual heart, made possible only by the death and resurrection of Christ.

2. *Suffering (Grief—pain—affliction)*

Example: *Josephs coat:*
My *joyes* to *weep,* and now my *griefs* to *sing.*

a. *Analysis*

   i. Joy: 5(a).
     Holy Spirit: 1.
     Peace: 1, 5(a).
     Mirth (Jest): 1, 5(a), 5(b), 7.

  ii. Grief: 5(a).
     Holy Spirit: 1.
     Repentance: 1, 5(a).

Pain:　　　　5(b), 7, 1.
　　Sighs (groans):　1, 5(b).
　　Breath:　　　1.
　　Tears (Man):　5(a), 5(b), 1.
　　Water:　　　3(b), 6.
　　Moisture:　　4.
　　Bottle (vial, cup):　7.
　　Baptism:　　1, 3(b).
　　Priest:　　　1, 7.
　　Church:　　　1, 7.
　　Drops:　　　3(b).
　　Sweat:　　　5(b), 1.
　　Wounds:　　5(b), 7.
　　Blood:　　　5(b), 7, 1.

iii. *Sing*
　　Music:　　　3(a), 7, 1, 4.
　　Creativity:　5(a).
　　Poet-musician:　7.
　　Words:　　　1, 7, 4.
　　Praise:　　　1, 7.

b. *Exposition*

My *joyes* to *weep*, and now my *griefs* to *sing*.

The central premise, as suggested by the inter-relationship of the imagery, would seem to deny suffering, in any form, as some means of divine punishment, retribution or wrath. In fact, the strong emphasis lies on the inherent Mystery of suffering, that it may not be explained by finite reasoning, in the direct association of suffering (grief—affliction—pain) with Joy: both derive directly from the Holy Spirit. Where Joy is consistently the manifestation of the Spirit present in the heart, grief can come—sin (enmity, war), but, equally, it is the direct outcome of repentance, that is, the work of the Holy Spirit in the heart in the over-coming of sin. Again: tears (the physical sign of grief/pain) are physical in consistency, being water and coming from the eyes of Man. But, Jesus wept and so tears are not only the property of Nature and of Man. Furthermore, tears are related to water and thus the outcome of grief is directly connected with baptism: the condition induced by repentance or by enmity is itself closely related to purification and the inspiration of Grace. Tears/water would be kept in a vessel of some kind. The love of God is at once suggested in his retaining our tears in a vial or bottle (Ps. 56). But, a cup, in itself, suggests the Eucharistic chalice, drops may be of blood as they are of tears, and blood is the direct outcome of the wounds of pain (Grief). Thus, grief is connected with Christ God, Christ Man, and our salvation in the Eucharistic Sacrament.

Singing is a vocal sound, pertaining to Man and to birds: the praise of Man, and the suggestion of the working of the Holy Spirit when Man prays (sings—worships). The angels praise God continuously and so the work of the Church on earth and the Church in heaven finds its common factor. But, it is a poet/ musician who sings, and so, once again the clear reminder that Herbert considers that the primary task of the poet is to use the words of his poetry as a gift of worship to God. So, in the positive acceptance of suffering, as a Mystery from God, directly emanating from the Holy Spirit, and equally directly related to Christ, God-Man, Herbert is released from any sense of guilt in the experience of grief, and can use it creatively, in the joyful experience of the presence, not the absence, of the Spirit.

Another example of this approach to the evil of suffering in Herbert may be seen in: *Making a scepter of the rod (Affliction* (III)).

The sceptre, the sovereign power of Man and of God: in the rod, Herbert sees the possibility of his own sovereignty, as the sceptre represents the King of kings. And the rod itself may appear as the instrument of pain, of punishment, but it is equally related to a staff on which it is possible to lean, and particularly (Ps. 23) of God himself. However, even as the instrument of pain, once again we return to the blood, and so to the redeeming blood of Christ, and thus to the Mystery of suffering, which, far from separating us from God, brings us nearer to him and so makes every man sovereign over his own sins and deficiencies.

The bird of Paradise (Prayer (I)) as the symbol of prayer is very interesting. A bird: the Holy Spirit. Of Paradise: Man before the Fall and hence in direct communion with heaven, now only partially possible through the Holy Spirit in prayer/praise: a bird: singing: praise. But the bird of Paradise is brilliant in colour. Blood is red: through the redemptive act of Christ we, in prayer, in the Holy Communion partake of his red blood: prayer: bird of Paradise: Christ: crucifixion (grief/pain): the Holy Spirit: the ascent to heaven.

3. *The Mystical Ascent: Some evidence of refutation*

Example: *The Pilgrimage:*
>   Save one good Angell, which a friend had ti'd
>   Close to my side.

a. *Analysis*

  i. Good: 1, 4, 7, 5(a).
  ii. Angell: 7, 3(c), 1, 4, 3(b), 2, 5(a), 5(b).
      (Gold coin)
  iii. Friend: 1, 3(b), 4, 5(a), 7.
      (Holy Spirit and Man)
  iv. Side: 5(b), 5(a), 1.
      (of Christ and of Man)
  v. ti'd: 3(c).
  vi. close: 4.

b. *Exposition*

> Save one good Angell, which a friend had ti'd
>   Close to my side.

This one line, in interpretation, can not of course be taken out of the context of the whole poem: it should not be forgotten that the pilgrimage entails the journey which includes the first hill, the seeming destination, the second hill, the next step of seeming destination, and then the discounting of the whole ascent in the one demand of the denial of any possibility other than death: the total renunciation of any claim of evaluation of the process of sanctification, or, indeed, of assurance of salvation. How, then, does this one line, in image, contribute to the full significance?

In the journey of the mystical ascent, Herbert was methodically deprived of every achievement and possession except, finally, *one good Angell:* the connotation, here, in its immediate significance would seem emphatically in favour of the possibility of his pilgrimage being successful: the Angell is a gold coin: the coin, the talent, practical and spiritual: the gift for deeds of charity, of fruitful and industrious putting to profit of whatever God had granted him, and, so too, the talent of the Spirit, his creative activity in praise (prayer and poetry). It was a *gold* coin, and, therefore, immediately related to the Holy Spirit with his golden wings. It was money, wealth, given to him so that he would not perish on his journey, that he might provide himself with the necessary nourishment, in soul and body. It was a *gold* coin, and gold is the symbol of sovereignty, of the crown, of king and of God. Thus, the presentation of the *gold* coin promised him victory. Gold: the aim of the Alchemist, of the Scientist. He was not left without his reasoning and speculative faculties to help him on his way. *The Friend* tied the coin to his side: the Friend, the Spirit of Truth, the Comforter. The Spirit of life, of creativity, and, hence, the promise that the Angell (the talent) would prove fruitful. The Friend: the source of purification through fire and water: thus the suggestion that Herbert had reached a particular stage of sanctification. The Friend was with him and so his heart was open and tender. The Friend tied the good Angell *close to his side*.

The Friend did not place the golden coin within the heart, but where it had access to the heart: the side of Christ: the blood of Christ: through the action of the Holy Spirit, the Mystery of the Eucharist was made available to him for this last part of the journey. Whatever else might be taken from Herbert, before he faced the Judgment, he retained the possibility, through the working of the Spirit, of salvation in the redeeming blood of Christ. The blood could not actually be inserted, for Herbert dogmatically would not accept the direct objective reality of the Eucharist, but the *way* was open for the reception of the sacramental Mystery of reality. The side: the side of Christ: if his own talent were insufficient, the deficiency, the lack in himself, could yet be remedied by the ransom paid by Christ: and is not Friend a human as well as a divine word? Christ, Man, was with him on his journey, the journey which he, as Man, had also completed.

The Angell was tied to Herbert's side: attached, but not imposed. The personal freedom of choice remained, and with it, no assurance. The gold, the wealth of the Temple of Solomon, the wealth of the Roman Catholic Church, was only attached to his side. The wealth of the assurance must be within the fabric of the heart, not of the Church.

So, the mystical ascent of sanctification would indeed seem blessed. This is apparent in the one image. How then was it a failure? Or, more precisely, at what point did it cease to be valid? The implications of the final point of invalidity accompany each point of validity at each stage, until the climax is reached.

The Good Angell: good is good, but goodness can smell and taste and sound good, as did the Apple. Goodness can be a temptation. Reason in Man is good, but not if he uses it without the acknowledgment of its limitation, and turns to speculation and hope which bring him to an immanent impasse. *Gold* is rich, but gold is of the earth, and gold corrupts and rusts and turns to dust. It is the treasure of the world and must end in the world and with the world. The search for gold and the retaining of gold draws the soul down to earth, not raises it to heaven. As for the *gold crown:* kingship: is not that ambition? and pride of human autonomous sovereignty? And the gold of the Temple, and the wealth of the Church, are they not both signs of corruption and promise of decay? It was *one* Angell: *one* talent: does this not suggest the talent and the one penny, both of which emphasise that we can not estimate the value of anything which we do? Nor, can we anticipate the reward. As for *the Friend,* if he were human, then the presence of potential treachery, of the Judas kiss, must be acknowledged. The Angell was tied to the *side,* to his body, not within the innermost heart, and both the body and the means of tying, rope—string—thread—are all corruptible. Did the tying only seem good cable? So, the antithetical argument may emerge from this one image. What, then, could be the synthesis?

It might well be that the synthesis lies in the actual contradiction. The way is indeed possible, and must be attempted. But, even as the effort is made, even as it is attempted, the knowledge must always be actively present of the non-achievement and, with this, the unceasing repentance and prayer. The clue: the side: the blood of Christ. There is no direct access from the finite into the infinite, from temporal to eternal life. There must be the preliminary work but always there must finally be death: the spiritual death of oneself in the acknowledgment that the work must be done but is not to be valued, that the contradictory series of images is in fact no contradiction: and, in the actual physical death of the body of each one of us: but, death ever springing from the redeeming death of Christ: the death of death.

4. *The Incarnation: The Mother of God*

Example: To all Angels and Saints:
    Thou art the cabinet where the jewell lay.

a. *Analysis*

  i. Thou: 5(a), 5(b).
 ii. art: 2.
iii. the cabinet: 3(c).
     carpenter: 7.
     family: 7.
     lay: 7, 4.
 iv. jewel: 3(c).
     crown: 1, 7.
     thorns: 3(c).
     crucifixion: 1.
     gold: 3(c), 5(b).
     death: 2, 5(b).
     life: 5(a).

Eucharist: 7.
obedience (disobedience): 5(a).
Annunciation: 1.
wings: 3(d).
The Word: 4.

b. *Exposition*

Thou art the cabinet where the jewell lay.

This image must of necessity be taken in conjunction with the whole apologetic trend of the poem, that, however reluctantly, Herbert feels that he can not offer the Mother of God the veneration, which he would obviously wish to offer. It is clear that he loves her and the argument goes, as it were, backwards and forwards within his own conflict. Herbert recognises the goodness of the Mother of God, he sees her as the Virgin Mother of the real baby, who is true Man and true God, and, yet, he must withdraw from his inner urge to venerate her: he must, therefore, insist on her normal humanity and mortality, even as he knows that, real as she was, she is beyond the Saints, and she has passed into heaven without corruption.

The opening *Thou art* immediately identifies the Mother of God as a real person, no mythological idea of some symbol of creativity. *Thou art:* she *is* the Mother of God. But, the present tense reminds us of her finite status, and, thence, her normal mortality: but, if she is subject to time, then the present tense also implies the eternal life in which she already participates. She is *the cabinet,* that is, the container of the child to be born, *the cabinet* is the womb which has conceived without seed, for a jewel derives from gold, precious stone, not from a living plant or creature. Yet, a cabinet would be manufactured in wood, and, here, delicately, St. Joseph is brought into the story of the birth, the carpenter, who did not put away his wife when she conceived and brought forth a child of whom he was not the father. Yet, the suggestion of St. Joseph brings with it the implication of husband, wife, child, and, hence, again, a strong sense of the reality of the Incarnation: a real baby in a real family. The incomprehensible conception and birth preceded an infant, lying in its swaddling clothes. The baby *lay* in the womb, and in the manger, a tiny, living creature created by Himself: God in his uttermost self-limitation of Love.

The baby is a jewel: the most precious of all stones, the material for a crown, a king, and the King of kings. But, if a crown, then so too already the promise of the crown of thorns, the Passion and the Crucifixion of One who was Man and God. Gold is the sovereign remedy, as the alchemists knew, and so the jewel, as a baby, and on the Cross, is seen as the remedy of all mankind by his redeeming death. The cabinet of wood is already the Cross of wood, and when he lay within the cabinet, he was lying already in the tomb. But, as he was born out of the womb into finite life, so, too, he resurrected into finite life, and, with him, all human-kind into life Eternal.

The baby was Christ-God; thus, when the Wise Men brought him gold as one of their offerings, the precious jewel was offered himself: the first occasion of the offering of himself to himself in the body and the blood of the Eucharistic Offering. How, then, can Herbert manage to refrain from venerating the Mother of God? Yet, as he feels dogmatically bound to refrain, perhaps the image of the cabinet may be a reminder that she was only the vehicle of the birth of God, that, in herself, she can claim no particular veneration. And, as the cabinet was of wood, she, herself, as wood, would decay and become ashes. Herbert would not accept the doctrine of the Assumption. For him the Mother of God, as any other mortal, must await the Resurrection of the body. But, his love reveals itself again in this same image of wood. How could Herbert not see her, who carried the baby within herself, when he lay within the wood of her body, now standing at the foot of the Cross, when he hung on the wood of the Cross? Nor could Herbert ignore her part in the redemption of Man: in her unqualified obedience, a Virgin, she accepted the decree to become a mother and, in her obedience, counteracted the disobedience of the first mother. She made it possible for the descent into hell of her Son that the first mother might be redeemed.

The Mother of God conceived of the Holy Spirit, the Spirit of the golden wings, the Spirit of Truth, and the baby was the jewel: God-Man: Christ: the Word.

Two further examples are interesting in this connection:

i. *Ungratefulnesse:* Herbert writes of Man's ingratitude to God and refers to God's *two rare cabinets full of treasure:* in the one, *the Trinity,* in the other, *the Incarnation.* Here, the jewels, the Trinity and Christ, are directly connected with the ring made of precious stone in the bridal image of their betrothal with their own creation: thus, again, the Virginity of the Mother of God is emphasised, but, so too, her mortality.

2. *Whitsunday:* the prayer to the Holy Spirit, the sweet dove, to *spread thy golden wings in me* and thereby: *hatching my tender heart so long, Till it get wing, and flie away with thee. Hatching:*

the connotation of the process of a birth, and so, the delicate suggestion in image of the Mystery of the presence of Christ in our hearts, through the action of the Spirit, even as the Mystery of the physical presence of Christ in the womb of the Holy Mother of God.

iv. *Key-words*

The following list of words, only a few from amongst the many, may be of some use, in conjunction with their synonyms and derivatives, for further analysis of idea and image in Herbert's poetry:

affliction	friend	raise
ascent	fruit	rest
beauty	gain	revenge
bird	gift	rich
blood	glory	ring
box	gold	rock
bread	grace	sceptre
breast	groan	side
breath	harmony	silence
busy	health	spirit
cold	heart	stand
contract	high	star
cross	hill	stay
crown	hive	stone
dark	hope	stretch
dear	hour	sudden
death	idle	sun
descent	journey	sweet
door	joy	sword
drink	king	tear
dry	life	tender
earth	light	thorn
eat	measure	treasure
faith	mother	tree
fear	music	warm
fight	nest	water
fire	noise	weep
flat	poor	wind
flesh	power	work
flower	praise	wisdom
free	quick	

Diagram 1

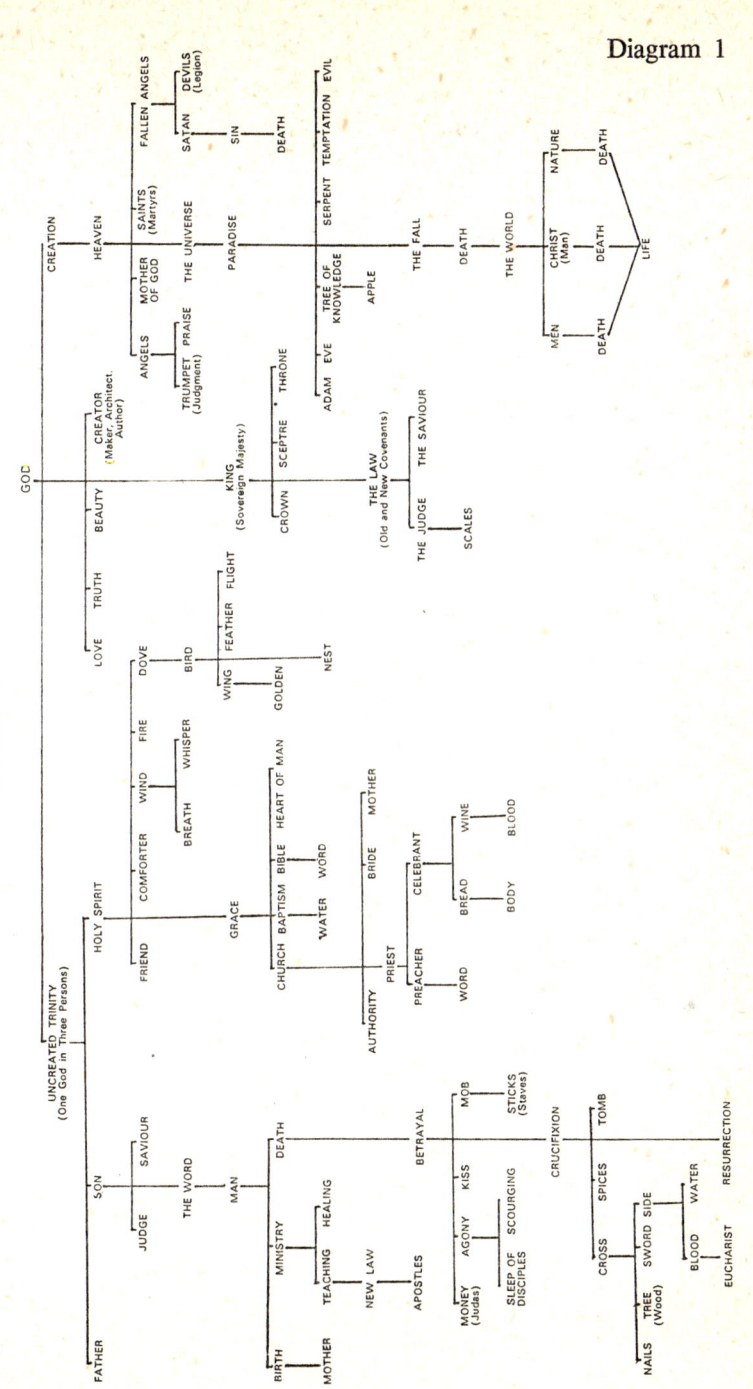

Diagram 2

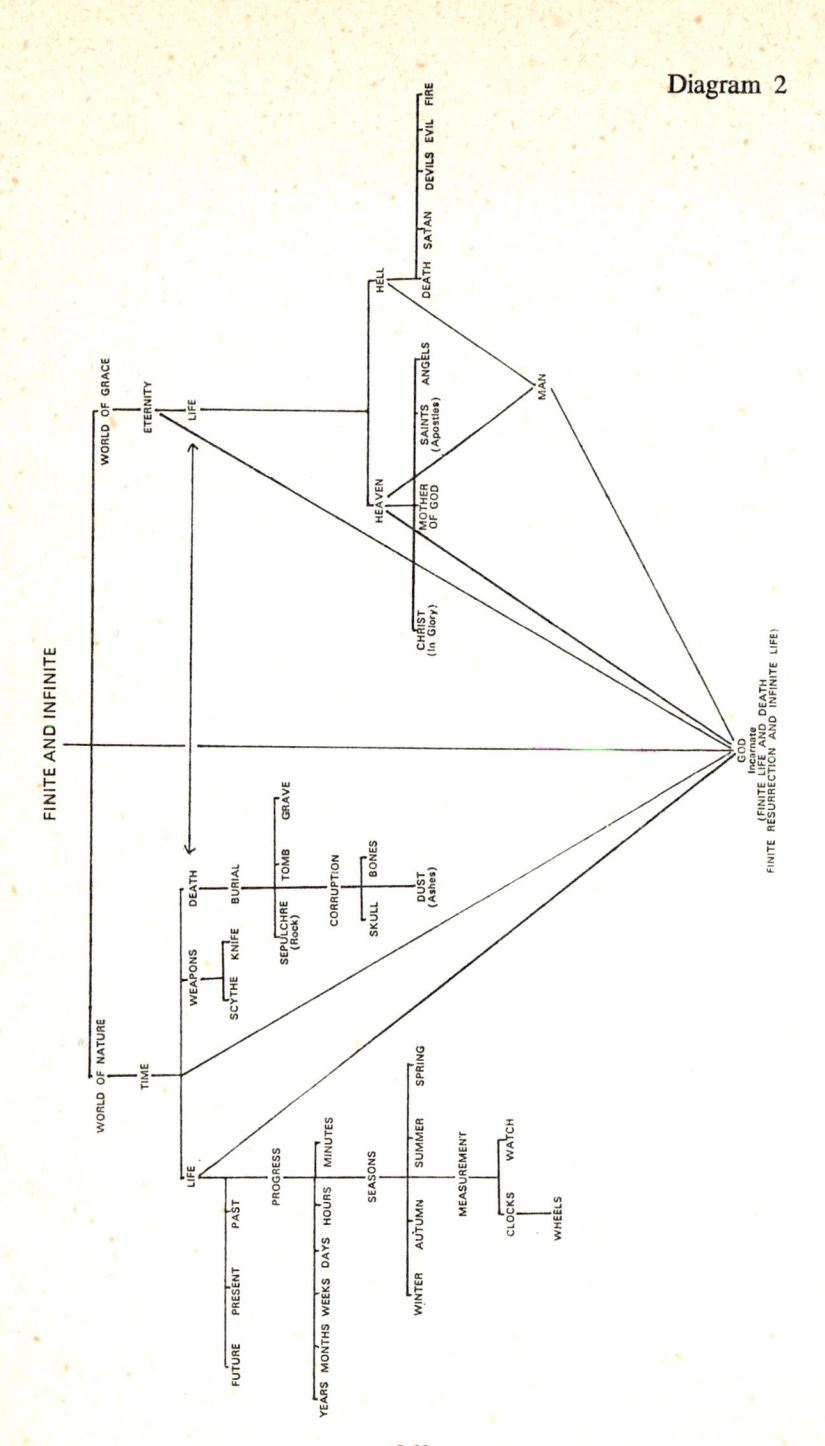

Diagram 3(a)

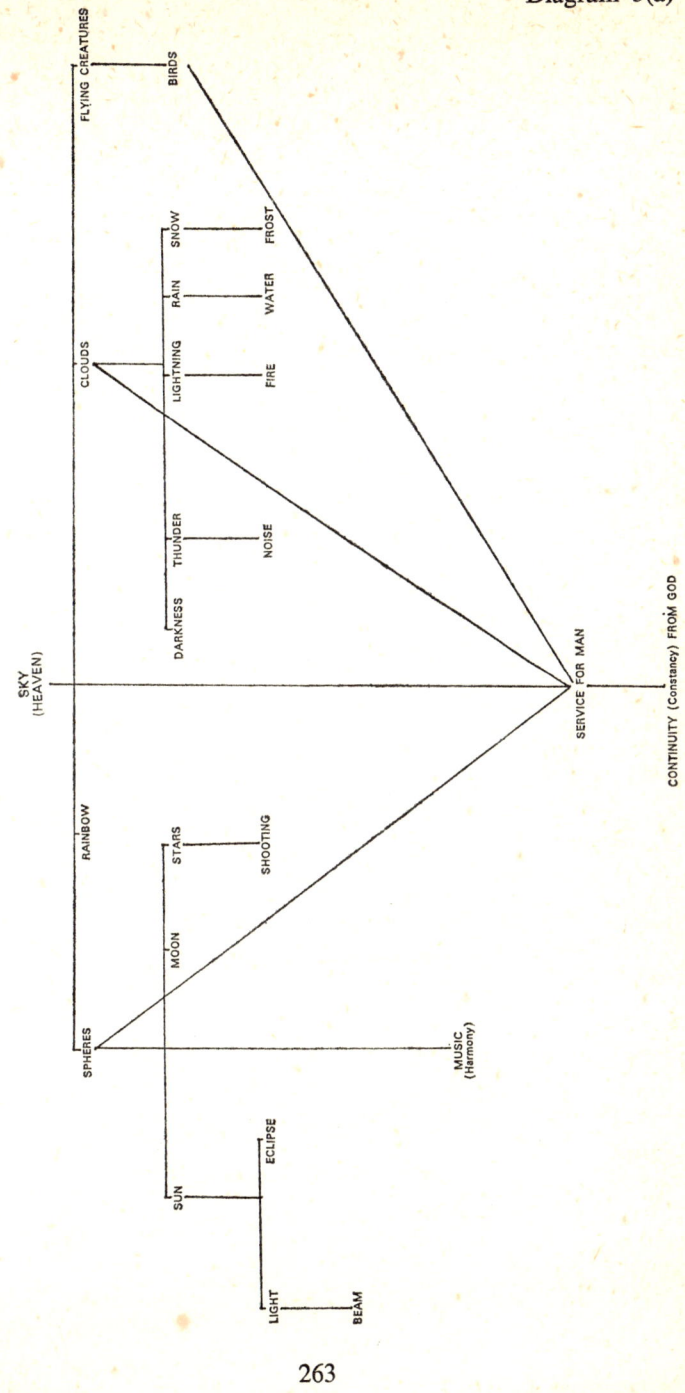

Diagram 3(b)

WORLD OF NATURE

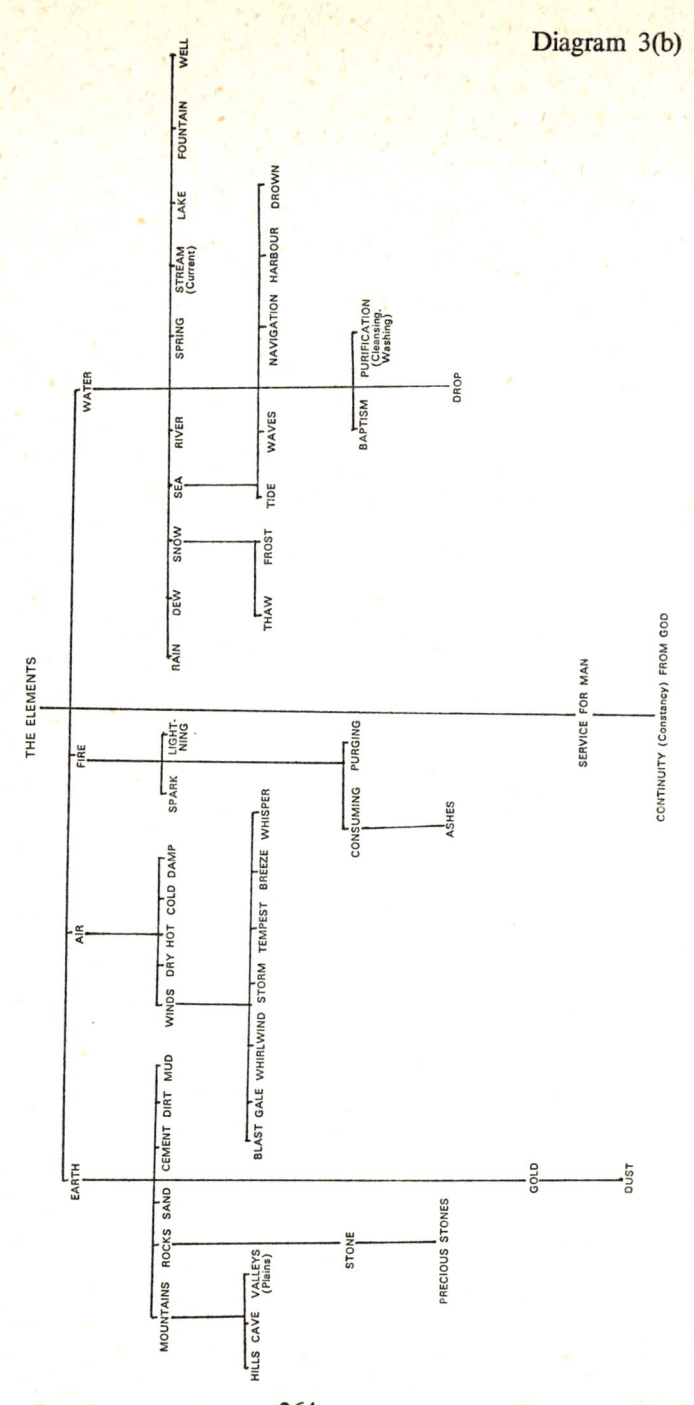

THE ELEMENTS

EARTH
- MOUNTAINS
  - HILLS
  - CAVE
  - VALLEYS (Plains)
- ROCKS
  - STONE
  - PRECIOUS STONES
- SAND
- CEMENT
- DIRT
- MUD
  - BLAST, GALE, WHIRLWIND, STORM, TEMPEST, BREEZE, WHISPER
- GOLD
- DUST

AIR
- WINDS
  - DRY, HOT, COLD, DAMP

FIRE
- SPARK
- LIGHTNING
- CONSUMING, PURGING
  - ASHES

WATER
- RAIN
- DEW
- SNOW
  - THAW
  - FROST
- SEA
  - TIDE
- RIVER
  - WAVES
- SPRING
- STREAM (Current)
- LAKE
- FOUNTAIN
- WELL
- NAVIGATION
- HARBOUR
- DROWN
- BAPTISM
- PURIFICATION (Cleansing, Washing)
  - DROP

SERVICE FOR MAN

CONTINUITY (Constancy) FROM GOD

Diagram 3(c)

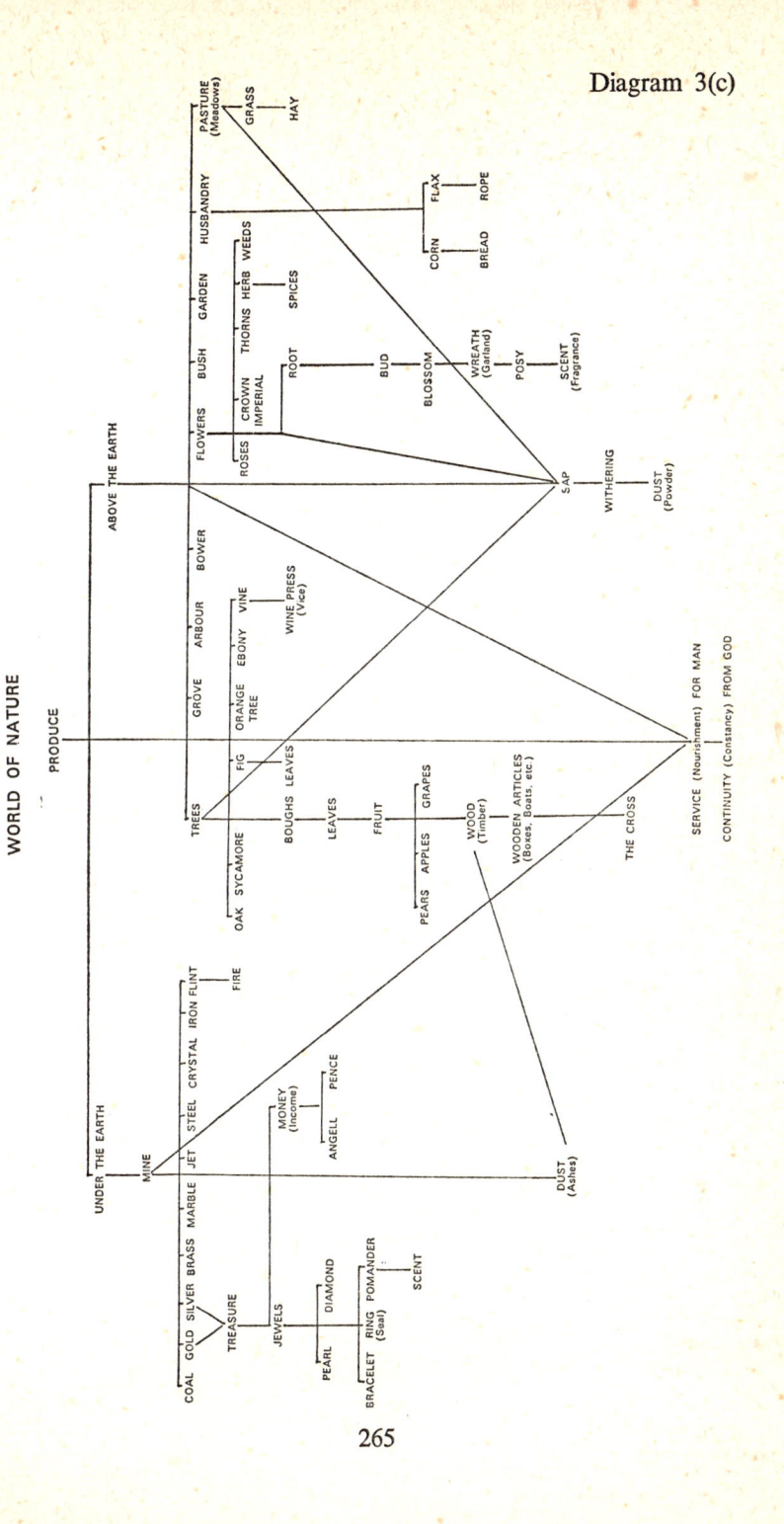

Diagram 3(d)

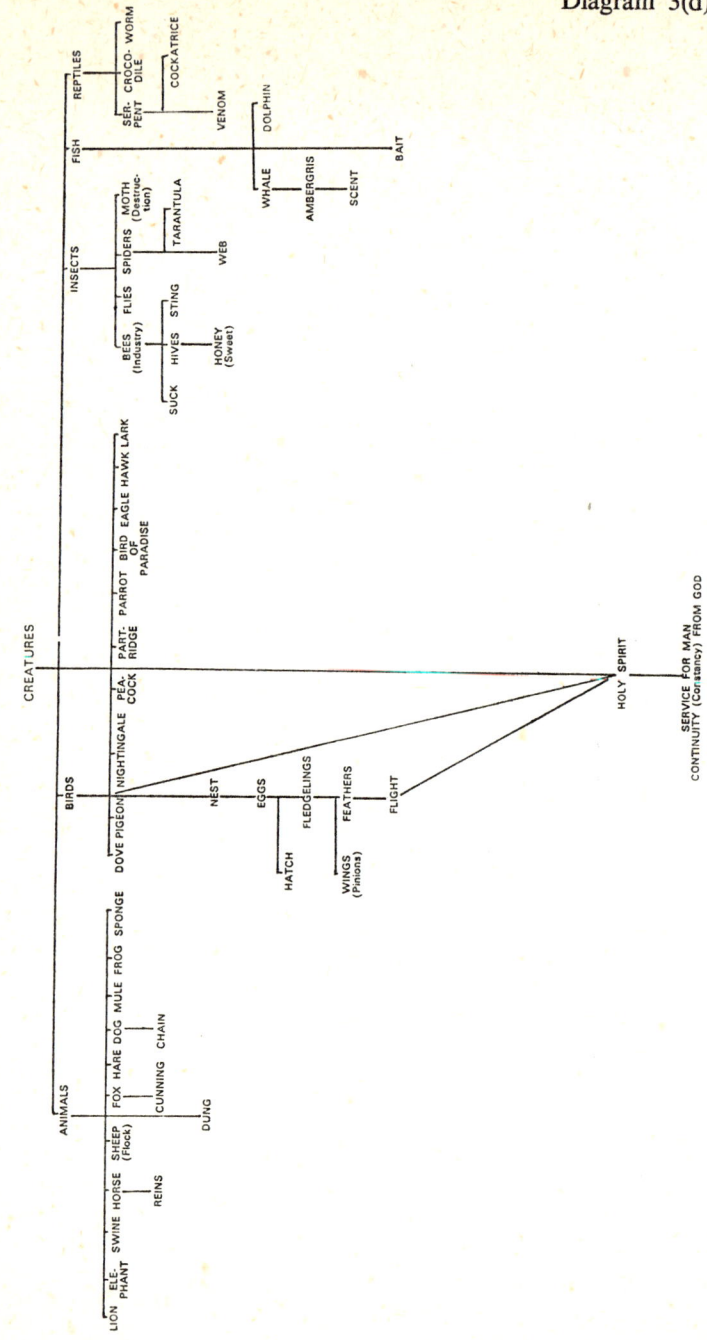

WORLD OF NATURE

- CREATURES
  - ANIMALS
    - LION, ELEPHANT, SWINE, HORSE, SHEEP (Flock)
      - REINS
    - FOX, HARE, DOG, MULE, FROG, SPONGE
      - CUNNING — CHAIN
      - DUNG
  - BIRDS
    - DOVE, PIGEON, NIGHTINGALE, PEACOCK, PARTRIDGE, PARROT, BIRD OF PARADISE, EAGLE, HAWK, LARK
      - NEST
      - EGGS
        - HATCH — FLEDGELINGS
      - FEATHERS
        - WINGS (Pinions)
      - FLIGHT
  - INSECTS
    - BEES (Industry), FLIES, SPIDERS, MOTH (Destruction)
      - SUCK
      - HIVES — STING
        - HONEY (Sweet)
      - TARANTULA
        - WEB
  - FISH
    - DOLPHIN, WHALE
      - AMBERGRIS
        - SCENT
      - BAIT
  - REPTILES
    - SERPENT, CROCODILE, WORM
      - COCKATRICE
        - VENOM

HOLY SPIRIT

SERVICE FOR MAN
CONTINUITY (Constancy) FROM GOD

Diagram 4

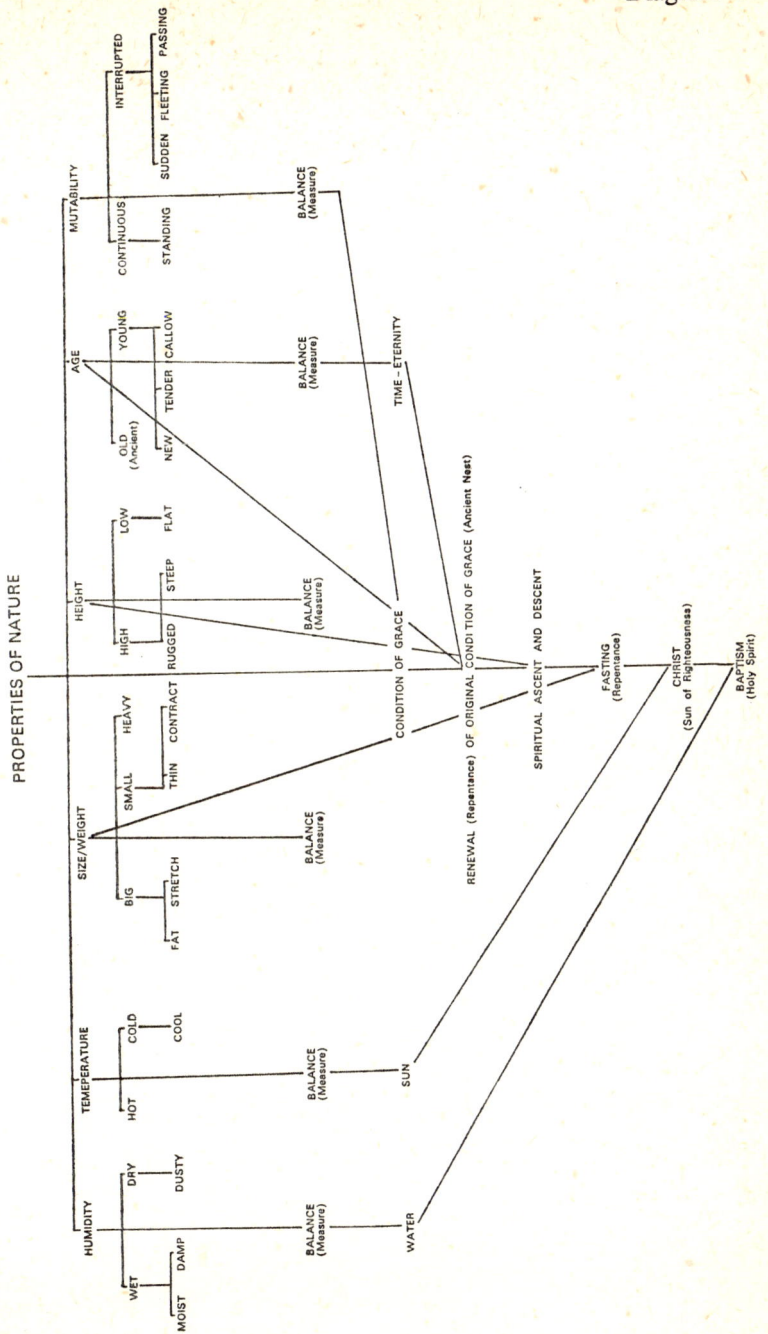

Diagram 4 (continued)

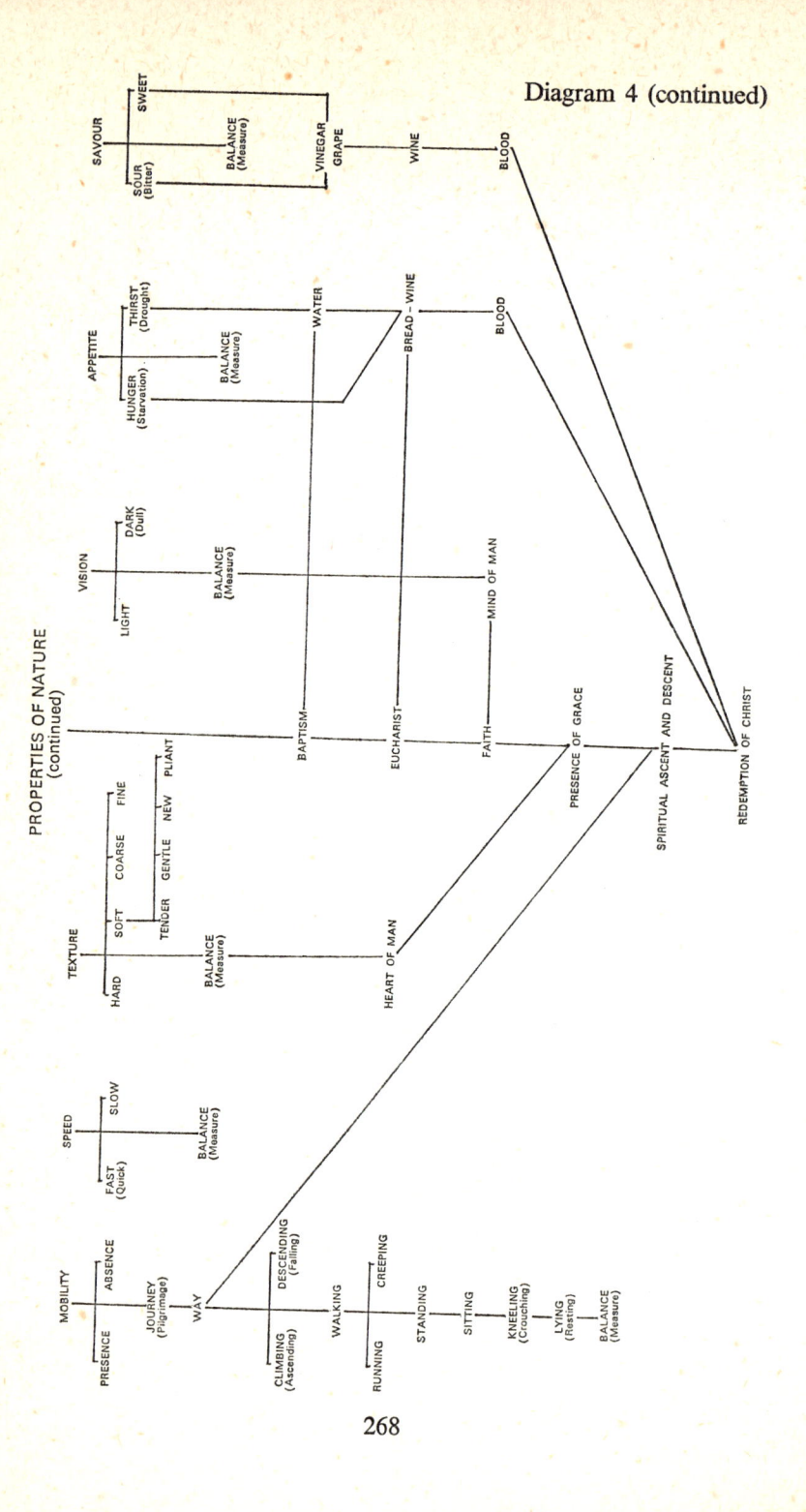

Diagram 4 (continued)

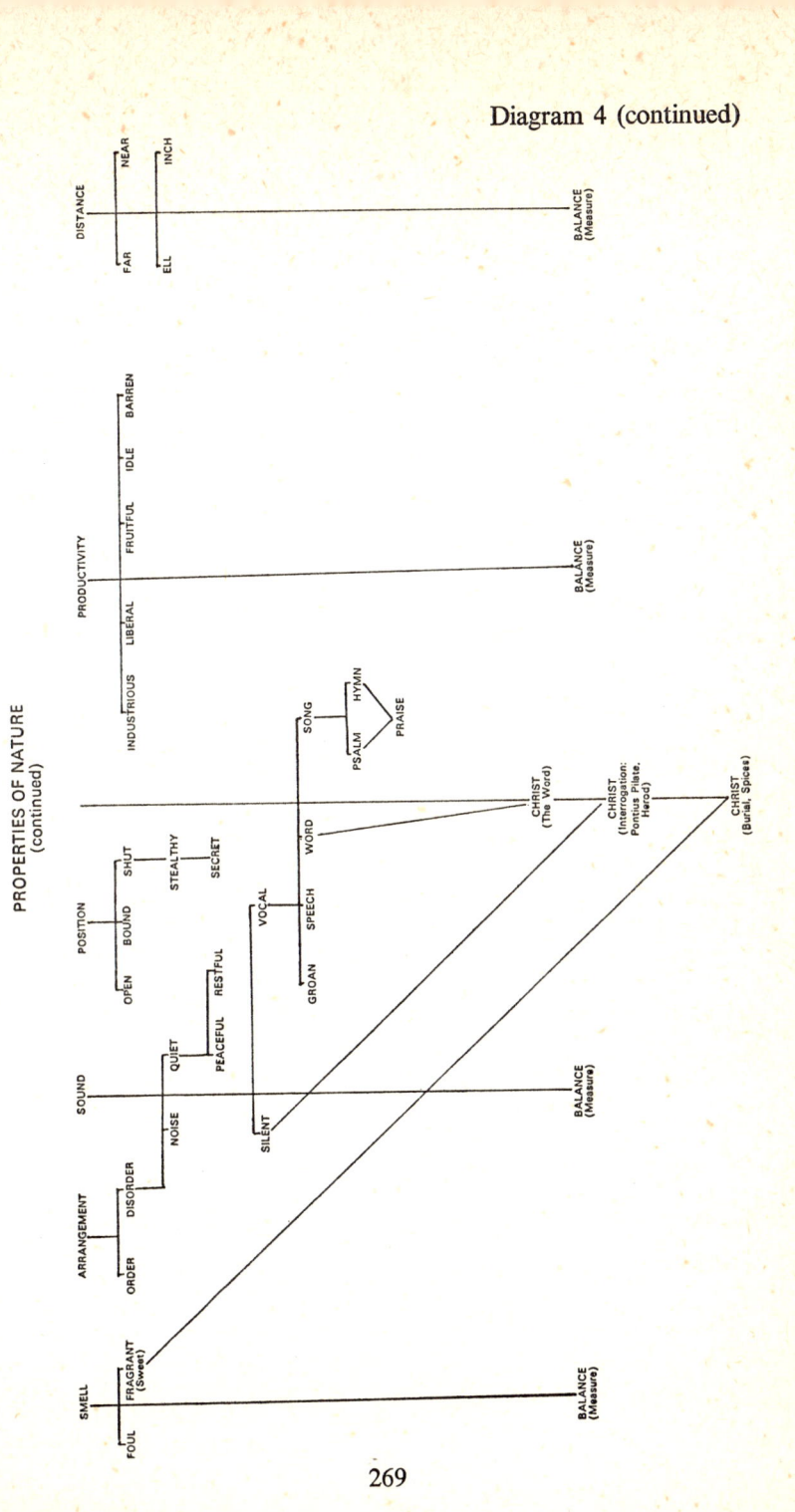

PROPERTIES OF NATURE
(continued)

- SMELL
  - FOUL
  - FRAGRANT (Sweet)
  → BALANCE (Measure)

- ARRANGEMENT
  - ORDER
  - DISORDER

- SOUND
  - NOISE
  - QUIET
    - PEACEFUL
    - RESTFUL
  - SILENT
  → BALANCE (Measure)

- POSITION
  - OPEN
  - BOUND
  - SHUT
    - STEALTHY
    - SECRET

- SPEECH
  - GROAN
  - VOCAL
    - WORD
    - SONG
      - PSALM
      - HYMN
      - PRAISE

- CHRIST (The Word)
- CHRIST (Interrogation: Pontius Pilate, Herod)
- CHRIST (Burial, Spices)

- PRODUCTIVITY
  - INDUSTRIOUS
  - LIBERAL
  - FRUITFUL
  - IDLE
  - BARREN
  → BALANCE (Measure)

- DISTANCE
  - FAR
  - NEAR
  - ELL
  - INCH
  → BALANCE (Measure)

269

Diagram 5(a)

CONSTITUTION OF MAN
SOUL
THE HEART
SOFT (Tender)
HARD (Callous)
PRESENCE OF SPIRIT (Grace)
ABSENCE OF SPIRIT (Grace)
CREATIVITY
GRIEF
TEARS
GROANS (Sighs)
LOVE
TRUST
BEAUTY
JOY
PEACE
REPENTANCE
ENMITY
NON-CREATIVITY
GRIEF (Sorrow)
TEARS
GROANS (Sighs)
SEAT OF CONFLICT
GOD (SPIRIT - GRACE)
SATAN (SIN - DEATH)
RESOLUTION OF CONFLICT (Harmony) (Christ conquers Satan, Sin, Death)
PRAYER (Praise)
LIFE
LOVE (For God)
APOSTLES (Disciples)
SAINTS
MOTHER OF GOD
VIRTUES (Love, Goodness)
REPENTANCE (Confession)
GRIEF
GROANS
TEARS
LAMENT (Pine)
GRATITUDE
CHASTITY
MEEKNESS
HOLINESS
JUSTICE
TEMPERANCE
LOYALTY
DUTY
OBEDIENCE
CONSTANCY
PATIENCE
CHARITY
LIFE
DAY OF JUDGMENT (CHRIST: JUDGE AND SAVIOUR)
ETERNAL LIFE
THE MIND
TRUTH
FOOLISHNESS
WISDOM
REASON
MIRTH
JEST
VANITY
CREATIVITY
POETRY
MUSIC
ART
CONSCIENCE
SCIENCE
DISPUTATION
WIT
HOPE
LIFE AND DEATH
SATAN
SIN (Evil, Enmity)
OBDURANCE
DISOBEDIENCE
INGRATITUDE
AVARICE
LUST
PRIDE
DISSENT
MURDER
THEFT
TREACHERY
COWARDICE
MADNESS
DEATH
DECAY
DUST

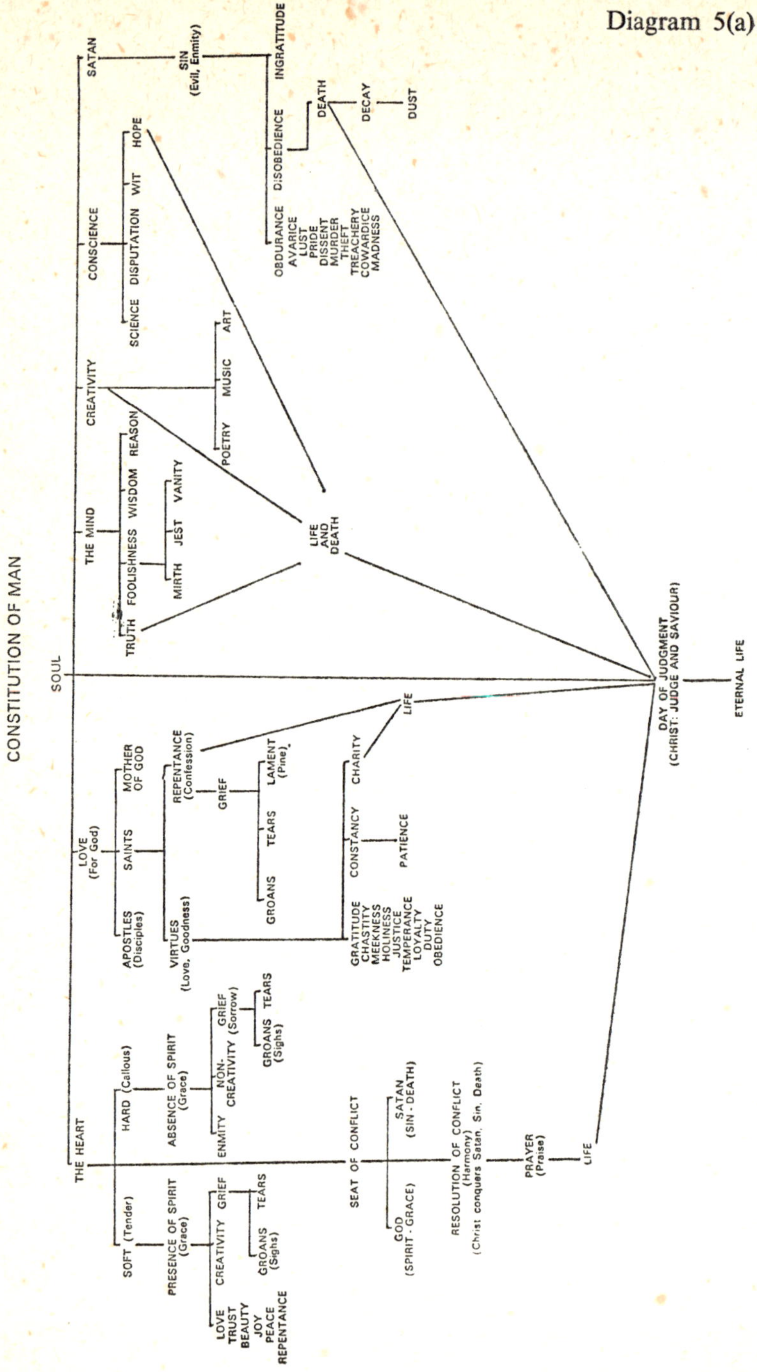

Diagram 5(b)

CONSTITUTION OF MAN

BODY
├── PHYSICAL (Earth, Clay)
│   ├── LIFE (Living, Quick)
│   │   ├── FLESH (Skin) — SWEAT
│   │   ├── BONES
│   │   ├── SINEWS — BROKEN (Fractured)
│   │   ├── JOINTS
│   │   ├── MEMBERS
│   │   │   ├── HAIR
│   │   │   ├── FACE
│   │   │   ├── HEAD — BEAUTY / DECAY
│   │   │   │   ├── FOREHEAD — FROWN
│   │   │   │   ├── EYES — SIGHT / TEARS / BLINDNESS
│   │   │   │   ├── EARS
│   │   │   │   ├── NOSE — SMELL
│   │   │   │   └── MOUTH (Lips)
│   │   │   │   ├── TONGUE
│   │   │   │   ├── TOOTH
│   │   │   │   └── KISS
│   │   │   ├── NECK — COLLAR
│   │   │   ├── SHOULDERS
│   │   │   ├── BACK
│   │   │   ├── BREAST — HEART
│   │   │   ├── SIDE
│   │   │   ├── STOMACH — DIGESTION
│   │   │   ├── ARMS — GALL
│   │   │   │   └── HANDS / FINGERS / NAILS — WRITE / STRIKE
│   │   │   ├── LEGS
│   │   │   └── KNEES
│   │   ├── BLOOD — STREAM / DROP
│   │   └── (Speech/Word branch)
│   │   ├── SPEECH
│   │   │   ├── ACCUSATION
│   │   │   ├── DEFENCE
│   │   │   ├── PRAISE
│   │   │   ├── INSULT
│   │   │   ├── OATHS
│   │   │   ├── PETITION
│   │   │   ├── PRAYER
│   │   │   ├── PREACHING
│   │   │   ├── QUARREL
│   │   │   ├── GROANS (Signs)
│   │   │   ├── JEST
│   │   │   └── SONG
│   │   ├── SILENCE
│   │   └── WORD
│   └── DEATH
│   ├── SKULL
│   ├── SKELETON
│   └── CORRUPTION (Decay) — DUST
└── IN EXPERIENCE
    ├── DANGER
    ├── SLEEP
    ├── GLUTTONY — NOURISHMENT
    ├── HUNGER — STARVATION
    ├── THIRST
    ├── ABSTINENCE — FASTING
    ├── DIRT
    ├── CLEANLINESS
    ├── WEARINESS
    ├── HEALTH
    └── SICKNESS
        ├── BLISTER
        ├── POISON
        ├── FEVER
        ├── AGUE
        ├── PLAGUE
        ├── RHEUM
        ├── PAIN
        ├── WOUNDS
        ├── FRACTURE
        ├── BRUISE
        └── PHYSICIAN
            └── MEDICINE (Physic)
                ├── PURGE
                ├── PLASTER
                ├── BALM
                ├── BALSAM
                ├── SALVE
                ├── OINTMENT
                ├── CORDIAL
                ├── PILL
                └── POTION

INCARNATE CHRIST (Body of Man through God-Man both in World of Grace and World of Nature)

CHRIST (The Word)

DEATH → RESURRECTION OF THE BODY OF MAN (Through God-Man)

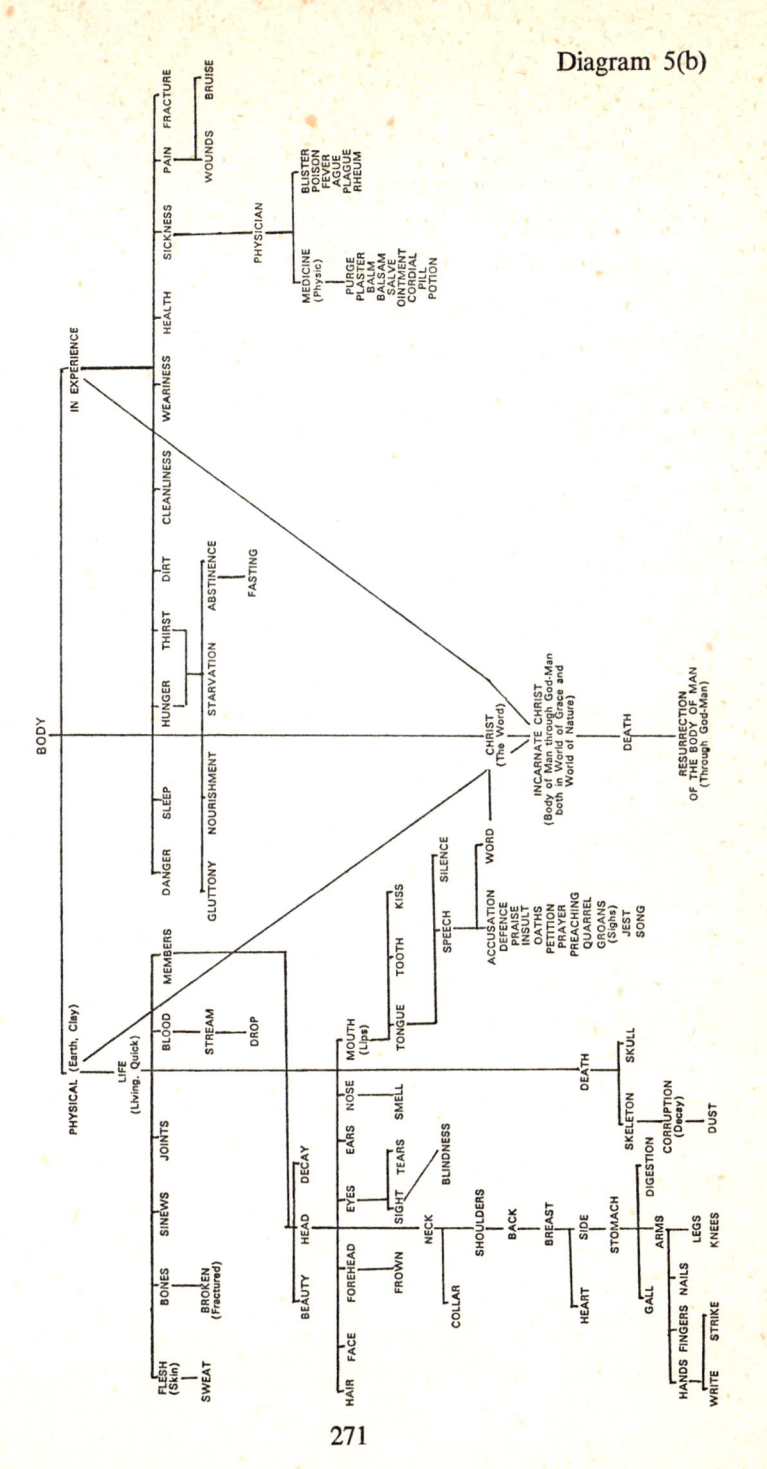

Diagram 6

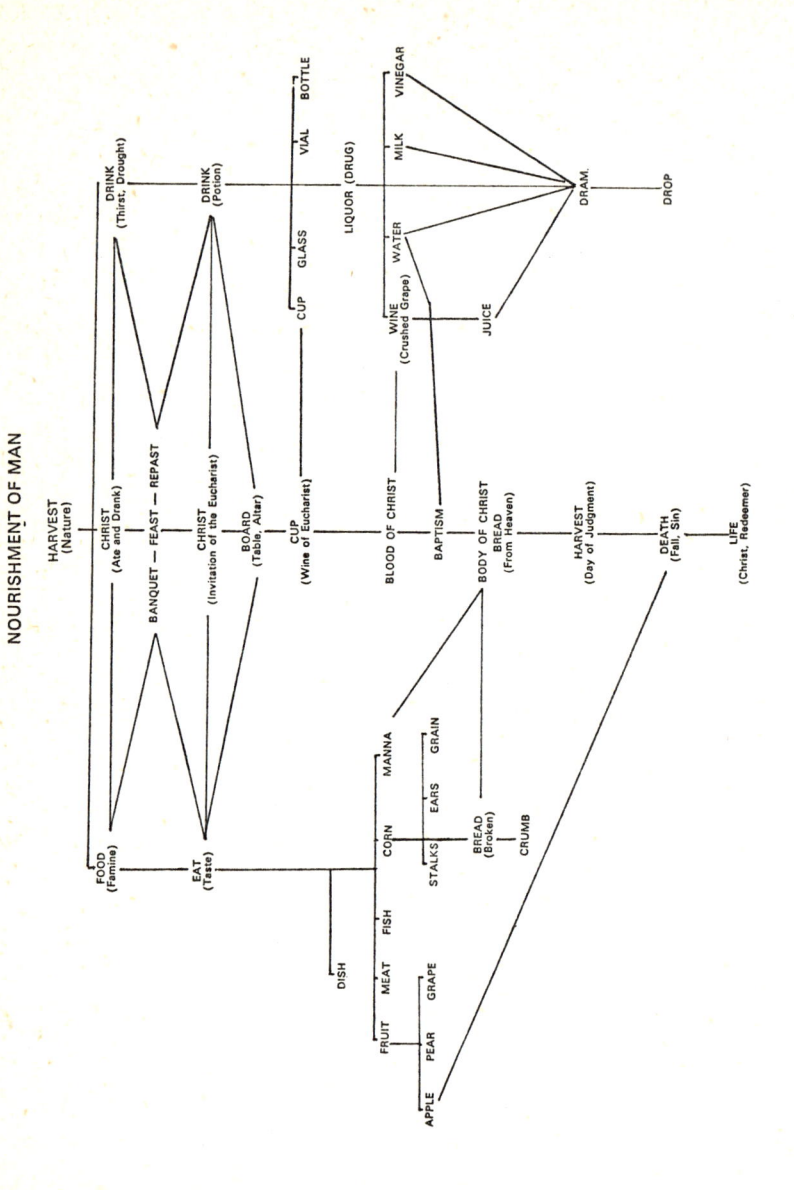

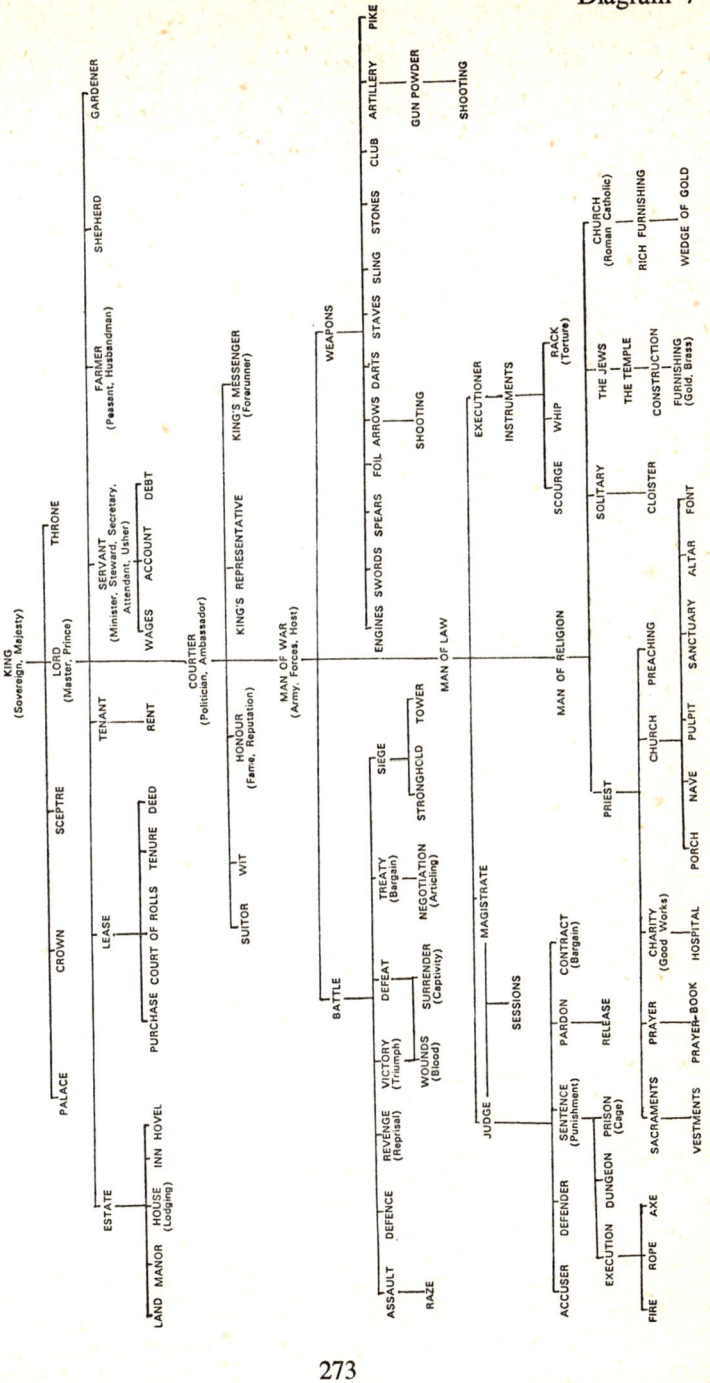

Diagram 7

MAN: RANK AND ACTIVITY

- **KING** (Sovereign, Majesty)
  - **LORD** (Master, Prince)
    - ESTATE
      - LAND
      - MANOR
      - HOUSE (Lodging)
      - INN
      - HOVEL
    - PALACE
    - CROWN
    - SCEPTRE
      - LEASE
      - PURCHASE
      - COURT OF ROLLS
      - TENURE
      - DEED
    - THRONE
    - TENANT
      - RENT
  - **SERVANT** (Minister, Steward, Secretary, Attendant, Usher)
    - WAGES
    - ACCOUNT
    - DEBT
  - **COURTIER** (Politician, Ambassador)
    - HONOUR (Fame, Reputation)
      - SUITOR
      - WIT
    - KING'S MESSENGER (Forerunner)
  - **FARMER** (Peasant, Husbandman)
  - **SHEPHERD**
  - **GARDENER**

- **KING'S REPRESENTATIVE**
  - **MAN OF WAR** (Army, Forces, Host)
    - BATTLE
      - ASSAULT
        - RAZE
      - DEFENCE
      - REVENGE (Reprisal)
      - VICTORY (Triumph)
        - WOUNDS (Blood)
      - DEFEAT
      - SURRENDER (Captivity)
      - TREATY (Bargain)
      - NEGOTIATION (Arbiting)
      - SIEGE
        - STRONGHOLD
        - TOWER
    - WEAPONS
      - ENGINES
      - SWORDS
      - SPEARS
      - FOIL
      - ARROWS
      - DARTS
        - SHOOTING
      - STAVES
      - SLING
      - STONES
      - CLUB
      - ARTILLERY
        - GUN POWDER
          - SHOOTING
      - PIKE

  - **MAN OF LAW**
    - JUDGE
    - MAGISTRATE
      - SESSIONS
    - ACCUSER
    - DEFENDER
      - SENTENCE (Punishment)
        - PRISON (Cage)
          - DUNGEON
          - EXECUTION
            - FIRE
            - ROPE
            - AXE
      - PARDON
        - RELEASE
      - CONTRACT (Bargain)
    - EXECUTIONER
      - INSTRUMENTS
        - SCOURGE
        - WHIP
        - RACK (Torture)

  - **MAN OF RELIGION**
    - PRIEST
      - SOLITARY
      - CLOISTER
      - CHURCH
        - PORCH
        - NAVE
        - PULPIT
        - SANCTUARY
        - ALTAR
        - FONT
      - PREACHING
        - PRAYER
          - PRAYER-BOOK
        - CHARITY (Good Works)
          - HOSPITAL
        - SACRAMENTS
          - VESTMENTS
    - CHURCH (Roman Catholic)
      - THE JEWS
      - THE TEMPLE
        - CONSTRUCTION
        - FURNISHING (Gold, Brass)
      - RICH FURNISHING
        - WEDGE OF GOLD

273

S

Diagram 7 (continued)

MAN: RANK AND ACTIVITY

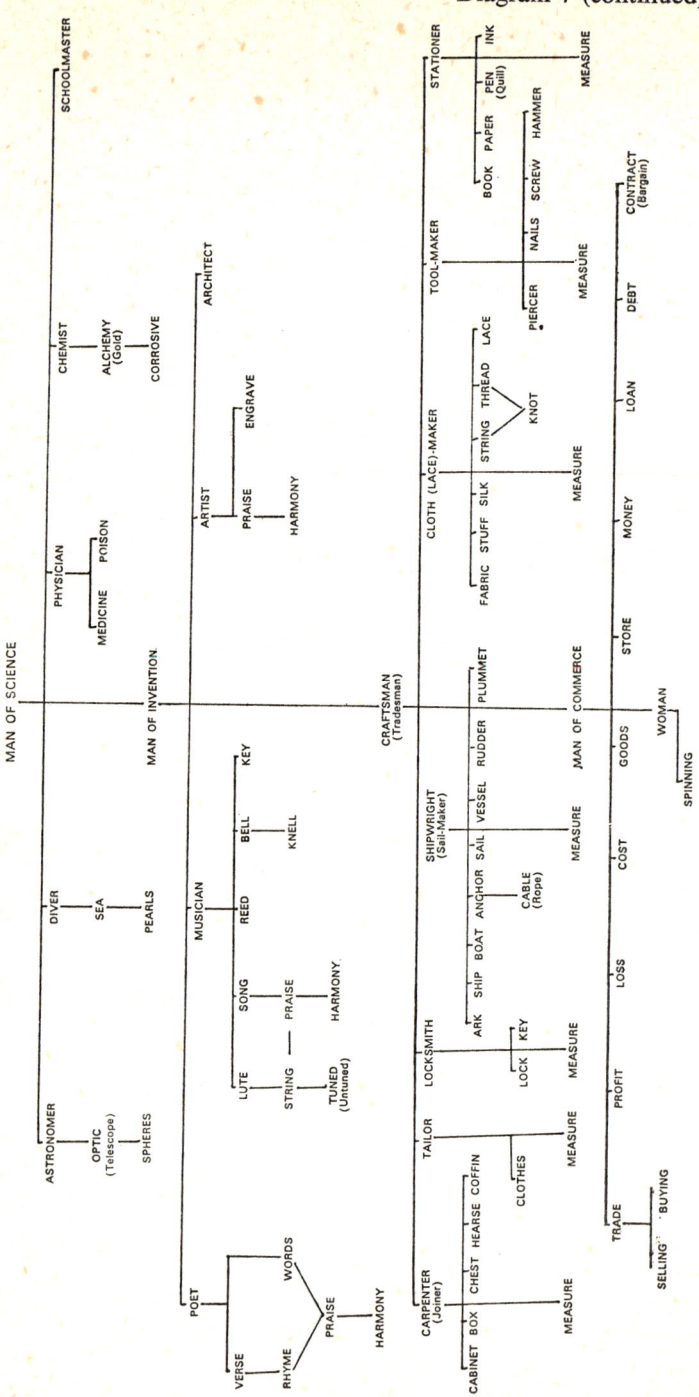

- ASTRONOMER
  - OPTIC (Telescope)
    - SPHERES
- POET
  - VERSE
  - RHYME
    - WORDS
  - PRAISE
  - HARMONY
- MAN OF SCIENCE
  - DIVER
    - SEA
    - PEARLS
  - MUSICIAN
    - LUTE
      - STRING — PRAISE
      - TUNED (Untuned) — HARMONY
    - SONG
    - REED
    - BELL
      - KNELL
    - KEY
  - PHYSICIAN
    - MEDICINE
    - POISON
  - CHEMIST
    - ALCHEMY (Gold)
    - CORROSIVE
  - SCHOOLMASTER
- MAN OF INVENTION
  - ARTIST
    - PRAISE
    - HARMONY
  - ENGRAVE
  - ARCHITECT
- CRAFTSMAN (Tradesman)
  - CARPENTER (Joiner)
    - CABINET BOX
    - CHEST HEARSE COFFIN
    - CLOTHES
    - MEASURE
  - TAILOR
    - CLOTHES
    - MEASURE
  - LOCKSMITH
    - ARK SHIP BOAT ANCHOR
    - LOCK KEY
    - MEASURE
  - SHIPWRIGHT (Sail-Maker)
    - SAIL VESSEL RUDDER PLUMMET
    - CABLE (Rope)
    - MEASURE
  - ARTIST
    - FABRIC STUFF SILK
  - CLOTH (LACE)-MAKER
    - STRING THREAD LACE
    - KNOT
    - MEASURE
  - TOOL-MAKER
    - PIERCER NAILS SCREW HAMMER
    - MEASURE
  - STATIONER
    - BOOK PAPER PEN (Quill) INK
    - MEASURE
- MAN OF COMMERCE
  - TRADE
    - SELLING
    - BUYING
  - PROFIT
  - LOSS
  - COST
  - GOODS
  - STORE
  - MONEY
  - LOAN
  - DEBT
  - CONTRACT (Bargain)
- WOMAN
  - SPINNING

Diagram 7 (continued)

MAN: RANK AND ACTIVITY

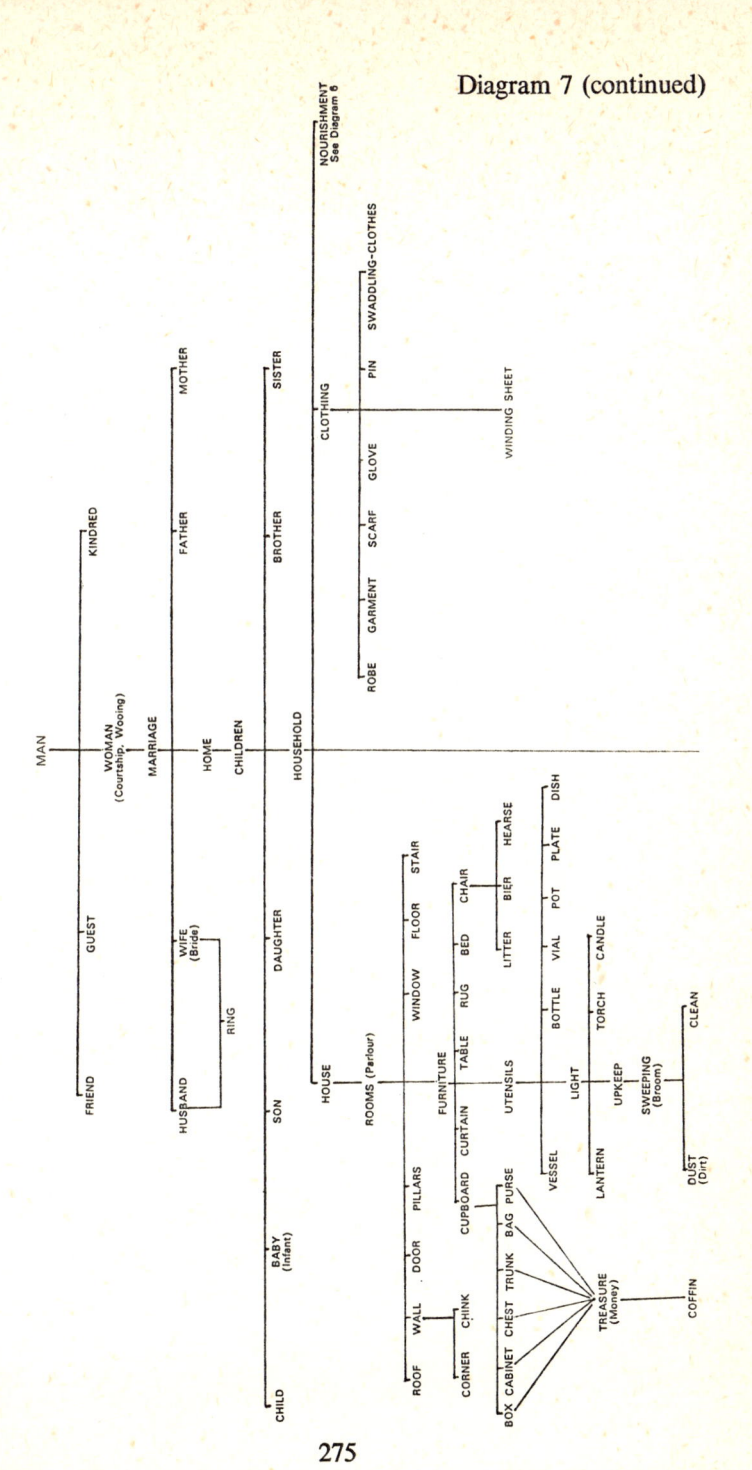

- MAN
  - WOMAN (Courtship, Wooing)
    - FRIEND
    - GUEST
    - KINDRED
  - MARRIAGE
    - HUSBAND
      - RING
    - WIFE (Bride)
  - HOME
    - FATHER
    - MOTHER
  - CHILDREN
    - CHILD
    - BABY (Infant)
    - SON
    - DAUGHTER
  - HOUSEHOLD
    - BROTHER
    - SISTER
    - CLOTHING
      - ROBE
      - GARMENT
      - SCARF
      - GLOVE
      - PIN
      - SWADDLING-CLOTHES
      - WINDING SHEET
    - NOURISHMENT (See Diagram 8)
    - HOUSE
      - ROOMS (Parlour)
        - WINDOW
        - FLOOR
        - STAIR
      - FURNITURE
        - TABLE
        - RUG
        - BED
        - CHAIR
        - LITTER
        - BIER
        - HEARSE
      - UTENSILS
        - CURTAIN
        - CUPBOARD
        - BAG
        - PURSE
        - BOTTLE
        - VIAL
        - POT
        - PLATE
        - DISH
      - LIGHT
        - VESSEL
        - LANTERN
        - TORCH
        - CANDLE
      - UPKEEP
        - SWEEPING (Broom)
          - DUST (Dirt)
          - CLEAN
    - ROOF
      - WALL
      - DOOR
      - PILLARS
      - CHINK
      - CORNER
    - BOX, CABINET, CHEST, TRUNK
    - TREASURE (Money)
      - COFFIN

CONCLUSION

A Note on the place of Literature in understanding between the Churches

I began this present exploration of Herbert's poetry with some misgivings and prejudice. I could hardly accept the possibility that the doctrinal differences, particularly where the realism of the Faith is concerned, between the Anglican and Orthodox Churches, would resolve themselves sufficiently to enable me to give the full and loving respect to Herbert's thoughts, without which it would not be possible to write. For a long time, I wasted my efforts in seeking some kind of compromise, some theological resolution. Of course, this proved nonsense; doctrine and dogma, as long as they remain doctrine and dogma, can not be resolved, if they could, they would cease to be doctrine and dogma. I found that efforts at such resolution, however tentative and personal, engendered irritation if not antipathy, a kind of hardening of the theological arteries as the differences, one by one, became more static and sharp in discussion. As far as I was concerned, and I could see no reason why some others might not be affected in the same way, I could only see, as a result of private theological discussion with a view to friendship, the contrary resulting in fact: either some kind of patronising toleration on both sides, or somewhere a mutual effort at conversion. This was distasteful. How, then, as Christians, can we make some kind of united front in the face of militant atheism? Reading Herbert, I wondered if we were not wasting our time, and worse, by talking theology at each other. Was there not another way? Did not, for example, most English people gain their impression of Russia from Dostoievsky, Tolstoy, and Chekhov? And did not Russians of Pre-Revolution times see England in Dickens?

It seems to me that we are far more likely to meet each other and love each other as Christians if we could only manage to live within each other's daily spirituality and whole attitude of life rather than float about on dogma. This is what I have found in diving deeply into Herbert's poetry. I have discovered a treasury of common Christian ground wholly unrelated to doctrine and, in the last count, hardly obscured by the few doctrinal assertions. When we leave doctrine and enter the field of *the heart* and of *the mind* of each other, then we can indeed become friends. And, where else but in Literature can we make friends with people either dead or not in our particular circle of acquaintance? So, I suggest that, in Literature, as in personal contact, we can still find strong, healthy and enduring ties of a common Christianity, which is so natural and instinctive, that it, rarely, if ever, becomes evident in explicit inter-Church discussion where the emphasis inevitably must lie on differences.

The study of Literature, however secular, still remains the most true passport to the greatest minds and spirits of the national culture and religion, and I am convinced that Literature may yet prove at least one source for a refreshing stream of true affinity between the divided Christian Churches, provided of course that it is real literature and not religious propaganda masquerading as such. I would suggest that it should not be forgotten that the divisions of the Churches, and I am speaking here particularly of the East and the West, derive as much from cultural as religious tradition, and, thus, again, the study of Literature reveals the customs and character of the people, and opens the door to warmth and to friendship.

THE ESSAY

GEORGE HERBERT: ASPECTS OF HIS THEOLOGY

Mother Maria

Herbert was musician, poet, and thinker. Beneath the weight of thought, his delicate health, again and again, threatened to break:

> . . . for he had a body apt to consumption, and to fevers, and other infirmities, which he judged were increased by his studies: for he would often say, "He had too thoughtful a wit; a wit like a penknife in too narrow a sheath, too sharp for his body."
> (Walton, *The Life of George Herbert*)

One theme pervades his whole work, in thousand-fold variations. It is the consciousness that this world stands in opposition to the world of grace, that the will of man stands opposed to the Will of God, and together with this consciousness, comes the incessant striving after unity. Harmony lies only in harmony with the world of God, and this harmony is the health of the soul.

In the harmony, we attain to perfect freedom and know the work of our life as unceasing praise:

> . . . *Mark the end.* (of purification)
> . . .
> *All did but strive to mend, what you had marr'd.*
> *Wherefore be cheer'd, and praise him to the full*
> *Each day, each houre, each moment of the week,*
> *Who fain would have you be new, tender, quick.*
> (*Love unknown*)

Herbert himself, characterised the movement of the poems as a progression from conflict to conflict between his soul and God, until, in the end, in the submission of his will, he attained to perfect freedom.

Shortly before his death, Herbert sent *The Temple* to Nicholas Ferrar and, with it, the following message:

> ... tell him he shall find in it a picture of the many spiritual conflicts that have passed betwixt God and my soul, before I could subject mine to the will of Jesus my Master: in whose service I have now found perfect freedom ...
>
> (Walton, *Life of George Herbert*)

There might, therefore, seem some justification in seeking a line of development in the sense of the mystical ascent. The mystic reveals himself, at the most convincing, where the shortest distance of inadequacy is felt as the widest separation from God, where the entering into the Will of God is in great measure, and, thereby, laborious. Repentance grows with sanctification, and the pain of abandonment in the measure of becoming one.

But, the scheme of mystical ascent, purification, illumination, the night of the soul, union, for Herbert is inadequate; to explain the apparently missing steps by his not having attained to union is equally unsatisfactory, for he, himself, on his deathbed, bears other witness: perfect freedom. Herbert died in the assurance of having reached the goal.

The reason for the inadequacy of applying any scheme of mystical ascent to Herbert should, therefore, rather be sought in his theological suppositions. And, I was repeatedly struck in the poems by the realisation of a rift or cleavage.

The rift, and the overcoming of the rift, are, in all the poems, discernible as being somehow present at one and the same time; they come in most delicate variations, and, often, only to be caught within the key. For Herbert, purification, the step by step progression towards the goal of sanctification, is inextricably linked and not unrelated to the unforeseeable irruption of the Divine presence into the immanent, of the experience ever anew and ever outside man's grasp, of the vertical descent of eternity into the *now*. In this experience of the *now*, there can be no progression of time and, therefore, purification, as a way, may almost lose its significance. The cry for the *now* to remain is the never-ceasing cry of agony in Herbert:

> But keep a standing Majestie in me.
> (*The Temper* (II))

> Thy life is Gods, thy time to come is gone,
>   And is his right.
> He is thy night at noon: he is at night
>   Thy noon alone.
> (*The Discharge*)

The Essay

The imputation of the righteousness of Christ as the outward or forensic justification of the soul and the inner grace, which guides and leads the soul in the daily work of progressive sanctification, stood vis-à-vis, the two uttermost poles of Catholic and Protestant theology. These two poles Hooker had recognised, picked up and integrated into the foundation of Anglican theology, the *via media,* and his writings allow no glimpse of the personal agony which might have gone into this resolution. Andrewes, again, did the same, the conflict in him raised into the supreme work of adoration. But, Herbert embodies in his poetry the mystery of the dialogue with God, which, as it were, the other two hid; he discloses the day-to-day work of building the *via media* between imputed righteousness on the one side, and in-dwelling grace on the other, and, thereby, he opens wide the inner torment and the overcoming of the torment in the Anglican faith, once and for all refuting the *via media* as a negative compromise. It is the faith which works before the distant majesty of God, and, at the same time, yields itself to him, in the most intimate familiarity. *Power and Love* of God is answered by man with *love and trus*t (*The Temper*—How should I praise thee).

Trust is the key-word of Anglican spirituality. It is the trust which, within the most intimate striving after unity, overcomes the terror of the transcendence, which opens therein, and bends it back into the union. The trust is the faith lived, which comprehends itself as love, and bears within itself the sovereignty of humility, the integrating power of reconciliation.

The conflict between the two poles of imputed righteousness and inner grace, founded on the premise arising from the relationship between the world of nature and the world of grace, persists in Herbert to the ultimate consequence of rift and painful cleavage.

Such a conflict is immediately apparent in Herbert's vision of Christ which does not allow for the full integration of the Body of Christ into Christ. Herbert opens himself wide to the saints, to the Mother of God, inspired and magnificent, but, forthwith, he also draws back, with the cold argument that every form of adoration is the royal *prerogative* of Christ. For him, the saints must remain *inferiour power,* independent entities, but still somewhere disjointed members of Christ, whence Herbert's anxious care lest the transcendence of God be violated if he were to acknowledge the total unity of Christ and his Church, in heaven and on earth, in the last consequence of love:

> I would address
> My vows to thee most gladly, Blessed Maid,

> And Mother of my God, in my distresse:
> . . . . .
> Thou art the cabinet where the jewell lay:
> Chiefly to thee would I my soul unfold:
>
> But now, alas, I dare not; for our King,
> Whom we do all jointly adore and praise,
>   Bids no such thing:
> And where his pleasure no injunction layes,
> ('Tis your own case) ye never move a wing.
>   (*To all Angels and Saints*)

Another point of cleavage comes in the doctrine of the Eucharist. Herbert confronts his accusing conscience with the purifying action of the Eucharist, but, he adds thereto, lest it be not enough, that he will cover himself with *the bloudie cross* of Christ, before which every assault must cease. The cross, here, symbolises for him the vertical irruption into time of the Saviour. Herbert, in effect, does for himself, what, according to the Calvinists, would only be done by God, in absolute power, upon his elect alone. But, even so, a rift is rent within the integral union of the Eucharist and the sacrifice of Christ:

> And the receit shall be
> My Saviours bloud: when ever at his board
> I do but taste it, straight it cleanseth me,
>   And leaves thee not a word . . .
>
>   Yet if thou talkest still,
> Besides my physick, know there's some for thee:
> Some wood and nails to make a staffe or bill
>   For those that trouble me:
> The bloudie cross of my deare Lord
> Is both my physick and my sword.
>   (*Conscience*)

The cleavage persists into the very heart of the Eucharist itself. The presence of Christ must be preserved as a mystery of grace and can not be asserted as an objective real presence in the elements: the grace descends vertically, not at our disposal, into whomsoever it will reveal itself. Manifoldly, wine and blood intermingle, one with the other: the one drinks wine, whilst the other receives *heavenly blood*. And, because the presence is an unsearchable Mystery, never to be defined by human words, the reality of the presence is thereby not diminished, but strongly heightened:

The Essay

> Indeed it's true. I found a callous matter
> Began to spread and to expatiate there:
> But with a richer drug then scalding water
> I bath'd it often, ev'n with holy bloud,
> Which at a board, while many drunk bare wine,
> A friend did steal into my cup for good,
> Ev'n taken inwardly, and most divine
> To supple hardnesses . . .
> *(Love unknown)*

    The strange inter-play of blood and wine, as divided and yet one, is suggested primarily in *The Odour*. The essential image in the poem is that of the crushed pomander, the broken bread, but the lasting sweetness of grace imbibed remains a matter of commerce between the master and the servant, who are thus finally ever two distinct entities within the union into one.
    Other passages more directly reveal this same contradiction within the non-contradiction:

> But he doth bid us take his bloud for wine,
>   Bid what he please; yet I am sure,
> To take and taste what he doth there designe,
>   Is all that saves, and not obscure.
> *(Divinitie)*

> Weep what ye have drunk amisse,
>   And drink this,
> Which before ye drink is bloud.
> *(The Invitation)*

> Love is that liquour sweet and most divine,
> Which my God feels as bloud; but I, as wine.
> *(The Agonie)*

    In *The H. Communion*, Herbert, for once, even emphatically, distinguishes between the elements, which nourish and purify the body, and grace, which penetrates into the soul through the elements:

> But by the way of nourishment and strength
>   Thou creep'st into my breast;
>   Making thy way my rest,
> And thy small quantities my length;
>   Which spread their forces into every part,
>   Meeting sinnes force and art.

. . . . .

The Essay

> Onely thy grace, which with these elements comes,
> Knoweth the ready way,
> And hath the privie key,
> Op'ning the souls most subtile rooms . . .
>
> (*The H. Communion*)

The split conception of the Church whereby the body of Christ is not integrally one with Christ Himself must inevitably give rise to the question of assurance of salvation. In this connection, Herbert defines imputation in very nearly the same words as Hooker. It is for both of them, the bulwark against fear, the objective making secure of the assurance of salvation. Imputation compensates for the cleavage in the conception of the Church:

> Thy hand above did burn and glow,
> Danting the stoutest hearts, the proudest wits.
>
> But now that Christs pure vail presents the sight,
> I see no fears.
>
> (*Justice* (II))

> . . . if such might be so far charged by error, as that the very root of faith should be quite extinguished in them, and so their salvation utterly lost it would shake the hearts of the strongest and stoutest of us all.
>
> (*A Learned Discourse.* p. 50.
> publ. Dent. ed. Morris)

Through the imputing of the righteousness of Christ, assurance of salvation, no longer fully borne by the Church, should be withdrawn from arbitrary subjective feeling or experience, and, thence, also from blind enthusiasm. Yet, in Herbert, as in Hooker, the religious experience remains deeply anchored in the Church, and has there its inalienable place. And, the Church is incorporated into the universal plan of the history of salvation since the creation. In this salvation, the Jews also participate:

> At which the Church falling upon her face
> Should crie so loud, untill the trump were drown'd,
> And by that crie of her deare Lord obtain,
> That your sweet sap might come again!
>
> (*The Jews*)

The Essay

It is an interesting side-light on Herbert's explicit and true conflict in the polarity of the theological foundation of his Church that he could be so deeply respected by members of its most extreme tendencies, from Baxter to Charles I.

In Herbert, the conflict of polarity, the world of nature and the world of grace, imputation of the righteousness of Christ and indwelling grace, the vertical and the horizontal, governs the very existence of man to the last particularity.

Herbert's poems might seem to have been conceived as a unity, even on a narrow, almost world-less basis, if not for the naked problematic of existence, as such, revealed in the recurring image of the confrontation of man with God.

Man discerns himself relentlessly as the meeting-point of heaven and earth, suspended between time and eternity, destined to be the dwelling-place of God, the agonised locality of conflict:

>   . . . now a wonder,
>   A wonder tortur'd in the space
>   Betwixt this world and that of grace.
>   (*Affliction* (IV))

>   But now thou dost thy self immure and close
>   In some one corner of a feeble heart . . .
>   (*Decay*)

>   Since then, my God, thou hast
>   So brave a Palace built; O dwell in it,
>   That it may dwell with thee at last!
>   (*Man*)

>   To this life things of sense
>   Make their pretence:
>   In th' other Angels have a right by birth:
>   Man ties them both alone,
>   And makes them one,
>   With th' one hand touching heav'n, with th' other earth.

>   In soul he mounts and flies,
>   In flesh he dies.
>   He wears a stuffe whose thread is coarse and round,
>   But trimm'd with curious lace . . .
>   (*Mans medley*)

The multiplicity of levels becomes overwhelming in Herbert's relationship to God.

Outwardly, Herbert's life was relatively little disturbed. The intensity of living was directed wholly inwards and unfolded, in immeasurable fullness, in his dialogue with God. He always considered that he wrote his poetry intimately for God alone, and even so, he would only communicate a small portion of the secret conversation:

> For all thy frame and fabrick is within.
> *(Sion)*

Herbert had a very fine sense for the poverty of God. Men are mean:

> How canst thou brook his foolishnesse?
> Why, he'l not lose a cup of drink for thee:
> Bid him but temper his excesse;
> Not he . . .
> *(Miserie)*

And in the consecration of his poetry to God, there is somewhere a note of reparation for this meanness:

> I am but finite, yet thine infinitely.
> *(Artillerie)*

This is the key-note of the dialogue: unequal partners.

Constantly exposed to the working of the transcendent in the vertical, Herbert experiences the torments of the widening. The laws of created life, as also the forms of space and time, can crumble into insignificance in the face of God: abandonment can be presence, and mourning, joy. Day becomes night; and distance, co-incidence. The immanence of grace can of a sudden be experienced as steep transcendence, at which man must break into fragments.

Herbert is conscious of the transcendence as the unforeseeable in divine creativity. The rational continuity of creation in the material world is not to be found in the world of grace. One might say that there God does not limit himself as carefully:

> The grosser world stands to thy word and art;
> But the diviner world of grace
> Thou suddenly dost raise and race,
> And ev'ry day a new Creatour art.
> *(The Temper* (II))

The Essay

God's working is *sudden*, so to speak outside time. *Suddenly* he hears:

> ... how suddenly
> May our requests thine eare invade!
> *(Prayer* (II)*)*

Suddenly his presence unfolds itself, great and supreme in the soul, activating all its faculties:

> ... O my onely light,
> It cannot be
> That I am he
> On whom thy tempests fell all night.
> *(The Flower)*

And *suddenly*, inexplicably, this presence is there no more:

> Whither away delight?
> Thou cam'st but now; wilt thou so soon depart,
> And give me up to night?
> *(The Glimpse)*

The soul remains perplexed in the abandonment which it can not understand. Herbert once contrasted such a discontinuity with the regularity of nature: wind, waves, and flowers keep a more constant rhythm *(The Glimpse).* The dew falls every night. Yet, he is fully aware that the inconstancy might prove constancy *if we could spell.*

Herbert frequently describes the working of God on the soul as a battle in which God engages with his creature:

> ... and thou dost deigne
> To enter combate with us, and contest
> With thine own clay ...
> *(Artillerie)*

In this combat, of seeming equality, God is, at the outset, at a disadvantage: one against two. His opponents are Sin and Satan who try to win for themselves God's small third of man's heart:

> But now thou dost thyself immure and close
> In some one corner of a feeble heart:
> Where yet both Sinne and Satan, thy old foes,
> Do pinch and straiten thee, and use much art
> To gain thy thirds and little part.
> *(Decay)*

But, on the other hand, this unequal combat between Creator and creature can end in no other way than in the submission of the creature:

> The fight is hard on either part.
> Great God doth fight, he doth submit.
>
> (*Sion*)

The image of battle holds the over-tone of the condescension of God, the very fact that he finds it worthwhile to enter into so ridiculous a situation. And, thereto, the touching joy of God over a single sigh of repentance:

> But grones are quick, and full of wings,
> And all their motions upward be;
> And ever as they mount, like larks they sing;
> The note is sad, yet musick for a king.
>
> (*Ibid*)

The combat is also experienced as taming:

> My stuffe is flesh, not brasse; my senses live,
> And grumble oft, that they have more in me
> Then he that curbs them, being but one to five:
> Yet I love thee.
>
> (*The Pearl*)

Challenge, yielding, resignation, *There is no articling with thee,* all possible strains of melody, but, the combat is ever fought out, even where it is most bitter, on the foundation of a unity deeply rooted and, in spite of all laments, in enthusiastic self-surrender. This can be clearly traced in *The Collar* and *Home*.

The Collar opens with rebellion:

> I struck the board, and cry'd, No more,
> I will abroad.

There is resentful defiance against divine imposition, against divine will:

> What? shall I ever sigh and pine?
> My lines and life are free; free as the rode,
> Loose as the winde, as large as store.

The grief, now almost akin to anger, is at the necessity of ever being in a condition of pleading, of imploring, there is no criterion whatsoever of stable assurance:

> Shall I be still in suit?

His only assurance as *fallen man* is the sacrifice of the cross, and even the Eucharist, as a permanent source of refreshment and cleansing, is barred for him. The efficacy of the Sacrament rests on grace, and grace descends only upon him who is worthy, the Sacrament has no objective validity or power divorced from grace:

> Sure there was wine
> Before my sighs did drie it: there was corn
> Before my tears did drown it.
> Is the yeare onely lost to me?

Into this rebellion of his exhausted soul, subjected day and night to uncertainty, committed to a faith based entirely on trust, allowing neither for reason nor doubt, comes the other voice of his inner consciousness. The voice pleads for his acceptance of the situation. It denies his incapacity to bear the burden of uncertainty. It claims the possibility of survival, of a harvest for the soul which accepts the condition of uncertainty, and remains ever awaiting the descent of grace:

> Not so, my heart: but there is fruit
> And thou hast hands.

The second voice calls him back from dispersing himself in the conflict, in the self-imposed duality of finding and holding the good for himself:

> Recover all thy sigh-blown age
> On double pleasures: leave thy cold dispute
> Of what is fit, and not; . . .

The voice urges that this rebellion and autonomous seeking is the real prison of the soul, that it hangs on a thin thread of sand and obscures the sight of the strong life-line to God.

Rebellion persists, denies the advice, sees the advice as cowardly fear before death and judgment:

> Away; take heed:
> I will abroad.
> Call in thy deaths head there: tie up thy fears.

The second voice warns, or perhaps it is still the first voice in despair, ready to bear the full terror of the insubordination to Omnipotence:

The Essay

> He that forbears
> To suit and serve his need,
> Deserves his load.

The wildness has reached its pitch, the soul is wrenched, torn asunder in its desire for peace, for some assurance whereon to lay its weariness, and the answer comes, but is it a solution? It comes, once again, from above, suddenly, descending, Divine, and in that moment the soul yields, sinks into the irruption of presence:

> But as I rav'd and grew more fierce and wilde
> At every word,
> Me thoughts I heard one calling, *Child!*
> And I reply'd, *My Lord.*

Home shows the same condition, as it were, in reverse, the rebellion here is gathered into the final point of longing. *Home* is a yearning for the submission, a cry for the last reconciliation:

> Come Lord, my head doth burn, my heart is sick,
> While thou dost ever, ever stay:
> Thy long deferrings wound me to the quick,
> My spirit gaspeth night and day.
> O show thyself to me,
> Or take me up to thee!

Again and again the cry is repeated of longing, the rebellion converges into reproach for the delay in the coming of the Beloved:

> What is this weary world; this meat and drink,
> That chains us by the teeth so fast?

The only joy, the only fulfilment, is the last joy, the vertical and horizontal meeting in the End:

> There is no fruitfull yeare, but that which brings
> The last and lov'd, though dreadfull day.

And so, in the last count, for Herbert, rebellion or submission, both are one, both collapse into insignificance, in both the sensible world is senseless:

> My thoughts and joyes are all packt up and gone,
> And for their old acquaintance plead.

The solution is not here, and continuity is established with another life, the Church in heaven where uncertainty will rest within the certainty itself.

The carrying force for this final senselessness of combat or submission is a unity, the unity at the very root of existence with the incarnate Christ.

In Herbert's vision, Christ, in his earthly life, has actually lived, as we ourselves, the life of each one of us in Truth, that is, the life in as far as it is related to God. Our whole existence is, as it were, anticipated, founded, and solved in every particularity, *each grief*, in eternity. We re-live it, but this means that we live it in eternity, and within the solution, which surrounds us on all sides although, in our consciousness, we seek it with tears. Hence the impetus and the work of praise, which makes us conscious of eternity:

> Thy crosse took up in one,
> By way of imprest, all my future mone.
> *(Affliction* (II))

But this means also that we live our life as Christ in us, and that means, in a higher degree, as we ourselves:

> Yet to be thine, doth me restore;
> So that again I now am mine,
> And with advantage mine the more.
> *(Clasping of hands)*

Herbert draws out this union in dis-identification to the uttermost consequence. At the Last Judgment, he will present the scroll of imputation instead of his own *book,* which he will simply refuse to show:

> But I resolve, when thou shalt call for mine,
> That to decline,
> And thrust a Testament into thy hand:
> Let that be scann'd.
> There thou shalt finde my faults are thine.
> *(Judgement)*

To the transcendent, dreadful Christ, Judge and Saviour, Herbert brings the transcendence of the life of Christ, in which his own is enclosed; thus, no more unequal partners.

There would seem not enough evidence here to suggest whether Herbert did think through, with all the implications, the question of the relationship between Power and Love, the significance of the

Potestas Absoluta in the cleavage between a theological stand on imputed righteousness on the one side, and on in-dwelling grace on the other. In this connection, the contribution of the Cambridge Platonists to Anglican theology is, undoubtedly, of the highest value.[1]

Man, according to Herbert, of his own, without the union with Christ, disintegrates into nothingness in the presence of God, into dust, clay, folly:

>Man is a foolish thing, a foolish thing.
>*(Miserie)*

He must die that, thereby, Christ may increase in him:

>My onely musick, striking me ev'n dead.
>*(Aaron)*

So Herbert bends forensic justification into inner grace, he thrusts his life into the transcendence of Christ and yields totally to Christ living His life in him; the two movements are synonymous but never one:

>I heard a friend expresse,
>That all things were more ours by being his.
>*(The Holdfast)*

Finely and delicately, he joins together, in his religious experience, the two poles of imputed righteousness and in-dwelling grace. The way of purification, that is for him the growing into the life of Christ, the becoming one with the Will of God, is solely built upon the foundation of this co-incidence.

This concept and act of joining causes everything to fall into union, *making two one (The Search)*. It gives rise to the flowing of the one into the other, but ever without fusion:

>His beams shall cheer my breast, and both so twine,
>Till ev'n his beams sing, and my musick shine.
>*(Christmas)*

No fusion, but rather the reciprocal influence of one upon the other is yet more strongly emphasised in:

>And thou with me dost thee restore.
>*(Clasping of hands)*

[1] See *Ralph Cudworth. Mystical Thinker.* Mother Maria: Pub. Greek Orthodox Monastery of the Assumption. 1973.

The Essay

There is another aspect to this union with Christ. Our life, which Christ has lived, we re-live as our own, as an integral part of his life.

In the life of Christ, we are only a part, but fully incorporated; the Whole is immeasurably greater and incommensurable, but, yet, we have a part therein; and, since we, ourselves, are a portion of the transcendent life of Christ, we can even say that he re-lives within us his own life; that is, according to our measure, he re-enacts his life on earth, and especially his passion and death, in us; whereby, in Herbert, there is also ever the suggestion of Christ's suffering for our sins, which he actually endures within us. Christ will realise his life within us to the measure in which we allow ourselves to be stretched. The wider we are ready to expand, the greater the size of his occupation. On his part there is no limit.

He, who has once grasped the consciousness of the occupation, no longer fears the cost:

> Thy life on earth was grief, and thou art still
> Constant unto it, making it to be
> A point of honour, now to grieve in me,
> And in thy members suffer ill.
> They who lament one crosse,
> Thou dying daily, praise thee to thy losse.
> (*Affliction* (III))

The inter-relationship with Christ, the *commerce,* once recognised and acknowledged, claims the whole person, constantly:

> Then let each houre
> Of my whole life one grief devoure;
> That thy distresse through all may runne,
> And be my sunne.
> (*Good Friday*)

Such a relationship gives rise to the image of the instrument in the hands of God. Herbert represents himself as a musical instrument on which God may play. It is the bliss of the instrument to be played upon, but, here also lies the inherent terror, the echo of the *sudden* of the vertical descent. When God chooses to cease to play, then the instrument becomes useless, of its own it has no volition, it remains *untun'd, unstrung*:

> Oh take thy lute, and tune it to a strain,
> Which may with thee
> All day complain.
> (*Ephes. 4.30*)

Again, it seems relevant to refer once more to the Cambridge Platonists, for whom to stop at this point could never have been satisfactory. For the Cambridge Platonist the soul of music inspires the instrument, so that henceforth it may play of its own accord, made alive from within. A time of dryness, therefore, need not be connected with Divine absence or desertion, when we are unfruitful it need not be that God has removed His grace from us, it is merely the inevitable accompaniment to the imperfection of finite existence.

Herbert demands that the earthly creature must learn, already on earth, to live according to heavenly measures. Thus, he may experience the boundless joy, as well as the boundless pain, of self-transcendence in Christ:

> Thou art my grief alone,
> Thou Lord conceal it not: and as thou art
> All my delight, so all my smart . . .
> *(Affliction* (II))

Herbert also experiences this pain as the being broken to pieces, with strong over-tones of the breaking of the bread in the Eucharist: *ev'ry part hath got a tongue!* Each separate member of the body prays. And, as pomander, which gains a higher potency through being crushed, so does the being broken in the spiritual life signify not obliteration but multiplication of strength. This image also pre-supposes the unity with the life of Christ, and draws out the line still further:

> Lord, Jesu, heare my heart,
> Which hath been broken now so long,
> That ev'ry part
> Hath got a tongue!
>   . . .
> Thy pile of dust, wherein each crumme
>   Sayes, Come?
>   *(Longing)*

So Herbert finds an all-embracing unity, on which, ultimately, the unity of the Church with Christ is founded; for, in fact, there is now only one grief (*Good Friday*), one death, and one victory (*The Dawning*), and the finite life is taken up into the eternal life of Christ as He, Himself, lives it within His creatures, in finite, and, at the same time, in eternal measures.

Herbert comes very close here to the concept of redeeming suffering within the Church of Christ. But, he does not take the step. Imputation bars the way. And, perhaps, for this same reason, there is, in Herbert, hardly any suggestion of bridal mystery. There are only a few distant notes:

> My God, what is a heart,
> That thou shouldst it so eye, and wooe,
> Powring upon it all thy art,
> As if thou hadst nothing else to do?
> *(Mattens)*

Or from man's part:

> My tears and prayers night and day do wooe,
> And work up to thee; yet thou dost refuse.
> *(Artillerie)*

It is strange how for Herbert the love, and the harmony, and the deeply hidden presence of God shine through most clearly not in the fulfilment, but in the desolation of abandonment. It is tempting to see here a true prophetic strain, even akin to Jeremiah, who speaks greatly in his lamentations. And it is most characteristic of the prophet in him that Herbert must rouse his soul from wholly losing itself in the contemplation of the one death, when God wishes to show him the victory:

> But thou dost still lament, and pine, and crie;
> And feel his death, but not his victorie.
>
> Arise sad heart: if thou doe not withstand,
> Christs resurrection thine may be . . .
> *(The Dawning)*

In the immediate presence of God, in the nearness which he experienced almost as co-incidence: —

> When thou dost turn, and wilt be neare;
> What edge so keen,
> What point so piercing can appeare
> To come between?
> *(The Search)*

—Herbert feels himself towards God as a servant face to face with his beloved lord. The relationship of servant-master, which determined his consecration to the priesthood, involves his total self-surrender, the tenderness and sovereignty of God: *Thy word is all.* And the joy, which hides therein, he stresses in *The Odour*, where servant and master so enter one into the other that they seem hardly separate any more, and, yet, a confrontation of persons remains.

It is interesting, however, that, on the other hand, *child* occurs only in moods of estrangement, in rebellion, or in doubt, whereby Herbert is reminded of the reality of baptism. For Herbert, childhood is the image of health, of the malleability wherein there is nothing hardened or stiffened. When God addresses him as *child*, He is calling him back to the foundation of his life. But, he does not answer with *father*, his answer is *my Lord*. In this connection, it may be relevant, although this is possibly going too far, that Herbert's father died when he was very young, and *father* would have remained for him a most intimate term, *my Lord* would retain a distance.

The question then arises of what, in fact, grace means for Herbert, and if he accepts a continuity of grace. It becomes immediately apparent that the two poles of imputed righteousness and in-dwelling grace, are, again, for Herbert, intertwined, the one of the personal meeting of the soul with God, and the other of the working of grace within are not antithetical or parallel for Herbert.

Grace and Holy Spirit flow into each other. The work of grace is the purification of the soul; and also here the emphasis lies on the vertical descent of divine force, which is not determinable by man's work and which can set in motion and activate the soul. Without the vertical descent of grace the soul remains barren. We have no harvests. The only harvest is the last loved day. But, this last day is already here, the day of grace.

Grace, not reason, because of this vertical descent, teaches, leads, and is the source of the knowledge of God. And, once again, such an exclusion of reason because of the inherent theological cleavage was not found equally unavoidable by the Cambridge Platonists. But, Herbert did not bridge the gulf, he suffered it to the very end:

> Yet through the labyrinths, not my groveling wit,
> But thy silk twist led down from heav'n to me,
> Did both conduct and teach me, how by it
>   To climbe to thee.
>   (*The Pearl*)

Science, honour, and earthly joys on the one side, and the world of grace on the other. Herbert makes his decision, a tormenting one, in the full consciousness of the magnitude of the sacrifice. He is tossed in the tempest of contrary good. How serenely, in comparison, the Platonists find their way on the same sea; for them there is no conflict, reason and grace do not exert a tug of war over their souls, there are not two worlds, but one, one world with many levels, and grace embraces all realms of human experience.

Herbert speaks of the Gospels and the whole Bible in the same context as he does of grace, that is, divorced from reason.

The Bible is health, purifying well, ambassador against death and hell:

> Thou art all health, health thriving till it make
> A full eternitie . . .
>   this is the well
> That washes what it shows . . .
>   thou art heav'ns Lidger here,
> Working against the states of death and hell.
>   (*The H. Scriptures.* I.)

The Bible is the only rudder; he will seek in it, until he has learned the art of love:

> Nay, I will reade thy book, and never move
> Till I have found therein thy love,
> Thy art of love, which I'le turn back on thee . . .
>   (*The Thanksgiving*)

> . . . heav'n lies flat in thee . . .
>   (*The H. Scriptures.* I.)

The only place of access to grace, which is always open to us, is here, in the Bible, *subject to ev'ry mounter's bended knee* (*The H. Scriptures.* I.). It is as if Herbert is extending the vertical arbitrary grace to the horizontal plane of the way of purification by means of the Gospel, that is, the word of Christ; thus, imputing of righteousness through Christ alone and indwelling grace once more converge but still do not become one. Heaven may lie flat, through the grace of the Gospel, but, it requires the supplication of the bended knee, the continual imploring, for the grace to descend, vertically, suddenly.

Grace acts on the soul in contradiction to sin. Sin makes the heart hard and impenetrable, immutable, *dry dust,* insensitive, coarse, dull, sick. But, grace rouses the soul, makes it *new, tender, quick,* so that it learns praise—harmony: grace supplies every lack, and generously makes good every failing, even in music:

> O let thy blessed Spirit bear a part,
> And make up our defects with his sweet art.
>   (*Easter*)

Herbert deeply longed for the feast of Pentecost to be brought back into the Church in its first splendour. From this, probably comes his strange predilection for the word *nest*. *Nest* is the essence of being sheltered, but, so too, the secret creative power. The Holy Spirit, *the sweet and sacred Dove*, has made the soul his nest, and hatches it out, until it is fledged, and flies to heaven:

> Listen sweet Dove unto my song,
> And spread thy golden wings in me;
> Hatching my tender heart so long,
> Till it get wing, and fly away with thee.
> (*Whitsunday*)

Christ leaves His nest with the Father that He might be born into the world:

> There lay thy sonne: and must he leave that nest,
> That hive of sweetnesse, to remove
> Thraldome from those, who would not at a feast
> Leave one poore apple for thy love?
> (*Home*)

And the human soul finds no rest until it attains to its *ancient nest* in heaven.

It is difficult to discern whether, and to what extent, Herbert thought that grace could be assimilated into the soul, and whether progress on the way of purification causes the growing of grace. He speaks, on one occasion, of the pre-conditions for the constant presence of God in the soul. Peace, silence, and order are the chief stipulations, no noise, especially that of grief:

> But, Lord, the house and familie are thine,
> Though some of them repine.
> Turn out these wranglers which defile thy seat:
> For where thou dwellest all is neat.
> (*The Familie*)

And, as for Plato, so for Herbert, there must be no heightened emotion to allow for the presence:

> Thy Saviour sentenc'd joy,
> And in the flesh condemn'd it as unfit,
> At least in lump: for such doth oft destroy . . .
> (*The Size*)

This is how the house must be prepared for God:

> Mark how the fire in flints doth quiet lie,
>   Content and warm t' it self alone . . .
>
> Gad not abroad at ev'ry quest and call . . .
> *(Content)*

And, the distance, also here, is still carefully preserved:

> This is thy house, with these it doth abound:
>   And where these are not found,
> Perhaps thou com'st sometimes, and for a day;
>   But not to make a constant stay.
> *(The Familie)*

On the other hand, he prays that the throne of grace may be set up in him for ever, that the powers of his soul would be directed to fruitful work, and would not be squandered uselessly:

> O fix thy chair of grace, that all my powers
>   May also fix their reverence . . .
> *(The Temper (II))*

Herbert was deeply concerned by the waste of time in the state of sadness when God does not play on him; these fears of uselessness constantly recur to him with the reproach that if he were anyone but himself he would not be as barren: as a tree, he would bear fruits, as a bee, he could gather honey. And, again, in contrast, in this same context, there can be traced the Platonist line in Anglican theology which is capable of integrating these times of seeming inability to work. But, on the other hand, Herbert, sick with consumption, with a body always feverish, always weary, found in the strength of his spirit the way to integrate this very pain of weariness into the plan of creation; he makes of it a grace and a loving call from God. All good things were apportioned to man, all, but rest, and so in the weariness lies the incentive to answer God's open embrace:

> Let him be rich and wearie, that at least,
>   If goodnesse leade him not, yet wearinesse
>   May tosse him to my breast.
> *(The Pulley)*

The Essay

In one short, cryptic poem, *Hope,* Herbert has characterised enigmatically the two streams which determined his religious experience. In the one stream, purification is a way. The goal is heaven, and the further he goes forward on the way, the more his whole being gravitates towards the goal, *The most of me to heav'n is fled: My thoughts and joyes are all packt up and gone* . . . (*Home*). In the second stream, the descent of eternity confronts progress within time, the presence of God through coherence with Christ, and, with this, the significance of the *now;* in the *now* of the presence of God, history is fulfilled. But equally with time, so space is also transcended in the *now* of the descent of the presence of God; multiplicity is gathered up into unity, *Thy power and love, my love and trust, Make one place ev'ry where* (*The Temper* (1)).

For Herbert, there is a double note in the one word *hope.* On the way of purification, in the growing gravitation towards the goal, towards unity, he would wish to be set free from hope, in as far as hope includes restlessness, and with the restlessness, weariness.

> I gave to Hope a watch of mine: but he
>   An anchor gave to me.
> Then an old prayer-book I did present:
>   And he an optick sent.
>
> With that I gave a viall full of tears:
>   But he a few green eares:
> Ah Loyterer! I'le no more, no more I'le bring:
>   I did expect a ring.

The watch: symbol of the progression in time, purification as a way, step by step, in direct contradiction to the anchor, symbol of the sole security through the imputation of righteousness, the anchor of Christ descending vertically in the *now* of eternity.

The prayer-book: medium of discursive adoration, within our narrower faculties, in contradiction to the lens, the gathering of multiplicity into the one focal point.

Viall of tears: broken-ness in the pains of purification, in contradiction to the broken bread of the Eucharist, the *green eares,* not yet come to full and sovereign maturity: the sacrifice as manifestation of the Eternal Love: the particular suffering bent into the suffering of Christ.

In three movements, the multiplicity in time, prayer, experience,

The Essay

are challenged and re-directed, bent back into unity and fulfilment in the *now* of the point without time or space, the point of the presence.

His answer: rebellion, analogous to the first deception in the aim set in *The Pilgrimage*. His hope was directed to redemption from out of suffering, not transfiguration within suffering.

Hope's answer: Hope had expected a ring. The bending back of the single straight line into the circle. The two streams may yet not be entirely separate. Hope's answer centres earthly events on to the *standing Majestie* of God within the soul. And man is not left to struggle alone, coldly bereft, for *ring* may yet have another significance, the trust in God's love irrespective of our merit, God woos His creature. It is possibly this image of the ring which Vaughan took up for his vision of eternity and bridal mystery.

Hope has led into the innermost heart of Herbert's mysticism, how he understood purification. Where he set the aim and purpose he suggests in several poems, particularly strikingly in *The Pilgrimage*.

The Pilgrimage follows the way of purification through the first stages of the overcoming of pride, despair, dreams, care, suffering, inner accidie, and, then, finally, a last ascent. But, after the uttermost effort, the aim and purpose reveals itself as deception. The way can ever only be a preparation, never the end. He breaks down:

> I fell, and cry'd, Alas my Kinge!
> Can both the way and end be tears?

He raises himself, recognises the deception, and knows the further goal. A voice calls, the vertical descends sharply, suddenly, this way goes through death. The call is a *now* and the way must be a *now*, from instant to instant, never continuous. This does not frighten him:

> My hill was further: so I flung away,
>   Yet heard a crie
> Just as I went, *None goes that way*
>   *And lives:* If that be all, said I,
> After so foul a journey death is fair,
>   And but a chair.

The over-tones to *chair* are throne, sceptre, king, or, simply, perfect freedom, that is the death inside this life, the *kill me not ev'ry day,* and the *Christ dying daily*. Perfection leads through death. The first goal set inevitably is one of deception, anxiety and despair. But, the second goal is the creative response to suffering, the *making a sceptre of the rod.*

The transformation, so longed for, may only be achieved in death, in the deaths within this life which mysteriously hold within themselves the living presence of God. The death must be died in such a way that this presence of God becomes the only reality, the inexpressible joy and fulfilment of all hope in the *now*. Thereby, the restless calls, the longing, and the *hope*, are gathered together into the fulfilment, into the unity.

Herbert suggests the same idea in another form in *Confession*.

Only an open heart, that is a heart which has accepted the daily death, escapes the torment of the afflictions which find their way into the innermost chambers and hiding places of self-defence:

> O, what a cunning guest
> Is this same grief! within my heart I made
>   Closets; and in them many a chest;
>   And, like a master in my trade,
> In those chests, boxes; in each box, a till:
> Yet grief knows all, and enters when he will.
>   . . .
>   We are the earth; and they,
> Like moles within us, heave, and cast about:
>   And till they foot and clutch their prey,
>   They never cool, much less give out.
>   . . .
>   Onely an open breast
> Doth shut them out, so that they cannot enter . . .

In the readiness to suffer, in the open heart, even if the afflictions enter, they can not stay, there is no resting place for them:

> Or, if they enter, cannot rest,
> But quickly seek some new adventure.

It is as if they can find no where to fix themselves, and they slide off impotently:

> Smooth open hearts no fastning have; but fiction
> Doth give a hold and handle to affliction.

Herbert, in *Confession,* challenges the enemies, he is not afraid:

> ... let them do their best,
> They shall be thick and cloudie to my breast.

And, Herbert is not afraid because the highest purpose and end can be none other than to learn the art of dying; for therein we attain to the deepest coherence with Christ:

> Yet Lord, instruct us so to die,
> That all these dyings may be life in death.
> *(Mortification)*

The drama of the violent conflict through death to life gradually enters, for Herbert, into the serenity of submission to the Will of God, in which he discovers the constancy of the presence, and the joy in suffering. It might seem that here Herbert is very near the Platonic trend in Anglican theology, but it is not quite so simple as that. However yielding and loving his submission seems, yet, there is always the implicit, if not explicit, hint of enduring the submission, of passivity rather than activity. God remains unforeseeable, and Herbert ever confronts an incomprehensible omnipotence, albeit in glad self-surrender. His reason is not concerned in the decision:

> Yet take thy way; for sure thy way is best:
> Stretch or contract me thy poore debter:
> This is but tuning of my breast,
> To make the musick better.
> *(The Temper* (I)*)*

The inner unpredictable up and down of *whether I flie with angels, fall with dust,* thereby loses significance. It is only a matter now of bearing the pain. He is no longer concerned with the immediate presence of God in the sense of the torment of experiencing God as near and then as far, in the sudden abandonment, in the unforeseen absence, because, with his personal surrender, he knows himself safe within the unity of the Power which created the world, and of the Love, which had led the world and would lead it to its consummation. This bending into unity is apparent and confirmed when he gathers together his creative power within the rending apart and the torment, and—can write. Now, he pierces through to the harmony of praise:

> Wounded I sing, tormented I indite ...
> *(Josephs Coat)*

The Essay

In the last count, prayer is the most potent work for Herbert since he sees it as actualising itself ultimately within eternity, it is the harmony which spans heaven and earth. Prayer is, therefore, so important, that, as Hooker, Herbert rates community prayer above private prayer for *where most pray* as in heaven, the harmony is intensified, and the reconciling power of praise the greater. And, as for Hooker, music for Herbert points the way to heaven since it frees us, for a while, from the limitations of our bodily being, and gives us back the strength to believe in the final harmony, and to live, as it were, the one reality in heaven and earth—*Pignus gloriae futurae.*

The peace and serenity, which radiate from Herbert, were dearly bought through the mastering of the tension in self-discipline and self-limitation. In their finality and validity as works of art, Herbert's poems reflect the suffering of the spirit, which if truly suffered, does not manifest itself as suffering but presents itself to man as goodness and to God as praise.

But, what then is the significance of imputation in this most delicate, lived inter-play of imputed righteousness and inner grace? Is it possible to assert that the total exclusion of justification through works might lead to a way of purification unassailed by cramping fear? But, is it not so, that where grace works, in effect justification through works is hardly more than a word, and of no practical significance?

For Herbert, imputation signifies the eternal foundation of his faith, and of his hope. Thence, he knows his salvation guaranteed, independent of deficiency and failure, and he can therefore overcome fear and despair. The way is made free for him for the work of purification. But, on the other hand, through the consciousness of the imputation of righteousness, the personal work of purification is also ultimately taken away from him. Then, he rests solely in the Will and working of God. Thus, he gains the strength to face his own narrow limitations, and to accept them peacefully: again, the serene humility founded on trust, the truest mark of Anglican spirituality.

This interplay of imputed righteousness and indwelling grace, not only in doctrine, but also in practical spirituality, throws a light on the significance and place of Anglicanism within the whole Church.

The Anglicans took up both extremes which, during the Reformation, had stiffened into the dilemma between the imputing of righteousness and in-dwelling grace, and dared to deliver the people up to this polarity, and to leave each person to find his own delicate balance in his own life:

> What, Child, is the ballance thine,
> Thine the poise and measure?
> *(Dialogue)*

Does not this passage suggest that the dilemma itself is erroneous, that, in fact, there need be no dilemma? It was the Anglicans who always found their way back to the Greek Fathers, and in them they would find no such dilemma. In the Fathers, the proportion is preserved of redemption without us, with us, and in us. There is no conflict of contradictory extremes. There is no mutually exclusive polarity. It is not unjustly that the Anglicans consider themselves in direct line of theological succession from the Fathers.

Can it be that the Anglican *via media*, far from being a compromise, in fact points the way in the West to the healing of the breach of the Reformation? In itself the *via media* can not be the solution, but it can be the first step. The Anglicans are foremost in recognising the vulnerability of their position and this has, from the outset, stimulated their deeper research into the Fathers. But, what also emerges is the close kinship of the Anglican Church to the Orthodox. The divergencies are many, but the fundamental conception, the attitude, is familiar and dear to both in the freedom of the Spirit.

INDEX OF POEMS

Aaron 31-33, 292
Affliction I 87-90
Affliction II 94-96, 291, 294, 301
Affliction III 147-148, 254, 293, 302
Affliction IV 197-198, 285
Affliction V 100-101
The Agonie 78-79, 283
The Altar 58-59
Anagram of the Virgin Marie 70-71
To all Angels and Saints 50, 71-73, 257-259, 281-282
The Answer 215, 216
Antiphon I 181-182
Antiphon II 137
Artillerie 104-106, 286, 287, 288, 295
Assurance 126-127
Avarice 170-171

The Bag 125-126
The Banquet 81-83
H. Baptisme I 120-121
H. Baptisme II 97-98
Bitter-sweet 90-91
The British Church 38-39
The Bunch of Grapes 79-81
Businesse 45

The Call 142
Charms and Knots 167
Christmas 195-196, 292
The Church-floore 168
Church-lock and Key 59-60
The Church Militant 36-37
Church-monuments 167
Church-musick 33
The Church-Porch 26-29, 163-167, 169
Church-rents and schismes 37-38
Clasping of hands 131-133, 291, 292
The Collar 216-219, 288-290
Coloss. iii, 3: 67-68
The H. Communion 83-85, 252, 283-284
Complaining 91-93, 94
Confession 160-161, 302-303
Conscience 61-63, 282
Constancie 169-170
Content 186-187, 299
The Crosse 108, 112-116

The Dawning 124-125, 294, 295

Death 173-175, 297
Decay 153-154, 162, 285, 287
Deniall 200-201
Dialogue 148-149, 305
A Dialogue-Antheme 173
The Discharge 122-124, 280
Discipline 108, 110-112
Divinitie 209-211, 283
Dooms-day 175
Dotage 22-23
Dulnesse 198-199

Easter 196-197, 297
Easter-wings 202-203, 251-252
The Elixir 171
Employment I 200
Employment II 182-183
Ephes. iv, 30: 60-61, 293
Even-song 141-142

Faith 42-44, 46, 47, 65, 77
The Familie 46, 298, 299
The Flower 212-214, 287, 295
The Foil 167
The Forerunners 187-189
Frailtie 169

Giddinesse 103-104
The Glance 106-107
The Glimpse 48-51, 287
Good Friday 63-64, 293, 294
Grace 51-52
Gratefulnesse 140-141
Grief 93-94

Heaven 177
The Holdfast 65-67, 292
Home 237-241, 288, 290, 298, 300
Hope 244-246, 300-301
Humilitie 168
A true Hymne 193-194

The Invitation 35-36, 283

Jesu 138
The Jews 35, 284
Jordan I 190-191
Jordan II 222-224
Josephs Coat 224-225, 252-254, 303
Judgement 68-69, 73, 291
Justice I 107
Justice II 121-122, 130, 284

Lent 138-140

306

L'Envoy 119
Life 172
Longing 129-131, 294
Love I 191-192, 193
Love II 191, 192, 193
Love III 149-151
Love-joy 138
Love unknown 225-232, 279, 282-283, 297

Man 98-99, 285
Mans medley 234-237, 285
Marie Magdalene 119-120
Mattens 140, 295
The Method 156-157
Miserie 219-222, 286, 292
Mortification 172-173, 303

Nature 107-108

Obedience 101-103
The Odour 108-110, 112, 283, 295-296
An Offering 127-128

Paradise 91
A Parodie 53-55, 157
Peace 85-87
The Pearl 142-143, 288, 296
The Pilgrimage 241-244, 245, 254-257, 301-302
The Posie 156
Praise I 199
Praise II 183-184
Praise III 184-185
Prayer I 178-179, 254
Prayer II 137, 138, 287
The Priesthood 29-30
Providence 179-181
The 23rd Psalme 149-150, 254
The Pulley 225, 232-234, 299

The Quidditie 190
The Quip 21-22

Redemption 57-58

Repentance 158-160
The Reprisall 146-147
The Rose 22

The Sacrifice 133-135
The H. Scriptures I 74-75, 84, 297
The H. Scriptures II 74, 75-77
The Search 55-57, 292, 295
Self-condemnation 24-25
Sepulchre 135
Sighs and Grones 145-146
Sinne I 155-156
Sinne II 153
The Sinner 157
Sinnes round 155
Sion 162-163, 168, 286, 288
The Size 23-24, 298
The Sonne 138
The Starre 52-53
The Storm 157-158
Submission 99
Sunday 136
Superliminare 28

The Temper I 203-205, 281, 300, 303
The Temper II 46-48, 53, 54, 64, 280, 286, 299, 301
The Thanksgiving 73-74, 194-195, 297
Time 175-177
Trinitie Sunday 161-162

Ungratefulnesse 143-144, 259
Unkindnesse 144-145

Vanitie I 41-42
Vanitie II 22
Vertue 42

The Water-course 158
Whitsunday 33-34, 259-260, 298
The Windows 30-31
The World 40-41, 252
A Wreath 189-190

307

Also by Sister Thekla:

John Keats: The Disinterested Heart
A Story of Babylon
Orthodox Potential (Essays I, II, III)
St Andrew of Crete: The Great Canon